The Poems of Robert Parry

Medieval and Renaissance Texts and Studies

Volume 303

Renaissance English Text Society

Seventh Series

Volume XXX (for 2005)

The Poems of Robert Parry

Edited by

G. Blakemore Evans

Arizona Center for Medieval and Renaissance Studies
in conjunction with
Renaissance English Text Society
Tempe, Arizona
2005

Library of Congress Cataloging-in-Publication Data

Parry, Robert, fl. 1540-1612.
The poems of Robert Parry / edited by G. Blakemore Evans.
p. cm. -- (Medieval and Renaissance Texts and Studies ; v. 303)
(Renaissance English Text Society ; 7th ser., v. 30)
Includes bibliographical references and index.
ISBN-13: 978-0-86698-347-1 (alk. paper)
ISBN-10: 0-86698-347-3 (alk. paper)
1. Parry, Robert, fl. 1540-1612.--Criticism and interpretation. I. Evans, G. Blakemore (Gwynne Blakemore), 1912- II. Arizona Center for Medieval and Renaissance Studies. III. Renaissance English Text Society. IV. Title. V. Medieval & Renaissance Texts & Studies (Series) v. 303. VI. Series: Renaissance English Text Society (Series) ; v. 30

PR2329.P14Z84 2005
821'.3--dc22

2005035244

∞
This book is made to last.
It is set in Adobe Minion Pro,
smyth-sewn and printed on acid-free paper
to library specifications.
Printed in the United States of America

Table of Contents

Acknowledgements

"And knowing how the debt grows, I will pay it."
The Comedy of Errors, 4.4.121

I am especially indebted to (1) the Trustees of the Huntington Library (San Marino, California) for permission to publish a facsimile edition of their unique copy of Robert Parry's poems; (2) the Bodleian Library (Oxford) and the Folger Shakespeare Library (Washington, D.C.) for permission to include in the collection twenty-two lyrics from their copies (the only extant copies) of Parry's chivalric romance, *Moderatus, The most delectable & famous Historie of the BLACKE Knight* (1595); and (3) the National Library of Wales (Aberystwyth) for permission to include passages from Robert Parry's Diary (manuscript) that are not transcribed by A. Foulkes-Roberts in his selections published in *Archaeologia Cambrensis* (1915).

Aside from an important article by Professor John Simons in 1996 and his valuable edition of *Moderatus* (2002), comparatively little attention has been paid to Robert Parry as either poet or romancer. The most significant earlier work, apart from Foulkes-Roberts' selections from Parry's Diary, appeared in Carleton Brown's *Poems by Sir John Salusbury and Robert Chester* (1914). Brown deserves great credit for being the first to untangle Parry's extensive use of acrostics in *Sinetes*, but his reason for the inclusion of a substantial number of Parry's poems from *Sinetes* in his edition of Salusbury's and Chester's poems arose from a misinterpretation of its title-page and other "evidence" that led him to attribute about a third of the poems in *Sinetes* to Salusbury (i.e., thirteen Posies, thirty-one Sonnettos, and, tentatively, "The lamentation of a Male-content"). However, as I believe I have been able to prove, none of these poems is by Salusbury (see Introduction, 11–23).

My editorial committee (Professors Steven W. May [Chairman], W. Speed Hill, Noel J. Kinnamon, Arthur F. Kinney, and Arthur F. Marotti) made many helpful suggestions and collected a fair crop of errors; their reading of my manuscript was meticulous and I was most fortunate to have have such generous collaboration.

I am deeply indebted to Dr. Stephen R. Tabor, Curator of Early Printed Books, Huntington Library, for a detailed bibliographical analysis of *Sinetes* and, for a similar analysis of *Moderatus*, to Dr. Mark Bland, Professor Randal McLeod and, once again, Steven W. May.

As many times in the past, the Reference Librarians in both Widener and Houghton Libraries, Harvard University, have with great patience and kindness endured my complete computer illiteracy and often assisted me at whatever need. As a result of this same illiteracy, I was forced to call upon my daughter and son-in-law (Pamela and J. G. Hook) and Marie Henson to transfer my untidy and difficult manuscript to immaculate floppy disks, a wearisome and demanding task for which I am most deeply grateful.

As always, it is a special pleasure to thank friends for ever-willing assistance at many moments of bafflement: William H. Bond, Steve B. Berkowitz, Heather Dubrow, John L. Klause, Randal McLeod, Thomas Moisan, John J. M. Tobin, Susannah Tobin, and Joseph Westlund.

In the Introduction (p. 24), I say that the derivation of Parry's pseudonym "Sinetes" has eluded explanation. Recently, however, two tempting explanations have been offered: (1) Dr. Steven Berkowitz and Ms. Irene Peirano, independently, have suggested that "Sinetes" may be derived from the Greek adjective συνετός (*synetos*) meaning "wise" or "intelligent," possibly in a nominative singular form as συνετής (*synetes*) with an extended sense of "one who knows from bitter experience what the world is like." (It should perhaps be noted that Greek upsilon is regularly transliterated as "y," which in Elizabethan usage was generally interchangeable with "i.") (2) Professor John Simons has suggested that, since we know almost certainly that Parry was familiar with Spanish and may have lived in Spain as a youth (see Introduction, 29), "Sinetes" may be derived from the Portuguese word *sinete* (plural, *sinetes*) meaning "a seal or signet." This would be appropriate, since, Simons suggests, "given the acrostics, and, no doubt, other covert or coded references in the poems . . . the idea of a title/name which carried notions of concealment and encoding [is] rather attractive."

I owe a very important debt to Dr. William Gentrup, Assistant Director of the Arizona Center for Medieval and Renaissance Studies, for his thoughtful work in preparing my manuscript for publication; he was forced to correct all too many typos while, at the same time, offering a substantial number of helpful critical comments. I am extremely grateful.

Finally, this little book is offered as a tribute to my wife, Betty, who has been an unfailing source of loving and sustaining support for more than sixty years.

G. B. E.

Abbreviations and References

Abbott	E. A. Abbott, *A Shakespearian Grammar*, 1869.
Brown	Carleton Brown, ed., *Poems by Sir John Salusbury and Robert Chester*, 1914. (Contains a text of Robert Parry's Posies and Sonettos)
CC	Christ Church (Oxford), MS 184
cf.	compare
Daniel	Samuel Daniel, *Poems and "A Defense of Ryme,"* ed. A. C. Sprague (1952).
Diary	Robert Parry's "Diary," ed. A. Foulkes-Roberts, in *Archaelogia Cambrensis: Journal of the Cambrian Archaeologica Association*, Sixth Series, 15 (1915): 109–39.
ed.	edited (by) *or* edition
fol(s).	folio(s)
Foulkes-Roberts	see Diary above
Greene	Robert Greene, *Complete Works*, ed. A. B. Grosart, 14 vols. (1881–86).
Honigmann	E. A. J. Honigmann, *Shakespeare: The Lost Years* (1985).
Lodge	Thomas Lodge, *Rosalynde* (1590), in *The New Variorum As You Like It*, ed. Richard Knowles (1977).
Moderatus	Robert Parry, *Moderatus. The most delectable & famous Historie of the Blacke Knight* (1595). (See also Simons below.)
MS Diary	Manuscript of Robert Parry's Diary in the National Library of Wales (Plâs Nantglyn, MS 1)
Nashe	Thomas Nashe, *Works*, ed. R. B. McKerrow, 5 vols. (1904).
O	octavo (siglum for *Sinetes*, 1597)
OED	*Oxford English Dictionary*
Ovid	Ovid, *Metamorphoses*, ed. and trans. F. J. Miller, 2 vols. (1916).
Powys Fadog	*The History of the Princes, the Lords Marcher and the Ancient Nobility of Powys Fadog*, ed. J. Y. W. Lloyd, 6 vols. (1881–87).

Q	quarto (siglum for *Moderatus*, 1595)
RES	*Review of English Studies*
Ringler	William A. Ringler; see Sidney
Shakespeare	*The Riverside Shakespeare*, gen. ed., G. Blakemore Evans, 2nd ed. (1997).
Sidney	*The Poems of Sir Philip Sidney*, ed. W. A. Ringler (1962).
sig(s).	signature(s)
Simons	John Simons, ed., *Moderatus by Robert Parry* (2002). (Also see M*oderatus* above)
Sinetes	Robert Parry, *Sinetes Passions vppon his fortunes . . .* (1597).
Speed	John Speed, *The History of Great Britain* (1623).
STC	*Short Title Catalogue* (revised ed., 1976).
Stow	John Stow, *Annals or Summary of English Chronicles* (in editions from 1565 to 1615).
Tilley	M. P. Tilley, ed., *A Dictionary of the Proverbs in England in the Sixteenth and Seventeenth Centuries* (1950).

General Introduction

I. Robert Parry's Life and Times

Robert Parry, Gentleman, belonged to the Parrys of Tywyssog in the parish of Henllan, Denbighshire, Wales. His father, Harri ap Robert, who married Elin, the daughter of Rhys Wynn ap Gruffydd ap Madog Vychan of Fynnogion (she died, according to Robert Parry's Diary, 2 November 1595),[1] was the fourth and youngest son of Robert ap Ieuan of Berain, a descendant of the Tudors of Berain, and his wife, Elen, the daughter of John Lloyd Rosendale of Foxhall in the parish of Henllan. In his Diary, Robert Parry himself tells us that "This yere [1564] the 30 daye of Iulie betweene 3 & 4 a clocke in the morninge I *Robert Parry* was borne."[2] Of Parry's youth we know nothing, in part, perhaps, because his Diary shows a substantial gap from 1572 to about 1582. The earliest entries that reflect personal involvement begin to appear in 1582: an outbreak of the plague in Denbigh, a city near to where Parry then lived, the slaying of a cousin, Thomas Iervis, and on "The fyrst Lady daye [i.e., 15 August, the Feast of the Assumption] my sister Lowrie died wth a fall from a Ricke of haye & the same daye my sister Sabell was maried &c."

---

[1] Robert Parry's MS Diary in the National Library of Wales (Plâs Nantglyn MS 1), on loan from the late Lt.-Col. J.C. Wynne-Edwards, is made up of sixty folios (120 pages), written recto and verso. It is arranged chronologically by year (and regnal year), month, and, frequently, day, beginning "1558 / Ao. 2 Eliz" and ending with a scribal copy of a letter from "Sigismond kinge of Polonia & Sweden" dated "the twelf of ffebruarie . . . 1613." A. Foulkes-Roberts edited and published a generous selection of entries (mostly in Parry's holograph) in *Archaeologia Cambrensis, The Journal of the Cambrian Archaeological Association*, XV, Sixth Series (1915), 109–39 (hereafter referred to as "Diary," with page reference to Foulkes-Roberts' edition [all quotations have been checked against the manuscript] or, if the passage quoted is not in Foulkes-Roberts' edition, as "MS Diary" and page number). Almost all dates are derived from the Diary or MS Diary.

[2] Robert Parry, who was the youngest son, had three brothers: Thomas, whose wife Ionett, died 21 June 1593, less than a year after her marriage (November 1592), leaving him childless; Richard, who by his wife Blanch (married 1593), the daughter of Edward Thelwall (or Theloall) of Plâs y Ward, High Sheriff of Denbighshire for 1592, had five sons and two daughters, whose line carried on the family name (Diary, 119); and John, who was injured 1 June 1595 and died, without issue, 2 July of the same year (Diary, 120). Official records give Robert six sisters: Alis, Alis Wen, Grace, Margaret (died in October 1593 of the plague in London, Diary, 120), Jane, and Catherine (married in 1583 to Owen ap John Owen, who died in 1601 in London, Diary, 114, 125). Parry, however, as referred to below, mentions two other sisters, Lowri and Sabell (see note 3 below). For further information on Robert Parry's family, see *Powys Fadog*, VI, 430–37; Brown, xl–xlvii.

Curiously, although his Diary records many other family marriages, births, and deaths, Parry fails to mention either his wife's name or the date of his marriage. She was, we learn from *Powys Fadog* (VI, 432), Dorothy, the daughter of John Wynn Panton, who served as Recorder of Denbigh and borough representative in the Parliaments of 1597 and 1601.[3] Parry does, however, record the births of his two children: a daughter, Luce, born 7 April 1593, who married John Vaughan *alias* Foulkes of Moelewig Park near Denbigh, and was still living in 1633[4]; a son, Foulk: "The 10th of Iulie [1596] beinge Saterdaye 2 Howres afore daye ffoulk parry my sonne was borne & christned by ffoulke lloyd esqr & Ric parry my brother & Mrs Conwaye my aunt for godmother &c."[5] Foulk must have died young and childless, because when Robert Parry died Luce was recognized as his heir. On 28 June 1612, Robert's brother, Richard, made his will, leaving Robert, at the insistence of Mr. Justice Townshend, four pounds "towards redeeming his tenement" (i.e., land tenure), and, by "reversion," returning "lands bought of my brother Robert in Eriviat, Bodleye, Dorwen, Llanarth, and Garth Gynau."[6] The date of Robert Parry's death is not known, but the latest date in his Diary is 12 February 1613.

Although Robert Parry fails to tell us his wife's name, the poems in *Sinetes* (1597), through a number of acrostics, associate him with Helena Owen, most personally and closely, with Frances Willoughby, Elizabeth Wolfreston, and, probably indirectly, with Dorothy Halsall. Except for Dorothy Halsall, who was the sister-in-law of John Salusbury, Parry's patron, to whom he dedicated *Sinetes*,[7] none of these women can be definitely identified, nor, indeed, aside from Helena Owen's, do we know anything of the nature of their relations with Parry. Brown suggests that Frances Willoughby may be the runaway daughter of Sir Francis Willoughby of Wallaton Hall, Nottinghamshire,

[3] Thomas Nicholas, ed., *Annals and Antiquities of the Counties and County Families of Wales* (1872), 403. The two sisters (Lowri and Sabell) not mentioned in *Powys Fadog* (VI, 432) may have been sisters-in-law (i.e., sisters of Parry's wife, Dorothy); if so, then Parry's marriage must have taken place before 1582, when Parry turned eighteen, a marriage without children until a daughter, Luce, was born in 1592/3 – on the whole, probably an unlikely order of events.

[4] Diary, (Foulkes-Roberts' annotation), 137.

[5] Diary, 121. There was a Foulkes family associated with Eriviat where Robert Parry lived from at least 1595.

[6] Diary (Foulkes-Roberts' annotation), 137.

[7] For Dorothy Halsall, see Brown, xliv–xlvi, and the headnote to Posie I; for John Salusbury, see *Powys Fadog*, IV, 330–39; Brown, xi–xxvii; Honigmann, 90–113; and Introduction, 8–10.

but Elizabeth Wolfreston evades even conjectural identification.[8] So far as Helena Owen is concerned, she may perhaps be connected with that branch of the Owen family into which Catherine, Parry's sister, married in 1583.[9] In any case, Helena Owen occupies a much more individual, possibly even intimate, position than any of the other women whom he celebrates. Both Sonettos 1, 15–31 and "The lamentation of a Male-content" are addressed to her,[10] and almost certainly the forty-six Passions, even though they are addressed to two other women, the mysterious Willoughby and Wolfreston, are about his unrequited "love" for the fair Helena, fairer than Helen of Troy.

Robert Parry is, I believe, the only Elizabethan poet for whom a day-by-day, month-by-month, and year-by-year diary has survived, a personal/impersonal record of his life and times. That it is much more about his times than his life and that it gives no hint that he was a published writer both in prose and verse and fails to make any reference to other contemporary writers is, of course, disappointing. Nevertheless, the Diary shows him to have been a man of wide and varied interests, one who kept his finger on the pulse not only of local and family affairs but also of national and even Continental events.[11]

---

[8] Brown, xlii–xliv. Another mysterious and ambiguous acrostic turns up in Sonettos 4 and 5: "Salusburye Elanor."

[9] Diary, 114, 125. Occasional references in "The lamentation of a Male-content" can perhaps be interpreted to mean that Helena Owen was Parry's social superior. In the dedicatory Epistle prefacing "The lamentation," Parry addresses her as "the Honorable minded," calls her "Patronesse," and laments that "my fortunes being so far inferior to my thoughts" makes him "doubt the sequell [of his love petition]." And in "The lamentation" itself, he speaks of her as his "noble patronesse" (line 217) and refers to her "noble brest" (line 137) and "noble beauties race" (line 245).

[10] For the evidence supporting Parry's authorship (*pace* Brown) of these poems, see Introduction, 11–23.

[11] Parry's Diary is a curious mixture of (1) national, Irish, even Continental news, much of it extracted from John Stow's *Annals* (dates ranging from 1592 to 1605) or *Summary of English Chronicles* (dates ranging from 1565 to 1607); English sea exploration; state and related court documents, including scribal copies of such matters as James I's progress from Scotland to London after Elizabeth's death (including Thomas Percy's petition on the behalf of English Catholics); scribal copies of James's general and free pardon at his coronation and his first address to Parliament; translation of a Spanish letter recounting the death of Philip II (see Appendix II for a transcription); an account of the assassination of the French king, Henry IV; continual reports of the deportation or execution of seminary priests and their Roman Catholic sympathizers and protectors, etc.; (2) local events concerning Denbigh, town and county; (3) immediate family-related entries (marriages, births, deaths, etc.); and (4) a long (29 folios) and detailed account (holograph) of Parry's six-month tour of Switzerland, Italy, and France.

Although there is no certain record of Parry's attendance at either Oxford or Cambridge,[12] his published works and his Diary show him to have been liberally educated, well-grounded in classical Latin literature, with a command of the language, and easily familiar with Greek and Roman mythology. "H.P." (sig. A4^{v}), in his commendatory verses, calls him "learned Parrye," a distinction repeated in two of the Latin commendatory poems prefacing *Moderatus* (1595), Parry's chivalric romance. He inserts, for example, a number of marginal Latin notes in his Diary, is relieved to discover that two of his "hostes" in Switzerland speak "latten" (MS Diary, 26), and in *Moderatus, The most delectable and famous Historie of the Blacke Knight* (1595), his chivalric romance, which he calls "this treatise of fancie," quotes (in Latin) Virgil, Ovid, and Cicero. Equally important, however, is Parry's defence of English as a literary language, the equal of any other language, including Latin:

> . . . I, though none of those that are rapt vp (as it were) into the second firmament, with some inspiration of heauenly furie, whose writings be as well replenished with wisedome and learning as pollished with a very fine and eloquent method, of which sort (in this age) our English soyle yeeldeth manie that might chalenge *Cicero* (if he were liuing) to the Lystes, writing in their owne mother tongue, which language is growne nowe to be so copious, that it may compare with most of the richest tongues in all *Europe*, such is the carefull industrie of our Countrimen (who in mine opinion deserue due praises,) to amplifie the same.[13]

[12] The following entry in Joseph Foster's *Alumni Oxoniensis* (1888) may refer to our Robert Parry: "Robert Parry of Flint Gent. Balliol Coll. matric 2 November 1582 aged 19. B. A. from St. Mary Hall 28 June 1588." Allowing for some possible confusion arising out of regnal and old and new style dating, our Parry would have been in his nineteenth year at matriculation in 1582—a concurrence of dates, since he was born in July of 1564. The principal catch, however, is that this Robert is described as "of Flint" rather than as "of Denbigh," the county, bordering on Flint, in which our Parry appears to have been born and bred. However, the commendatory poems (six in Latin and one in Greek) that preface *Moderatus* (1595; sigs. A3^{v}–A4^{v}), Parry's chivalric romance (see Introduction, 28–34), strongly suggest some kind of academic or Inns of Court connection. One of these poems, signed "Th. P." may be by Parry's brother, Thomas, and another, signed "H.T.," by Henry Townshend, to whom the book is dedicated.

[13] *Moderatus*, sig. A3. Parry's praise of English as a literary language worthy of attention echoes Richard Mulcaster's *Elementarie* (1582), which, in addition, strongly criticizes Elizabethan schools for failing to train students in the use of syntactic English, sacrificing

As a landed gentleman, Robert Parry had no need to pursue any particular calling, but he shows an informed interest in law and may, perhaps, have had some connexion with one of the Inns of Court, as so many country gentlemen then did. In any case, he was closely associated with Henry Townshend, "one of her Maiesties Iustices of Assise of the Countie Pallatine of Chester, and one of her Highnesse honourable Counsell, established in the marches and principality of Wales," to whom he dedicated "these first fruits of my simple trauels," *Moderatus* (1595), describing him, in a two-page "Epistle Dedicatorie," as "his singular good Master," to whom he owes "so many fauors," and himself as "Your Worsh. most bounden seruant." Then, in 1599 (about September or November), his Diary notes: "I brought the p^{r}vie Counsells l'r'rs [i.e., letters] purportinge the Queens commandement vnto my Mr Mr Iustice Townshend to supplie his place [i.e., the position then occupied by Sir Richard Shuttleworth, Justice of Chester, who was either dead or dying]."[14] Some years earlier (1587) Parry had been appointed by the Queen as one of twenty-five capital burgesses for the borough of Denbigh.[15]

Parry must have had substantial private means. In 1599, for example, "The thyrde daye of Ianuarie I had po*essio*n in the landes wch I bought of m^{r} Will*ia*m Myddelton in Eriviatt & bodeliog."[16] And he records several trips to London, the first visit probably in 1584, the second in 1588. There he appears to have mingled in somewhat aristocratic company, probably because of his apparently close association with his patron, John Salusbury, Esq. (later, Sir John), who, as he tells us in the dedicatory Epistle to *Sinetes* (1597), was appointed

---

too early their native language to Latin, a complaint later repeated by John Brinsley in *Ludus Literarius, or The Grammer Schoole* (1612), a sacrifice that Parry apparently escaped. For a list of Parry's use of new and rare words, see Introduction, **26–28**.

[14] Diary, 123. Parry's interest in, and knowledge of, legal matters is further suggested by his account (not taken from Stow), employing technical legal terms, of the trial of Edward Morgan, a Welshman, who, in May of 1605, killed John Egerton, the challenger, in a duel with short swords: "Morgan was brought to his triall to the Kinges benche on teusdaye the 12 of Iune graced wth the Compeny of the L. Walden sonne & heyre to the L. Chamberlaine & two or three other Lordes wth 500 welshmen most of the Innes of Coorte" (Diary, 132). (Was Parry perhaps among them?) The trial was postponed, but Morgan was later found guilty of murder, though pardoned by King James. It is also, perhaps, significant that Parry twice notes that Michaelmas term of the High Court of Justice was held out of London, in 1583 at Hartford and in 1593 at St. Albans. In *Moderatus* (sig. K2^{v}) he quotes (in Latin) a "Maxime in the Ciuill lawe."

[15] See John W. Williams, ed., *Ancient and Modern Denbigh* (1856), 121.

[16] Diary, 123.

"Esquier for the Bodie to the Queenes most excellent Maiestie" in March of 1595 and was later knighted by the Queen in June of 1601.[17] Parry's association with Salusbury and his circle must have begun some time before 1591, the year in which Salusbury's mother, the widely-known and much married Catherine of Berain, died, for whom he, among a number of others, wrote a long "Epitath" (*sic*) in jogging fourteeners.[18] Parry was in attendance at Court in 1593: "This was a yere of great sicknes [i.e., plague] in london so that my self beinge at the Coorte at Wynsor vpon a sondaye the bill*es* that weeke were nineteene [score *crossed through*] hundred fewe townes in England were free this yere. So that mychaelmas terme was kept at S^{ct} Albones."[19] On 6 (Stow says "8") of February 1601, Parry was again in London, and witnessed the Essex rebellion ("I haurd hym proclaymed traytor by Temple barr in ffleet street . . .").[20]

About a year earlier (1599), Parry had set off on what he calls his "Iter in Italia": "In ffebruarie I Robert parry traveled beyond the seas to Italie & retorned agayne wthin sixe monethes &c the true discourse of Iorney I have here sett downe."[21] Parry was accompanied by two friends, Thomas Parton and William Lloyd, and two servants, one of whom became ill and had to return to England shortly after reaching the Continent. Before setting out, however, Parry and Parton applied jointly for, and received, what Parry terms a "lycence" for foreign travel from Sir Robert Cecil, Secretary of State.[22] This license "lycencd [them] to travell into foreyn p*ar*tes in amitie wth her ma^{tie} only to atteyne langueges, thereby the better to enhable themselves to doe theire Contrey service thereafter."[23] The license then orders all officials, from constables to ambassadors, to protect and give them all aid both before embarking and when abroad.

---

[17] Diary, 125.

[18] In Christ Church MS 184, fols. 179–180^{v}; the poem is transcribed in Appendix I.

[19] Diary, 120.

[20] Diary, 125. Foulkes-Roberts transcribes less than half of Parry's first-hand account of the Essex rebellion; the full text may be found in Appendix II.

[21] Diary, 124. The "true discourse" occupies 59 pages (fols. 21–50) in Parry's hand, recto and verso. Foulkes-Roberts transcribes almost nothing from the MS Diary account.

[22] The "lycence" is dated "at Richmond the viith of ffeb: 1599" (see MS Diary, 21). How important it was to procure such a license is shown by what happened to the Earl of Arundell, who was imprisoned in the Tower (25 April 1585) "for attemptinge to dep*arte* out of the land wthout lycence"; on 17 May 1586, he was "condemned in the Starrchamber to paye 10000^{li} fyne for his Contempte & to remayne in prison at the Queens pleasure" (Diary, 115–16).

[23] MS Diary, 21.

Sailing from Dover, they landed at "Cales" on 22 February only to discover that their planned route south through France had to be abandoned because of plague in "Savoye & Pimont," thus making their approach to Italy through Switzerland necessary, because, as Parry tells us, "the Italians are very curious & circumspect in receavinge any strayngers into theire Contreyes wthout Bulletynes wch could not be had but in places free from, disseases the meanynge wherof in place more apte I will declare for that I nothinge doubt but that this worde bulletyne is straynge to our nation especially those that have not travelled in foren contryes."[24] Parry was right! The earliest citation of "this worde" in any sense in the *OED* is 1645.

We may now leave Parry and his friends launched on their Italian "Iorney." His account, written strictly in plain style, offers nothing that sheds further light on Parry as a writer, however interesting it might be to social historians, to whom it appears to be unknown. Parry tells us, often in some detail, what he is told and sees, particularly in Florence, Rome, and Venice, and, homeward bound, in Paris, but rarely what he feels, except to express wonder and admiration or annoyance with poor lodgings.

One further important aspect of Parry's life that finds a reflection in his Diary deserves some notice: his religious position. The second half of the sixteenth century in England was a period in which a person's religious affiliations could be a matter of life or death. Three choices faced someone like Parry: accept the state church, the Protestant Anglican establishment, in many ways a middle ground between the other two, the old Catholicism most probably that of his parents, or the newly emerging and already influential fundamentalist extreme Protestantism of the several Puritan sects. Whatever his inner leanings, Parry's choice was almost certainly influenced by his "apprenticeship" to Henry Townshend and the justice system and by his close association with John Salusbury, his patron, who, in order to achieve a profitable position at court, had to emphasize his Anglican adherence to offset the dangerous implications of the fact that his elder brother, Thomas, had been executed for his role in the Babington Plot (1586) to murder Queen Elizabeth.[25] Whether Parry's apparent acceptance of the Anglican establishment was personal or more or less politic, we may never know, but there is some evidence in his Diary that he was personally disturbed by the harsh and deadly measures

---

24 MS Diary, 22. Parry's comment about "bulletyne" may, perhaps, suggest that he had visited the continent at an earlier date (see Introduction, **29**).

25 See Introduction, 8.

used by the government against Catholics and Catholic sympathizers. The large number of entries throughout the Diary memorializing their execution or, occasionally, deportation, would seem best explained as genuinely sympathetic, if unstated, concern. Indeed, on two occasions he, unguardedly perhaps, allows such personal feeling to escape: (1) he refers to a Catholic priest, William Day, who had been executed in Anglesey, as having been "martired"; and (2) apparently witnessing the execution of an avowed Catholic, he contrasts his death with that of some "heretickes" (i.e., Puritans): he died "very resolutly his face vncov*er*ed wth a most myld & sweet countenaunce wheare the other [i.e., the "heretickes"], beinge dead dyd looke most horrible & vgly."[26] Nor, when in Rome, does Parry give vent to what might be called Protestant comments when he is shown such reliques as "a great piece" of the true cross, the spear that pierced Christ's side on that cross (and the resulting blood and water that issued from the wound), the table used at the Last Supper, the first shirt the Virgin Mary made for Jesus, or the two pillars that upheld the veil of Solomon's temple and the veil that was "rented" when Christ was crucified.[27]

Several aspects of Parry's personal and literary association with John Salusbury (created Sir John in 1601) have already been touched on, but considering his position as Parry's patron, to whom he dedicated *Sinetes* and the central figure in the opening dedicatory Epistle as well as in the so-called Patron-series (a part of the Posies), in both of which Parry paints Salusbury in almost heroic terms, a more focused account of his life may be helpful in filling out the larger picture of Parry's own life and times.

John Salusbury of Lleweni, Esq., known as "The Strong," was born in 1566. He was descended from Adam de Salzburgh, who came to England with William the Conqueror. Edward I granted Adam's great great grandson, Sir Henry Salusbury, the estate of Lleweni, formerly a hunting seat of the Prince of Wales. Many generations later our John Salusbury became heir to Lleweni when his elder brother, Thomas Salusbury, an ardent Roman Catholic, was executed in 1586 for his role in the Babington Plot, which aimed to assassinate Queen Elizabeth and, through rebellion, place Mary, Queen of Scots, on the throne.[28]

---

[26] Diary, 119; MS Diary, 101 (see Appendix for the full text). In this connection it may be recalled that Parry includes a scribal transcript of Thomas Percy's "peticōn in the behalf of the Catholiques of Englande," which was "p*re*ferred to the kinges mat^ie^ at Yorke or Berwicke," when James I, after Queen Elizabeth's death, was coming from Scotland to London in 1603 (MS Diary, 60–63).

[27] MS Diary, 45.

[28] This brief account of John Salusbury is drawn from *Powys Fadog*, IV (1884), 330–39; Brown, xi–xxvii; Honigmann, 90–113.

Comparatively little is known of John Salusbury's early years. His father, another John Salusbury, probably died before his son's birth, and his mother, the beautiful and much elegized Catherine of Berain, remarried three times before her death in 1591. Robert Parry's "Epitath" (Other Poems, 309–13), one among many, evidences such an easy familiarity with her extended marital relations (and their offspring) that Parry, and probably his brother Richard, had already been among Salusbury's circle of adulatory "friends" somewhat earlier than 1591, even though the report of her death marks the first reference to the Salusbury family in his Diary. In his own marriage, Salusbury acted with what may have been a measure of social foresight by marrying Ursula Stanley, the natural (but acknowledged) daughter of Henry Stanley, fourth Earl of Derby, by Jane Halsall.[29]

Salusbury, at the age of fourteen, matriculated at Jesus College, Oxford, in 1581, although there is no record that he remained there long enough to receive a degree. And, like so many country gentlemen who wished to become active in local and national politics, he was admitted as a student of the Inner Temple in March of 1594–95, where he might pick up some rudimentary training in the law. Then, in the same month, having apparently sufficiently reassured the government, despite his brother's earlier execution for treason, that he was a staunch and vocal adherent of the Church of England, he was "sworne the Queens man as squir for the bodye," and in June 1601, he "beinge before sworne to be the Queens man was by her ma^{tie} knighted."[30] In 1597 Salusbury had been appointed Deputy Lieutenant for the county of Denbigh by the Privy Council, and in 1601, he (now Sir John) was elected to represent the county of Denbigh in the Parliament of 1601 as Knight of the Shire together with John Panton as borough representative, who, it will be recalled, was the father of Robert Parry's wife. It was, indeed, a small and tight-knit world!

With the death of Queen Elizabeth, Sir John's political fortunes declined sharply and finally. King James, whose mind had been poisoned against him by a powerful pro-Catholic faction, refused Salusbury any court appointment and, in ill health and financially embarrassed, he was forced to retire to country living at Lleweni, where he died on 24 July 1612.

A word must be said about Sir John's real-life character, if only somewhat to balance the kind of fulsome praise lavished on him by Parry in *Sinetes* as well as by other "admirers," praise that he would appear to have eaten up with great relish.[31] According to his enemies (and he seems to have generated a number of

[29] On the Halsall connection, see Introduction, 2.

[30] Diary, 120, 125.

[31] See Introduction, 13, 18.

powerful ones), he had the reputation of one who "cannot be pleased except he rule the country, and judges and justices also."[32] He was aggressive and litigious, with some touch of violence if crossed, but, as E. A. J. Honigmann suggests, probably no more so than his enemies, personal and political.[33]

Finally, two more small links between the Parry and Salusbury families. In making his will on 24 June 1613, Richard Parry, Robert's brother, devotes a paragraph listing various debts that the "late deceased" Sir John Salusbury owed him. Among others he notes: ". . . where also I lent my lady his wife, by the hands of my brother Robert Parry, the sum of five pounds as by her letter may appear."[34] This may suggest, perhaps, that Robert Parry's connection with the Salusburys was more personal and intimate than his brother's. The second link, of uncertain date, would have, if Parry were then still alive, doubtless greatly pleased him: the marriage of Richard Parry's eldest son, John, with Oriana Salusbury, the daughter of Sir John.[35]

II. *SINETES Passions vppon his fortunes (1597): a question of authorship*

Before we turn to consider Robert Parry's position among other Elizabethan poets, an important question needs to be faced and so far as possible answered. Although neither the title-page of *Sinetes* (1597) nor two subtitles mention any author other than Robert Parry, Carleton Brown in his edition of Sir John Salusbury's poems (1914) argues that all but one ("Posie IIII") of what may be called the Patron-series, including the seven other Posies, all of the thirty-one Sonettos, and, perhaps, "The lamentation of a Male-content," which Brown claims "In tone as well as theme . . . resembles much of Salusbury's verse," are, in fact, by Salusbury, Parry's patron, to whom *Sinetes* is dedicated.[36] Brown would thus reduce Parry's part in the volume to the dedicatory Epistle, the forty-six Passions, Posie IIII, and "Sinetes Dumpe."

---

[32] Quoted by Honigmann, 97.

[33] Honigmann, 97.

[34] Quoted by Honigmann, 111.

[35] *Powys Fadog*, VI (1887), 433, but *Powys Fadog*, IV, 336, gives Oriana's name as Uricina. Oriana is the name of a character in the chivalric romance *Amadis de Gaulle*.

[36] Brown, xl–xlvii. Brown reprints the Posies and Sonettos without commentary (47–78).

Brown draws upon two kinds of evidence to substantiate his claim for the Salusbury attributions. First, the title-page, the second division of which reads:

The Patrons patheticall Po-
sies, Sonets, Maddrigals, and
Rowndelayes. Together with
Sinetes Dompe.
Plena verecundi culpa pudoris erit.
By Robert Parry
Gent.

Brown interprets the wording here to mean that the poems there listed, except "Sinetes Dompe," were written by "The Patron," John Salusbury. Many years earlier, Alexander Grosart, in his New Shakspere Society edition (1878) of Robert Chester's *Loves Martyr* (1601), a volume also dedicated to Salusbury, wisely comments that the title-page statement "is somewhat ambiguous, for one is left in doubt whether the "patheticall Posies, Sonets, Maddrigals, and Rowndelayes" are Salisburie's, as his production, or by gift of Parry."[37] He then moots the possibility, which he admits is improbable, that the Patron-series, at least, may be by Salusbury.

Second, noting Grosart's tentative suggestion, Brown comments: "Had he recognized the acrostics which they contain his joy would have been full, for these supply positive proof of Salusbury's authorship."[38] The acrostics to which Brown refers may be found in Posies I–IV, VI, and VIII, in which the name DOROTHY HALSALL, Salusbury's sister-in-law, is spelled out (see the commentary headnote to each poem). Posie IIII, which Brown allows to be by Parry, is an extremely elaborate example of acrostic fever and contains not only Dorothy Halsall's name but four other names: (1) IOHN SALESBURY; (2) FRANSIS WILOWBI; (3) ELIZABETH WOLFRESTONE; and (4) ROBERT PARRYE. The last three names also appear as acrostics in Parry's Passions (see commentary headnote to Passion I and Brown, xlii–xlvi).

Brown then considers the thirty-one Sonettos, which follow the Posies in *Sinetes*, and argues that they too should be attributed to Salusbury. Again he appeals to the front title-page and to acrostics, though none of the names connected with the Passions or the Posies, except that of Salusbury, recurs in

[37] Grosart, ed., *Loves Martyr*, xvii.
[38] Brown, xliv–xlv.

the Sonettos. He concludes that the acrostic in Sonetto 3 (i.e., IS HIS VALENTINE) furnishes proof of Salusbury's authorship, but the two other names that appear (SALVSBVRYE ELANOR) in Sonettos 4 and 5 and HELENA OWEN in Sonettos 16–18, he is unable to relate to either the Salusbury or the Parry circles.

In building his case for Salusbury's authorship of the Sonettos, Brown curiously fails to notice what is surely an important difference distinguishing Sonettos 2–14 that might be interpreted to support their attribution to Salusbury: a capital "S" is appended below the last line of each of these sonettos. This distinctive "S" can only be explained in one of two ways: (1) Sonettos 2–14 (hereafter referred to as the S-Sonettos) are indeed by Salusbury; or (2) they were written by Parry for Salusbury. These alternatives will have to be examined later.

I have now, I believe, fairly stated Carleton Brown's case for assigning substantial parts of *Sinetes* to John Salusbury. My view of the authorship question is significantly different and is based on both external evidence (i.e., the front title-page and the capital "S" appended to each of the Sonettos 2–14) and a large body of internal evidence (i.e., statements of intent and verbal and thematic echoes) linking poems that Brown attributes to Salusbury with Parry's unchallenged work: the opening dedicatory Epistle, the Passions, and "Sinetes Dumpe"; *Moderatus, The Most Delectable & Famous Historie of the BLACKE Knight* (1595); and "The Epitath [*sic*] of mistris Katheryn Theloall" (1591), preserved in CC, fols. 179–180^{v}, a manuscript closely associated with the Salusbury circle. My view, as it will be developed in the discussion that follows, thus reclaims for Parry the Patron-series and the other seven Posies, Sonettos 1–31, with the other poems preceding "Sinetes Dumpe," and "The lamentation of a Male-content," a poem at least questioned by Brown.

Before the evidence supporting the case against Brown's Salusbury hypothesis is considered in detail, there is room, perhaps, for what might be called a commonsense observation: Is it not, indeed, quite aside from any evidence pro or con, seriously threatening the bounds of credibility to postulate the publication of a book under a single author's name, of which something in the range of one third, essentially unacknowledged, is by a second hand, particularly when the identity of that other hand is the same as that of the person to whom the volume is dedicated?[39]

[39] Professor Steven May suggests (privately) that the absence of any reference to Salusbury as part author or collaborator in the seven commendatory poems (sigs. A3^{v}–A7) may be taken to indicate that Salusbury had made no significant contribution to *Sinetes*.

Parry makes three statements about the intentions underlying his publication of *Sinetes*: (1) in the top division of the title-page, he tells us that his "Passions vppon his fortunes" are "offered for an Incense at the / shrine of the Ladies which gui- / ded his distempered / thoughtes"; (2) in the opening dedicatory Epistle, he promises that Salusbury will gain lasting honor and immortal fame from what is said about him in *Sinetes*; (3) in the dedicatory Epistle prefacing "The lamentation of a Male-content," he announces that "the Name-lesse" (i.e., Parry) is writing the poem to wish "*the Honorable minded* vnknowne" (who will shortly be identified as Helena Owen) "perfect health and / perpetuall happines." The second and third statements will prove to be important in helping to establish Parry's authorship of the Posies, Sonettos, and "The lamentation of a Male-content."

In the opening dedicatory Epistle, Parry claims that Salusbury will gain a kind of immortality through the publication of *Sinetes*: Parry's "breathing Muse . . . vowed hath, to manifest thy worth, / That noble fruites to future age bringes foorth" (lines 7, 11–12); and later he proclaims (lines 37–46):

> Tis only that, which thou mayst clayme thine owne,
> Deuouring time, cannot obscure the same [i.e., fame],
> In future age by this [i.e., "my rime"] thou mayst be knowne,
> When as posterities renue thy fame:
> Then thou being dead, shalt lyfe a newe possesse,
> When workes nor wordes, thy worthynes expresse.
>   Then shall my rime a fort of strength remaine,
> To shielde the florish of thy high renowne,
> That ruin's force may neu'r graces stain,
> Which with fames sound, shall through the worlde bee blowne: . . .

The Patron-series in the Posies is the only part of *Sinetes* in which Salusbury is held up to us as an icon for the ages. If, then, as Brown argues we should, we assign the authorship of the Patron-series, except for Posie IIII, to Salusbury, how can we account for Parry's lavish, if conventional, promises to Salusbury in the dedicatory Epistle? That we can't is manifestly borne out by further examination of the Posies, using, however, a different kind of internal evidence.

"Posie I. The patrones conceyte" offers clear evidence of Parry's hand, furnishing thematic and verbal echoes, a number of them what may be called distinctive Parryisms, from *Moderatus* (1595) and the poems unchallenged by Brown, as well as from some of the other Posies, Sonettos 1–31, and "The lamentation of a Malecontent," all of which will later be shown to be unquestionably by Parry.

Line:	
2 Heau'ns erected trophies of thy prayes [this unusual spelling of "praise" also appears in Parry's "Epitath" in CC, 90]	Male-content, 57: The Gods built vp a trophie of renowne
3–4 Aurora / blush / smile / shine	Posie IIII.78: Aurora's blush that decks thy smile Sonetto 16.5: Auroras shine doth blush to see her grace *Moderatus*, sig. K1: Auroraes first blush
5 Natures chiefe pride	Posie IIII.33: Natures pride *Moderatus*, sig. B1: the verie pride of Nature *Moderatus*, sig. R2: the pride of Nature
5 beauties grace	Posie IIII.1: beauties grace Sonetto 17.3: beauties grace Sonetto 31.12: beauties grace
13, 17–18 Adon / ardent / Venus / loue [implied]	Posie IIII.15–17: Adon / Venus / ardent loue Sonetto 23.10: ardencie of loue *Moderatus*, sig. M1: ardent and loyall loue
15–16 eies . . . doe hide a bayted hooke: / Which doth intrap by force of Goulden hue	Sonetto 17.8: bayted hooke Male-content, 199: bayted hooke *Moderatus*, sigs. L1–L1v: Beautie alone . . . [is] but a pleasant bayte to intrappe the minde . . . [is] of great force to procure loue . . . would with that glorious hewe and fading gloze vanish away *Moderatus* sig. M2: Vnder a baite doeth hide a hydeous hooke
20 shining beam's doe light the westerne Isle	Posie IX.13: Phoebus drawe his shining beam's away Male-content, 48: for to light this Isle set out this lampe *Moderatus*, sig. G3: Cupid . . . / Whose shining beames doeth plainly show
22 stealing time	Passion XXII.19: stealing time Dedicatory Epistle, 49: steling tyme

Line:	
23 breath so doth perfume the ayre	Posie IIII.13: Touch of breath perfumes the same (i.e., her "fayrest frame") Male-content, 106: sweete bed, perfum'd by her sweete breath
25 purest die	Posie IX.25: purest Indian die Male-content, 86: purest die on earth
26 With honours Equipage long liue thy fame	Sonetto 27.2: hope doth march with honours equipage Sonetto 11.12: March wee must with swiftest Equipage
27 Christall skie	Posie IIII.47: Christall skie *Moderatus*, sig.B2ᵛ: Christall skie
31 earth's possessed wonder	Posie XII.5: worldes faire admiring wonder
33 Ioves loue that kills with thunder	Posie XII.6: Ioves loue that kills with thunder
34 Thy memorie her beautie doth deface	Posie IIII.36: Helens beautie is defac'd
37 Ympe graft with vertue	Posie IIII.55: Ympe with natures vertue graft Epitath, 36 (in CC): frutfull Impes, in vertues soyle that plantes
48 match-lesse Paragone	*Moderatus*, sig. R2: matchlesse Parragon Epitath, 21 (in CC): pearlesse paragones

Some of the above parallels are, or course, common coin of the period, but their frequency in other Parry poems lends some corroborative weight to those parallels that are idiosyncratic or distinctive Parryisms (see lines 2, 5, 23, 26, 31, 33, 34, 37). Moreover, none of these parallels, commonplace or distinctive, appears in what may be considered Salusbury's few extant poems.[40] And who but Parry himself, for the most part unconsciously, would be capable of pillaging his own work, in verse and prose, so over-generously?

If we now examine "Posie IIII. The Patrons Pauze in ode," the only one of the Posies that Brown allows to be Parry's, we can see how characteristic of Parry such self-plagiarism, as in Posie I, frequently is. Parallels common to Posie IIII and Posie I, already noted above, have not been included.

[40] See Brown, 3–43.

Line:	
16 sweetest flower	Sonetto 1.6: sweetest flowers
21 Hope of our time	Dedicatory Epistle, 1: Hope of these, and glasse of future times
30 newe-spronge woe	Passion XV.1: new-sprong charge Passion XXVIII.18: New-sprong effects Passion XLI.15: thy woes are sprong
31 Tuned notes of care I sing	Passion XXV.21: tune your trebled notes of care Passion XXXIII.20: naught can tune but solemne notes of care Dedicatory Epistle, 26: And tun'd the note
45–46 Resting by the siluer streame, / Tossing nature seame by seame	*Moderatus*, sig. G3^{v}: Fishes swamme in siluer streame, / And I vnripped seame by seame
50–51 Hayre of Amber, fresh of hue, / Wau'd with goulden wyers newe	*Moderatus*, sig. B2^{v}: Her Amber hayres with wyers of golde *Moderatus*, sig. H1^{v}: His amber lockes so gaily twyn'd / like crysped wyers of golde
52–53 Riches of the finest mould, / Rarest glorie to behould	*Moderatus*, sig. G3^{v}: Circumstance of natures mould, / Which rare seemed to behold
62 Queene desier	*Moderatus*, sigs. D2^{v}, G2^{v}, H1^{v}, H4: Queene desire
73 deck'd with honours worth	Dedicatory Epistle, 32: honours worth, may reape a due rewarde *Moderatus*, sig. G2^{v}: WHo aymes at honours worthy name
80 Where curious thoughts built the nest	*Moderatus*, sig. C4^{v}: In whose high thoughtes I wish to builde my nest *Moderatus*, sig. L3: Loue in my secret thought hath built his nest

If Posie I and Posie IIII have, credibly, been shown to come from Parry's pen, it would strongly suggest that all the Patron-series should be attributed to Parry. And, indeed, all but one of them, short as most of them are, afford us one or more Parryisms. In "Posie II. The Patrone's affection," compare "Launterne of loue . . . / Light some beame my affection to guide" (lines 1–2), the "Launterne" metaphor being picked up from the "Lampe" image in the next to last line of Posie I, with Passion XI.1, "O lampe that guides"; with Posie I.20, "Whose shining beam's doe light"; and with *Moderatus*, sigs. 2A3 and R2, "lanthorne of true and perfect nobilitie"; sig. F1, "lantherne of perfect nobilitie, beautie, and vertue"; and sig. X2^{v}, "lanterne of vertue." In "Posie III. The patrones phantasie," compare "I yeilde to fate, and welcome endles Smart" (line 8) with Passion XXXVII.24, "Inforst by time, to end my endlesse harme." In "Posie VI. The patrones Dilemma" (i.e., between hope and despair), compare with *Moderatus*, sig. F4: "euerie sigh ministring a thousand doubtfull Dilemmas . . . thus bathing him selfe in a sea of confused thoughtes, betweene hope and despaire he rested speechless"; *Moderatus*, sig. Cl^{v}: "*Priscus* a verie long time houered betweene hope and despaire"; and *Moderatus*, sig. R2^{v}, "resting in a *Dilemma* betweene feare and hope"; "th' emperiall skie" (line 4) with "The lamentation of a Male-content," 54, "th[e em]pire skie"; and "The Topas chast . . . / The Lupinar hath not more chast affects" (lines 13, 21) with *Moderatus*, sig. E2^{v}, "if you haue not the vertue to be chaste, carrie about you the hearbe *Lupinar*, or the *Topaze* stone, which cooleth desire." Posie VIII offers no distinctive Parry clue, but, in its eight lines, it contains four Parry commonplaces not occurring in Salusbury's acknowledged verse: "loues desire," "quench my fire," "salue the sore" ("salue," as here, being associated with "cherish" in Passion XXXIII), and "feruant zeale." Even more extensive verbal and thematic parallels can be cited, a significant number of which may be termed distinctive Parryisms, in the other seven Posies, making it clear that all the Posies should be attributed to Robert Parry.

Carleton Brown's use of the Dorothy Halsall acrostics as evidence of Salusbury's hand in the Posies requires further comment. Since Dorothy Halsall was John Salusbury's sister-in-law, any relationship of even a comparatively intimate nature with Parry would seem not only unlikely but dangerous given Salusbury's position as both social superior and patron. If, however, we see Parry's role as a kind of poet-in-waiting or ghostwriter, as John Klause has suggested,[41] to Salusbury, Parry's authorship of the Posies (and, as we shall see, of Sonettos 1–31) is explained and the Posies become eulogistic gifts honoring Salusbury's apparently not so secret relations with Dorothy Halsall. If this sounds farfetched, one has only to consider a manuscript collection of poems now preserved in the library of Christ Church, Oxford (MS 184) to recognize that Salusbury was surrounded by a small bevy of admirers, some of whom may probably be described as flattering patronage seekers. In MS 184, six persons offer poems in praise of Salusbury, and five others (including Parry) write elegies lamenting the death, in 1591, of Salusbury's mother, the celebrated Catherine of Berain. Among the first six, the name of Robert Chester is particularly prominent. He is responsible for at least eight poems, among which three contain acrostics naming Dorothy Halsall, and a fourth, a longer poem almost as acrostically sophisticated as Parry's Posie IIII, contains the names of Dorothy Halsall and John Salusbury. Like Parry, Chester sought the patronage of Salusbury and dedicated his long, confusedly wandering, and enigmatic poem *Loves Martyr* (1601) to him. Some lines from a Christmas poem by Chester and addressed to Salusbury suggest the kind of social atmosphere out of which Parry's Posies arose:

> In signe of honor and obedience
> to the whight Lyon of Arcadia [i.e., Salusbury]
> that doth defend our liues from ravenous beares
> and feeds vs with the pray that he persues

[41] In "*The Phoenix and Turtle* in Its Time," *In the Company of Shakespeare: Essays in Honor of G. Blakemore Evans*, ed. Thomas Moisan and Douglas Bruster (2002), 214–15, John Klause suggests that Parry and Chester may have been ghostwriters for Salusbury and that Thomas Dekker in *Satiromastix* (1601) satirizes Salusbury in the character of a Welshman, Sir Vaughan ap Rees, who hires Horace (i.e., Ben Jonson) to write verses for him to use in his wooing of the widow, Mistress Miniver. (Salusbury's maternal grandfather was Tudor ap Robert Vychan [Vychan is a variant form of Vaughan]; see also Brown, xiii.) That such ghostwriting was a not uncommon practice is amusingly reported in the anonymous *The Penniless Parliament of Thread-bare Poets* (1608), reprinted in modernized spelling in *The Old Book Collectors' Miscellany*, ed., Charles Hindley (1872), II, 13: 27.

> Moreover, for the further increase of foolish humours, we do establish and set down, that fantastic devices shall prove most excellent [referring, perhaps, to anagrams and acrostics] and some shall so long devise for other men, that they will become barren themselves; some shall devise novelties to their own shames, and some snares to entrap themselves with.

A homely cuntry hornepipe we will daunce
A sheapheards prety Gigg to make him sport
and sing A madringall or roundelay
to please *our* Lordlike sheapheard lord of vs
take hands take hands *our* hartes lett vs Advaunce
and strive to please his hum*our* with A daunce.[42]

The Parry/Chester analogy lends some weight to viewing the so-called S-Sonneto series (2–14), like the Dorothy Halsall acrostics written by Chester mentioned above, as complimentary verses composed by Parry for use by Salusbury in his presumably amorous pursuit of Dorothy. Such a view is very strongly supported—and I believe proved—by the substantial number of thematic and verbal parallels between the S-Sonettos and what is certainly Parry's work in both *Sinetes* and *Moderatus*, at least seven of them characteristically distinctive Parryisms; and by the absence in the S-Sonettos of any such significant parallels in the poems assigned to Salusbury in Christ Church MS 184, a collection that constitutes his known corpus. These parallels occur in ten of the thirteen S-Sonettos:[43]

Sonetto	
2.17 Farewell long stay for winde to fill the sayle	Passion XXVI.2: Whole armies of reproches fill my sayle. *Moderatus*, sig. O1: yet sayled in effecting his desire [all three uses are metaphorical]
3.13–14 So shall my muse your name ay coronize, / I will it blaze to all posterities	Dedicatory Epistle, 39–40: In future age by this thou mayst be knowne, / When as posterities renue thy fame
4.6 Enforced loue dislikes which is not meete	Sonetto 31.1: I Loue enforst by loues vnlouing charmes

[42] CC, fol. 46v; Brown, 20 (No. XII, lines 19–28).

[43] The S-Sonettos generally employ, in fourteen-lines, a rhyme scheme that limits the number of rhyme words to five (i.e., a/b/a/b/b/c/b/c/c/d/c/d/e/e); Sonettos 1 and 15–31 generally use, in fourteen-lines, a rhyme scheme with seven rhyme words (i.e., a/b/a/b/c/d/c/d/e/f/e/f/g/g). The S-Sonetto rhyme scheme does not appear in Salusbury's verses in CC where he usually writes in rhymed couplets.

Sonetto	
4.7 Equalitie of loue doth neuer paine	*Moderatus*, sig. C1: So, as nothing is to be respected in amitie and friendship, more then equitie *Moderatus*, sig. H3: And others cryed for equality [in love] *Moderatus*, sig. K4^{v}: true and perfect loue can not bee but betweene equales
5.11 Bearing in my heart the wish of heartie deede.	Posie V.1–2: The wound of hart . . . / And sighes doe oft report my hartie sore [both with play on "heart"]
5.13 Vnspotted trust and truth ty'd to the same	*Moderatus*, sig. T3^{v}: a faithfull and vnspotted league of true and perfect friendship *Moderatus*, sig. T3^{v}: so perfect a map of pure and vnspotted loyalty *Moderatus*, sig. N3: proceeding rather of lust, then of any pure and vnspotted loue
7.1–2 Marching in the plaine field of my conceyte, / I might behold a tent which was at rest	*Moderatus* sig. M1: affection is Generall of the field, there alwayes either Plentie pitcheth his pauilion [both use a tent metaphor]
8.7 To fancies hest thou art a stately chaire	Passion IIII.20: Your gentle brests is mercies chaire of state *Moderatus*, sig. H2^{v}: he vaunc'd him selfe, / vnto a stately throne
8.9 More bright then sun thou stand'st in window bay	*Moderatus*, sig. F2: *Cornelius* standing in a Bay window [both, like the following, surveying a flower garden] *Moderatus*, sig. F2^{v}: my selfe stood heere in this windowe, viewing . . . this delightfull and pleasant garden

We may now turn to consider the authorship of Sonettos 1 and 15–31. Brown, having interpreted the second division of the title-page (its wording essentially repeated on the first subtitle, sig. D6^{v}) to mean that "The Patrons pathetical Po- / sies" were necessarily by Salusbury, was naturally misled into concluding that the other poems there listed following the Posies ("Sonets,

Maddrigalls, and / Rowndelayes") were also by Salusbury.[44] He thus ignored the fact that the above list is, without any break, followed by "Together with / Sinetes Dompe." all included in the same division of the title-page, which, following a short Latin quotation, also includes the author's name: "By ROBERT PARRY / Gent." If, indeed, as I have shown, "The Patrons patheticall Po- / sies" are by Parry and addressed by him to Salusbury, the supposed title-page evidence for Salusbury's hand in this section of *Sinetes* simply disappears.

Parry's authorship of Sonettos 1 and 15–31 is supported and, I believe, established by a body of interlocking evidence. The central key is the Helena Owen acrostics in Sonettos 16–18 and the repeated comparison of Helena Owen, who unfortunately cannot be specifically identified, to Helen of Troy. The first definite reference appears in Sonetto 1.14, "Liue Helens peere eternized thy fame" (cf. *Moderatus*, sig. M4^{v}, "thy name be eternized in the booke of memorie"; sig. R2^{v}, "it also eternized your fame"; and sig. X2^{v}, "to eternize your owne worthines"; as well as Sonetto 31.13, "your worthes eternished remaine"). In Sonetto 16.10, a sonetto addressed acrostically to Helena Owen, we find "Helen the faire was not so faire as she" (cf. *Moderatus*, sig. B3^{v}, "The beautie of this pearelesse peece, / Surpasseth farre the Queene of Greece"; and "The lamentation of a Male-content," 59, "The Queene of beautie must resigne her Crowne [to Helena Owen]").

The first line of Sonetto 18, the third of the sonettos addressed, acrostically, to Helena Owen, reads, "Namelesse the flower that workes my discontent," a line that links this sonetto with Parry's dedication of "The lamentation of a Male-content" to "*the Honorable minded* / vnknowne, the Name-lesse/ wisheth perfect health and / perpetuall happines," thus neatly transferring "Name-lesse" to the "vnknowne." Again, in a short poem entitled "To Paris darling," which follows Sonetto 31, Parry, referring to Helena Owen writes, "Were I sheapheard as I am a woodman, / Thy Paris would I be if not thy goodman." And, finally, "The lamentation of a Male-content," 153–56, makes Parry's unrequited love for Helena Owen explicit:

> Why shall not I her loue hope to obtayne,
> Though Venus peere, or yet rather peerelesse,
> Paris a sheaphard I a homely swayne,
> He wanton, I chast Helen would possesse.

[44] Brown, xlvii.

If the above interlocking evidence is not thought sufficient to establish Parry's authorship of Sonettos 1 and 15–31, some eighty Parryisms, many of them distinctive, can be cited, each of the sonettos having at least two and eleven having five or more.

Only "The lamentation of a Male-content" remains to be considered.[45] Despite Brown's suggestion that "The lamentation" "in tone as well as in theme . . . resembles much of Salusbury's verse,"[46] there can be no question that it is by Parry, and, like Sonettos 1 and 15–31, is addressed to Helena Owen. Drawing only, except in two instances, on work unchallenged by Brown (i.e., opening dedicatory Epistle, Passions, "Sinetes Dumpe") and *Moderatus*, "The lamentation" contains at least twenty-five Parryisms, fifteen of them distinctive. A selection of the distinctive parallels will be sufficient to establish Parry's authorship.

Line (prose dedication):	
14–15 I heard a voyce from / a Cloude [in a dream]	*Moderatus*, sig. G4v: [in a dream] I heard a voyce that lowd did crie
18 my fortunes being so far inferior to my thoughts	Sinetes Dumpe, 5: My thoughtes were far aboue my fortunes bent
Line (the poem):	
28, 122 wearied mindes / wearied minde	Passion I.1: wearied minde Passion XIX.4: wearied mind *Moderatus*, sig. A2: wearines of their minds *and* wearied mind *Moderatus*, sig. I2: wearyeth the minde
72 Semy-goddesse	*Moderatus*, sig. 2A4: Semi-goddesse *Moderatus* sig. B4: Semi-goddesse
117–118 heate of my desire, / Whose accents banish'd reason	Passion XXXI.9: accents of desire
119 My bed beares guilt of this my burning fire	Passion IIII.3: The sheetes beare guilt of my distressed soule

45 The subtitle (sig. 2Ar) expands the title of "The lamentation": "The / lamentation of / a Male-content v- / pon this Enigma. / *Maister thy desier or / liue in Despaire.*"

46 For a discussion of Parry's probable identity with the "R. P." who translated parts of Diego Ortúñez de Calahorra's *Espejo de Principes y Cavalleros*, under the general title *The Mirror of Knighthood*, see Introduction, 26–34.

Line (prose dedication):	
121 ech place denied me scope of thought	Sonetto 1.11: Of all my thoughtes here shalt thou finde the scope
145–146 Ought Palmers come and sit in Princes throane, / To beg for Dole to satisfie there want	Posie VII.10–11: If Dole I had to satisfie my minde: / Then I for Dole a Palmers name would craue
181 she reade these ruin's of my time	Passion XXVIII.19: Sing Muses, sing, the ruines of my time [both in reference to his verses]
207, 264 my little hope deface my fates hope to deface	Passion X.9: for then did hope deface *Moderatus*, sig. P1^{v}: yet feare but nearly defaced with hope
213 abrupted ayre	Passion XI.18: abrupted ayer [earliest citation of "abrupted" in *OED* is 1633]

In examining the extent of Parry's hand in *Sinetes* it has been argued and, I believe, proved that John Salusbury has no part in what may once again be properly called Robert Parry's *Sinetes*.

III.
Parry as poet, romancer, and (?) translator

Robert Parry, as a poet, may properly be ranked with a group of Elizabethan-Jacobean poet-versifiers, who, occupying what may be called a third level, wrote more from a sense of satisfying a fashionable mode, sometimes, to be sure, with happy effect, than from any deeply-felt emotional involvement, particularly those who wrote in the sonnet and complaint traditions. Parry, then, may fairly be placed in the company of Thomas Watson, Abraham Fraunce, the Earl of Oxford, John Davies of Hereford, Thomas Churchyard, Robert Chester, Bartholomew Griffin, Richard Linche, and Robert Tofte. Thomas Nashe, in his novella *The Unfortunate Traveller* (1594), catches perfectly what it was that drove most of these poets:

> Who would haue learned to write an excellent passion, might haue bin a perfect tragick poet, had he but attended halfe the extremitie of his lament, Passion vpon passion would throng one on anothers necke [Parry wrote forty-six poems under the title "Passions"], he wold praise her beyond the moone and starres, and that so sweetly

> and rauishingly as I perswade my self he was more in loue with his curious forming fancie than her face; and truth it is, many become passionate louers onely to winne praise to theyr wits.[47]

"T.S.," in his commendatory verses in *Sinetes* ("In prayse of the Booke," sig. A6), refers to what he feels is a new note in Parry's voice:

> OF loue of ioy of solace sweete and pleasant vaine,
> That wonted was thy sugred muse to write and sing,
> Both Sonetts Maddrigals with dainty ditties playne,
> What sudden chaunce hath moued to chang thy stile what thing. (1–4)

His comment points to what Parry terms "SINETES / Passions vppon his fortunes" (see title-page), a series of forty-six poems entitled "Passions," and seems to suggest that the Passions are among Parry's most recent compositions. They do, indeed, strike a more hopeless and "tragic" note and appear to offer a lament for the loss (through death?) of a long-sought and loved mistress,[48] most probably Helena Owen.[49] That, indeed, the Passions may be recent work is also suggested by the fact that only in the Passions, and in the title "Sinetes Dumpe," does Parry refer to himself as "Sinetes," a Greek-sounding sobriquet, the meaning of which has successfully eluded interpretation. See, however, my "Acknowledgements."

Parry's use of the term "passion" to describe a poem that treats of a lover's affliction and unbearable suffering arising out of an unrequited or lost love was influenced by Thomas Watson's *Hekatompathia or Passionate Centurie of Loue* (1582). Watson calls his poems "my Loue Passions" and usually refers to them as "passions" in the headnote to each of the hundred poems that make up the collection. Like Watson, Parry employs a six-line stanza form, a "Sixaine" as Puttenham calls it,[50] rhyming a/b/a/b/c/c, a stanza form that he also uses in many of what he calls Posies. Again like Watson, who divides his "Centurie" into what may be called love (nos. 1–79) and anti-love (nos. 80–100) poems, Parry writes what may be considered an anti-love poem in "The lamentation of a Male-content," each poet using an anti-love motto: "MY LOVE IS PAST" (Watson) and "Maister thy desier, or liue in Despaire" (Parry).

---

47 Nashe, II, 262.

48 See Passions V, XXIV, XXVII, XXXVII, XLIII, XLVI. Parry uses the phrase "tragick notes" in Passion XXVIII.21.

49 See Introduction, 2–3. A reference to "beauties Queene" (i.e., Helen of Troy) in Passion XXIX.19 may allude to Helena Owen.

50 George Puttenham, *The Arte of English Poesie* (1589), ed. Edward Arber (1895), 101.

In one respect the Passions are, I believe, unique. Although they mourn the loss of a mistress, they are actually addressed to two other women, whose names, along with Robert Parry's, are encrypted in acrostics, Francis Wyloughby and Elyzabeth Wolfreston,[51] to whom the Passions, as the title-page informs us, are "offered for an Incense at the / shrine of the Ladies which gui-/ ded his distempered / thoughtes." These "Ladies," then, serve as advisors and mother-confessors. The nature of their relationship with Parry is otherwise unknown.

The concept behind the thirteen Posies, which follow the Passions in *Sinetes*, is also, at least to some extent, original with Parry. Among these Posies is what may be called the Patron-series (nos. I–IV, VI, VIII), in which, practising a kind of ventriloquism, Parry presents John Salusbury, his honored patron, in the role of a would-be lover speaking of his mistress, Dorothy Halsall, a device that enables Parry to lavish "glorious" praise on both: on Salusbury, for having such high thoughts and ardent feelings, and on Dorothy Halsall, his sister-in-law, for her dazzling beauty and extraordinary virtues, catching, as it were, two birds with one rhetorical device.[52]

A collection of thirty-one Sonettos follows the Posies. Alone among English sonnet writers, Parry uses the Italian form "sonetto" instead of "sonnet" throughout the sequence.[53] Seven Sonettos contain either more (2, 4, 5, 6) or less (16, 17, 18) than fourteen lines, a length we now consider as technically standard for the sonnet, but, since the Elizabethans also used the term "sonnet" to describe short lyrics of different lengths, such formal variety would not have appeared anomalous and can be paralleled in other sonnet sequences.[54]

Following Sonetto 31 is a small group of poems that may fairly be characterized as anacreontic: "To Paris darling," "Buen matina," two madrigals, and two roundelays. These are immediately followed by "Sinetes Dumpe" and, allowing for the insertion of Hugh Gryffyth's eulogy of Salusbury (sig. H4), by "The lamentation of a Male-content," apparently a late addition to the volume, both of which fall into the complaint tradition. This sonnet /

---

[51] See headnote, Passion I. The same names appear again as acrostics in Posie IIII.

[52] For an account of the acrostics involved, see Introduction, 2–3, and the headnotes to each of the Patron-series Posies. On Parry's authorship of the Posies, see Introduction, 11–19.

[53] On Parry's authorship of Sonettos 1 and 15–31 and the so-called S-Sonettos (2–14), see Introduction, 20–22.

[54] Compare, for example, Giles Fletcher the Elder's *Licia* (1593), Barnabe Barnes's *Parthenophil and Parthenophe* (1593), Shakespeare's *Sonnets* (1609), etc.

anacreontic / complaint arrangement may be paralleled, as Katherine Duncan-Jones has shown,[55] in six other contemporary sonnet-sequences, including Shakespeare's *Sonnets* (1609).

Before the publication of *Sinetes* in 1597, Parry had already made his appearance as a poet in *Moderatus* (1595), where, following the tradition of a number of sixteenth-century chivalric romances, he interspersed the prose narrative with twenty-two lyrics, many of which he calls "ditties," with occasional use of such terms as "fancy," "ode," "madrigal," or "cansong." And, unlike *Sinetes*, *Moderatus* may have achieved contemporary notice. Francis Meres in his *Palladis Tamia* (1598), fol. 268^{v}, among a list of twenty-five romances that may be deemed "hurtfull to youth," includes one he calls "the blacke Knight," referring, perhaps, to the subtitle of *Moderatus, The most delectable & famous Historie of the Blacke Knight.*

Parry's interest in English as a literary language, essentially inferior to none,[56] is reflected to some extent in his own writing. Despite what might be termed "vices of style"—(1) unthinking self-plagiarism, i.e., all too frequently expressing the same ideas in identical or closely related language; (2) use of "for to" too often as a metrical crutch; and (3) the lazy trick of using "the same" to avoid the trouble of referring specifically to something recently expressed concretely—Parry can, on occasion, show his interest in expanding English usage by introducing words or word forms apparently new to, or rare in, literary English. Since the *Oxford English Dictionary* (*OED*) failed to include either *Moderatus* (1595) or *Sinetes* (1597) in the "List of Books Quoted" (*Supplement*, 1933), something of Parry's contribution to the vocabulary of his contemporaries deserves to be noticed. In the following list Parry's use of a word is set against either its absence from, or earliest citation in, the *OED*.

abrupted:	Passion XI.18, Male-content, 213; earliest citation in OED 1633.
actrix:	*Moderatus*, sig. H2; not in *OED*.
begin:	MS Diary, 100; used as a noun (=beginning); only citation in *OED* 1597 (from Sidney).
bulletin:	MS Diary, 21; earliest citation in *OED* 1645; see Introduction, p. 7.

[55] "Was the 1609 *Shake-speares Sonnets* Really Unauthorized?" *RES*, new series, 34 (1983): 151–71. Duncan-Jones does not include a discussion of *Sinetes*.

[56] See Introduction, 4.

Camber: Epitath, 7, 66; form of "Cambrian"; no citation between 1586 and 1626 in *OED.*

cansong: *Moderatus*, sigs. D2, G2; a variant of "canson" not recorded in *OED.*

cartesman: *Moderatus*, sig. Q4; only eighteenth- and nineteenth-century citations in *OED* under "cartman."

complaint: Epitath, 59; used as a verb; not in *OED.*

complease: Sonetto 6.12; earliest (printed) citation in *OED* 1604.

contingent: *Moderatus*, sig. R1; in *OED*: (1) earliest citation, meaning "a thing coming by chance," 1553, next citation 1637; (2) earliest citation, meaning "a thing that may or may not happen," 1623.

deluge: Sonetto 27.2; no adjectival use cited in *OED.*

diapered: *Moderatus*, sig. P4; no citation between 1400 and 1656 in *OED.*

edict: Passion XXXV.8; used as a verb; earliest citation in *OED* 1652.

gloring: Sinetes Dumpe, 8; earliest citation in *OED* 1632.

immit: Sonetto 6.10: no citation between 1578 and 1652 in *OED.*

instimulation: *Moderatus*, sig. E1^{v}; earliest citation in *OED* 1638.

invest: Sonetto 23.3; "invest"= to besiege; earliest citation in *OED* 1600.

lathe: Passion XLIIII.18; "lathe"= to invite; no citation between 1450 and 1854 in *OED.*

Lestrigonian: *Moderatus*, sig. S4^{v}; used adjectivally; no such use cited in *OED.*

opal: Posie IIII.8; first cited as an adjective in *OED* 1649.

oppose: Sonetto 29.8; used as a noun; not in *OED.*

overmatch: Epitath, 76; used as a noun; no citation between 1589 and 1667 in *OED.*

presaging: *Moderatus,* sig. S2; earliest citation in *OED* 1606.

protect: first dedicatory Epistle, 20; used as a noun; not in *OED.*

radian: Posie I.25; used in the sense of "radiating"; possibly a misreading of "radiant"; not in *OED.*

ransack: *Moderatus*, sig. E4^{v}; used as a noun; first cited in *OED* 1589, but "R. P."(i.e., probably Robert Parry) uses "ransack" as a noun in *The Second Part of the Myrror of Knighthood*, sig. B7^{v}, in 1583; no citation between 1589 and 1635 in *OED.*

short-taken: dedicatory Epistle, 9; not in *OED*.
socering: *Moderatus*, sig. L4; earliest citation in *OED* 1640.
sopor: Passion XL.15; earliest citation in *OED* 1658.
soul-sick: Sonetto 3.5; earliest citation in *OED* 1598.
stanchless: Sonetto 3.5; earliest citation in *OED* 1605.
surflow: Sonetto 6.7; not in *OED*.
terred: Epitath (1591), 16; aphetic form of "inter"; not in *OED*.
thirstless: *Moderatus*, sig. E4v; no citation between 1591 and 1883.
understand: MS Diary, 18; used as a noun (=understanding); no citation after 1444 in *OED*.
unspected: Male-content, 51 ("spect"=see. look on); not in *OED*.
valens: Sonetto 3.3; probably a variant form of "valency"; not recorded in *OED*.
warlylike: MS Diary, 52; meaning "as in a warlike manner"; not in *OED*.
whey-white: Sonetto 6.11 (describing "waves"); not in *OED*.

The twenty-two lyrics, mostly song lyrics, in *Moderatus*, which have been included in the present edition of Robert Parry's poems, indeed *Moderatus* itself, are perhaps a personal reflection, a kind of mirror image, of earlier work that Parry may have undertaken. Indeed, nearly a hundred years ago, it was suggested that Robert Parry was the "R. P." who translated three parts of Diego Ortúñez de Calahorra's *Espejo de Principes y Cavalleros* under the general title of *The Mirror of Knighthood*, with its continuations by other hands (two of which "R. P." translated), an interminably long Spanish chivalric romance.[57] This identification of "R. P." has been more or less accepted by the *Dictionary of National Biography* (Vol. XLIII, 1895, but with a "perhaps"), by the revised *Short Title Catalogue* (1976), and by John Simons, who considers Parry's hand as "almost certain."[58]

[57] See *Short Title Catalogue* (revised ed., 1976), 18862 (by Ortúñez); 18864 (by Ortúñez); (?) 18871 (continuation by Martinez). The last part (18871), proposed as a possibility in *STC*, does not name (i.e., by initials) the translator; it contains only one longer lyric (twenty-four lines), which is stylistically awkward and metrically incompetent, as are the two- or three-line versicles scattered throughout. It is unlikely to be the work of "R. P.," if we may judge by the verse translations in the other two parts (18866 and 18868). Francis Meres (*Palladis Tamia* (1598), fol 268v), along with "the blacke Knight," also includes the "Myrror of Knighthood" among romances "hurtfull to youth."

[58] John Simons, "Robert Parry's *Moderatus*: A Study in Elizabethan Romance," in *Romance Reading on the Book: Essays on Medieval Narrative Presented to Maldwyn Mills*, ed., Jennifer Fellows, Rosalind Field, Gillian Rogers, and Judith Weiss (1996), 242. Very

The second part of The Myrror of Knighthood, the first part that claims to be translated by "R. P.," appeared in 1583; although not entered on the Stationers' Register, it was published by Thomas Este, who was the publisher of three of the five parts attributed to "R. P." However, another part, *The second part of the first Booke of The Myrrour of Knighthood*, not published until 1585, was entered on the Stationers' Register on 24 August 1582. This suggests that that part had been translated by "R. P." as early as 1582, when Parry was only eighteen.

If this "R. P." was, indeed, Robert Parry, when and how did he become familiar with Spanish? Unfortunately, there is a substantial gap in Parry's Diary covering the years 1572–79 and 1580, a period beginning when he was about eight years old. The two most likely possibilities would seem to be: either he lived for a long enough time in Spain to acquire at least a reading knowledge of Spanish or he had a tutor from whom he gained a sufficient command of the language.

In addition to a single poem in *Sinetes* with a Spanish title ("Buen matina," sig. G6^{v}), two other sources afford us some evidence, if only circumstantial, that Parry may qualify for the role of "R. P.": (1) a fairly pervasive interest in Spanish affairs throughout his Diary; (2) as himself the author of a chivalric romance, a work that shows familiarity with the Spanish romance tradition represented by *The Mirror of Knighthood*.

The most significant piece of evidence in the Diary is a letter, in Parry's holograph, "Trulie translated" and "written in a Spanishe l'tt're" concerning "the sicknes last wordes, & death of the kinge of Spaine Philipe the seconde" on 13 September 1598.[59] The phrase "trulie translated," attached to the letter by Parry certainly seems to imply, though it does not, of course, prove, that Parry himself is the translator. Earlier in 1598, a peace treaty had been arranged between Spain and France, an event that interested Parry because

recently (2002) Professor Simons has published an old-spelling edition of *Moderatus*. He has changed his mind (wrongly, I think) on equating "R. P." with Robert Parry, and he calls attention, for the first time, to a number of Parry's borrowings particularly from Robert Greene's *1 Mamillia* (1583) and Thomas Lodge's *Rosalynde* (1590). On *Moderatus*, see also John J. O'Connor, *"Amadis de Gaule" and Its Influence on Elizabethan Literature* (1970), 221; Elaine V. Bailin, *The Uses of Mythology in Elizabethan Prose Romance* (1988), 223–33. In her edition (1968) of Bartholomew Yong's translation (published in 1598, but translated sixteen years earlier) of Montemayor's *Diana* and Gil Polo's *Enamoured Diana*, Judith M. Kennedy, lxi, suggests that *Moderatus* may show some influence from both these works.

[59] MS Diary, 18–19. See a transcript in Appendix.

he, at considerable length and in his own hand, details the "Reasons for the peace" (how the treaty might advantage England), "Reasons agaynst the peace," and "The last reasons agaynst."[60] There is also an eight-page scribal copy, in Latin (Stow gives an English translation) of a treaty (1604) involving, among others, James I and Philip III of Spain, [61] and an account of the elaborate celebration staged in London in April 1605 by the Spanish ambassador upon the birth of a son and heir to Philip III.[62]

Moderatus, The most delectable & famous Historie of the BLACKE *Knight* (1595), as Simons shows, moves beyond the Spanish *Amadis* cycle, of which *The Mirror of Knighthood* is representative, by incorporating "the more refined pastoral ethos of courtly romance and *novella*," thus combining, in plain style, the typical chivalric adventures ("a state of order disturbed, complex love affairs, fights with powerful enemies, false accusations, disguises, journeys, honourable behaviour, and a final reconciliation") with, in Euphistic style, the kind of pastoralism found in Sidney's *Arcadia*.[63] There is, then, no question that Parry was well learned in the kind of literary background that gave birth to *Moderatus*.

An examination of some fifty-four lyrics scattered throughout two parts of *The Mirror of Knighthood* that claim to be translated by "R. P." (STC 18866 [1583] and 18868 [1598]) has turned up a number of thematic and verbal parallels with *Moderatus* and *Sinetes*. Since no one, so far as I know, has examined these lyrics (or parts of the prose texts) with Parry's authorship in mind and since the evidence these parallels offer lends positive, if not indisputable, support for Parry's hand as translator, they should, at least, be noticed.

Second Part (1583, STC 18866):

Sig. B6: with his hand ingrau'de him [i.e., buried] in this ground . . . He did ingraue these lines	Passion XX.23–24: SINETES hope though in his graue, / That in your mindes his worthes you will ingraue *Moderatus*, sig. S1: These lines I graue, / . . . though dead I be in graue

[60] Diary, 121–22.

[61] MS Diary, 89–97.

[62] MS Diary, 100–1. See a transcript in Appendix.

[63] Simons, 241, 243–44.

Sig. B7: may know in life I die Sig. C7^{v}: And liuing die Sig. AA8: For onely death will lasting life prouide, / Where liuing thus I sundry deaths abide	Passion V.13–14: The liuing doth presage his dying dole, / His life is death Passion VII.7: Life is a death Maddrigall [II].13: I liue, yet still dying Male-content, 221: Yet haue remorse on him that liuing dyes *Moderatus*, sig. 2A3^{v}: and liuing thus to die *Moderatus*, sig. H4: And though I liue, yet liuing daily dye *Moderatus*, sig. M3: Dye had I leuer, then liue and liuing so Epitath (1591), 83: cheeff desire was here to lyve, by lyvinge soe to die
Sig. B7^{v}: And leau'st me now to ransacke of defame [earliest use of "ransack" as noun in *OED* is 1589]	*Moderatus*, sig. E4^{v}: there wanted in them nothing but sufficient audacitie, to recouer the ransacke of thy person, and spoyle of thine honour
Sig. B7^{v}: my eyes more cleare then starres in frost that show	Posie I.14–15: Thy Christall-pointed eies (like Saphyres blue, / Set in the snowe)
Sig. B7^{v}: My haires excell bright Phoebus golden raies	Posie I.3–4: thy smile, / Shines far more bright then Phoebus goulden rayes
Sg. C5^{v}: kindling the aire with fire, with that burning cholar wherein he was wrapped, vnhappie had he bene	*Moderatus* sig. A3: Euen so I, though none of those that are rapt vp . . . into the second firmament *Moderatus*, sig. I1^{v}: the more to wrappe this young nouice in a Laberinth of his owne fonde conceits *Moderatus*, sig. L2^{v}: *Verosa* began to feele her heart warmed, with a secret and priuie flame that lay wrapped in her bosome *Moderatus*, sig. T2: wrapped in a mind ful of impatient thoughtes
Sig. C8: fond conceit	Posie X.6: fond conceyte in sorrows ioy I fare Sonetto 15.1: fond conceyt doth moue the wauering minde

Sig. D1: And for the sweete which then by thee I felt / I founde sharpe sowre Sig. E5^{v}: turn his sweete to most detested sour Sig. DD5: Cupid . . . turnes his sweete to most detested sower Sig. Ii3^{v}: I hold that lyfe in great despight, / That hath not sower mixt with sweete among	Posie V.18: Thus without sower the sweete is neuer had Posie X.1: SOwre is the sweet that sorrow doth mainetaine Sonetto 21.10: Makes sweete proue sower
Sig. F5^{v}: And sith I seeke in siluane shade to shroud / my selfe	*Moderatus*, B2: sitting . . . vnder a broad Beech tree, the hanging boughs whereof shadowed and shrowded them
Sig. F6: the burden of my song, / It's sighs and sobbes that are constraind by wrong Sig. BB5: They will with sobs assist the sighs of me	Passion XXXI.1: hart breath no sighing sobs Male-content, 96: In sighes, in sobbs *Moderatus*, sig. E1^{v}: sighing sobbes stopping the passage of his speech *Moderatus*, sig. M3: what meaneth these sighing sobbes *Moderatus*, sig. P4^{v}: I sobbe and sigh with sobbing care
Sig. N3: headlong tumbled into Cupides snare Sig. P1^{v}: twice caught in Cupides snare Sig. NN7^{v}: Cupide himselfe within his snare is caught	Posie X.5: enthraulde in blind CVPIDOS snare *Moderatus*, sig. G4: And to intrap, he [Cupid] snares doeth lay
Sig. Q1^{v}: fortune frownes . . . / Whose double face when smoothest it doth smile / Then meanes she most the mightie to beguile	*Moderatus*, sig. 2A2: *Ianus* double faced daughter [i.e., Fortune] . . . began to flatter them a little, turning her late frownes vnto smiles *Moderatus*, sig. N4: submitted her selfe, . . . to the stormy blastes of double faced fortune

Sig. BB4: For therein thou shalt finde reliefe / And blaze thy Faith by Fame	Sonetto 3.13–14: your name . . . I will it blaze to all posterities *Moderatus*, sig. C4: Fame carefull then for to perfourme her charge, / . . . Venus ouer-match, she blazed then at large *Moderatus*, sig. E1: not to be credulous of those thinges which are blazed by common report *Moderatus*, sig. I1v: this instimulation proceeding only vpon bare report of her rare beautie, blazed by a silly shepheard in a song [earliest use of "instimulation" in *OED* is 1658]
Sig. BB5: Caliope from Pernasse hill proceede . . . / O mournfull Muse assist / My wailing song	*Moderatus*, sig. B2v: CAliope assist my quill, / . . . For to describe this pearelesse Dame [both are the opening lines of a lyric]

Sixth Book (1598; STC 18868)

Sig. E1v: Nor earth nor sea my fury can asswage	Sonetto 29.3–4: The force of fier . . . / Makes all thinges weake his furie to asswage *Moderatus*, sig. H3v: All sought that night . . . , / Of raging heate the furie to appease
Sig. X8v: Where loue lackes can be no life	Posie V.4: That loue is lacke and I doe grieue therefore *Moderatus*, sig. M1: beleeue this Maxime to be true, that in loue there is no lacke
Sig. OO1: song with refrain: "Lullaby Lulla Lullaby'	*Moderatus*, sig. 2A3v: song with refrain: / "Sing lullabie, lullie, lullabie, / sing lulla, lull, lullie'

And, finally, in the *Second Part of the First Book* (1585; *STC* 18862; sig. [A3]) in "To the Reader" signed "T. E." (i.e., Thomas Este, the publisher), we find: "Whereby the quaint beginning, and the quoy [i.e., coy] abruption shall be brought to a concord." Even if "To the reader" was actually written by Thomas

Este and not, indeed, by "R. P.," the use of the word "abruption," the earliest citation of which in the *OED* is in Shakespeare's *Troilus and Cressida* (1601–2), is intriguing because Parry twice uses the related phrase "abrupted ayer" (Passion XI.18; "The lamentation of a Male-content," 213), the earliest citation of "abrupted" in the *OED* being 1633.

Who first proposed that "R. P." and Robert Parry shared a common identity is uncertain. William Herbert, in his greatly enlarged edition of Joseph Ames's (1749) *Typographical Antiquities* (1786), II, 1050), was the first bibliographer even to notice *Moderatus*, but he suggests no connection between Parry and "R. P." the translator. In 1802, however, Joseph Ritson (*Bibliographica Poetica*, 293), repeating Herbert's notice, observes that Richard Farmer, an antiquarian and Shakespearean commentator, had mistakenly attributed *Moderatus* to "Rich'd Parre, Gent." in a manuscript note in his copy (now in the Folger Shakespeare Library) of Parry's romance. He based his attribution, the title-page being lacking, on a fudged manuscript title-page, which is headed by what appears to be the name "Parrs" (the "s" is uncertain), and on the colophon (sig. X3^{v}), which reads "FINIS. R. P. Gent.," Ritson corrects Farmer, but then adds to the confusion by identifying Richard Parre as "a writer of romancees," a writer unknown to the *Dictionary of National Biography*, the *Short-Title Catalogue*, or the *New Cambridge Bibliography of English Literature* (1974). The short account in the *Dictionary of National Biography* (1895), which labels him as a "translator," may, then, be the first to propose the "R. P.=Parry" equation, perhaps under the combined influence of Farmer's mistake and Ritson's "writer of romancees."

Although Robert Parry's identity with "R. P." cannot, perhaps, be considered as certain, the evidence reviewed above suggests, even if we allow for the fact that we are dealing with translations, that we may accept such an equation as, at least, probable.

IV. Bibliographical analysis.

i

The volume here reproduced in facsimile is unique, only a single copy of SINETES / *Passions vppon his fortunes* (1597), now in the Huntington Library (RB51800), having survived what Parry calls the "force of time." This copy was discovered in 1867 at Lamport Hall in Northhamptonshire, the seat of the

Isham family, and, in 1893, became part of Wakefield Christie-Miller's important Britwell Library.

Sinetes was entered on the Stationers' Register by William Holme (#3), the publisher, on 5 October 1596: "Entred for his coppie vnder the hand of master HARTWELL a booke intituled SINETES mournfull maddrigal vpon his Discontented fortune &c" (see *A Transcript of the Registers of the Company of Stationers of London 1554–1640*, ed., Edward Arber, III [1896], 14). Note that the title of the "booke" differs significantly from that of the published volume. This would seem to suggest that Parry was in London and altered the title after his manuscript had been turned over to the printer, Thomas Purfoot the Elder (see below). *Sinetes* is the only book published by Holme in 1597 (see the revised *STC*, ed., Katharine Pantzer, III [1991], 84–85).

Collation: 8°: A–G^{8} H^{4}; 2A^{8}. All quires are signed through leaf four, except for title-page, B2, 2A1; E2 missigned F2; H, being a half-sheet only the first two leaves are signed; 2A2–4 are missigned 2A1–3; the volume is unpaged.

Volume size: 12.4 x 8.2 cm.

Watermark: a hand surmounted by some kind of figure, the figure being joined by a short line to the tip of the third finger and split at upper margin of A1, 4; B2, 3; C2, 3; D2, 3; E2, 3; F1, 4; G1, 4; 2A2, 2, 3; no countermark; no watermark in half-sheet H.

Paper-fills affecting printing on A1, A8, E2, H4, 2A1–3. A piece of leaf 2A3 bearing a bit of text is stuck to the recto of 2A4. Paper-fills not affecting printing on A2–5, 7; E13–8; 2A8. The last leaf is repaired at the inner margin, so chain lines do not line up with 2A5, but apparently no cancel is involved.

Binding: very dark olive crushed morocco, signed on front lower turn-in by W. Pratt, gilt fillet around edges, two gilt fillets around turn-ins, spine in six panels, the second gilt-stamped "PARRY / SIN- / ETES," the third gilt-stamped "LOND. / 1597." Front and back gilt-stamped with the arms and initials of Wakefield Christie-Miller. All edges gilt.

Provenance bookplate: "This volume discovered in 1867 at Lamport Hall, Northhamtonsire, the seat of the Isham family was added in 1893 to the Britwell Library," Wakefield Christie-Miller (binding); Britwell shelfmark "34 A 35" in pencil on front pastedown; Britwell sale, 15 March 1923; #529 bought by Rosenbach probably as agent for the Huntington Library.

The title-page is bordered by a rectangle (14.4 x 9.4 cm.) built up by printer's ornaments (nine joined ornaments on the right and left sides joined at the top and bottom by bars of four printer's ornaments, thus forming a closed rectangle). The printer, Thomas Purfoot ("T.P." on title-page), employs the same kind of title-page border in several other books printed around this date (1597). The two subtitles (sigs. D6^{v} and 2A1) make use of a truncated woodcut title-page (i.e., the lower quarter has been cut off) used uncut by Purfoot in 1592 (see R. B. McKerrow and F. S. Ferguson, eds., *Title-page Borders Used in England & Scotland 1485–1640*, No. 211).

'The lamentation of a Male-content" (sigs. 2A2–8) is not listed among Parry's other poems on the title-page (sig. A1) or on the first woodcut subtitle (sig. D6^{v}), but is attached following sig. H4^{v}, with its own woodcut subtitle (sig. 2A1, unsigned and verso blank). It would appear, therefore, that "The lamentation" was a last-minute addition, a conclusion further borne out by its position following Hugh Gryffyth's commendatory verses addressed to John Salusbury (sigs. H4–H4^{v}), a fitting enough end-piece to a volume dedicated to Salusbury. It has been suggested that "The lamentation" was a separate, anonymous publication (no author's, printer's, or publisher's names appear on its subtitle) that somehow got tacked on to *Sinetes* (see the revised *STC*). Aside from the fact that "The lamentation" can, from internal evidence, be shown to be unquestionably by Parry (see Introduction, 22–23), bibliographical evidence also makes such a view untenable. (1) The use of "FINIS" at the end of "The lamentation" (sig. 2A8^{v}) does not necessarily imply the end of a separate volume. A similar "FINIS" appears at the end of Passion XLVI (sig. D6), of Posie XIII (sig. E7), and of "Sinetes Dumpe" (sig. H2^{v}). (2) The same woodcut subtitle that prefaces "The lamentation" (sig. 2A1) is also used to introduce the section called Posies, etc. (sig. D6^{v}), again without author's, printer's, or publisher's names. These two subtitles are also linked by "THE" (large caps), which in both begins the listing of the contents of that section, and the exactly same positioning of "THE" in "THE lamentation" subtitle shows that it derives from the subtitle of the Posies.

As the title-page of *Sinetes* tells us, the book was printed in the print-shop of "T. P." (i.e., Thomas Purfoot the Elder), a long-established printer (?1566–1605). As a piece of printing, it is, I believe, somewhat poorer than average for a volume of this size (68 leaves); it contains 133 errors, for the most part compositorial, twenty five of which result from a turned *n* or *u*. These figures, of course, do not include errors in punctuation, most of which may also be considered compositorial, since verse manuscripts at that time left most of the pointing, particularly line-end pointing, to the often faulty interpretation of compositor or proof-reader. Because, except in comparatively rare instances, errors in pointing may easily enough be adjusted as one reads, I have let the punctuation stand. But where the pointing renders meaning ambiguous or confused, the line (or lines) is discussed in a Commentary note.

The handling of the printer's copy for *Sinetes* in Thomas Purfoot's printing house is a matter of some interest but one that, despite analysis, remains uncertain in several respects. The copy that Parry finally turned over to William Holme was probably scribal rather than holograph. Very few of Parry's characteristic spellings, frequent in the holograph parts of Parry's Diary (e.g., "lyef"; "prayes"=praise, once each only; "doeth," where "doth" is intended; "-ing" forms, regularly "-inge"), survive both scribe and compositor. If the spelling in *Sinetes* were only compositorial, I would argue that more of Parry's idiosyncratic spellings would have come through. Moreover, Parry employed a scribe to transcribe, as part of his Diary, a number of longer documents, manuscript and printed. There is a similar uncertainty about how the copy was set: was it set seriatim or by cast-off copy? The printer's copy in this case was of a kind ideal for casting-off: it was wholly in verse, except for one short prose dedication (sigs. 2A2–2A2^{v}), and, using an octavo rather than a quarto format, Purfoot could afford to allow the great majority of the poems one page each. Cast-off copy was prepared either to cut substantially the time needed to produce a book (i.e., two compositors were able to set concurrently the outer and inner formes, the two formes then being printed off on different presses at the same time), or to remedy a type shortage (i.e., the outer or inner forme once printed off, type would be distributed and used to set the other forme). An examination of the running-titles (mostly single words, i.e., PASSION. I., POSIE, I, Sonetto. 1.) and the ornamental bars composed of printer's ornaments which are placed, as space-fillers, both above and below many of the shorter poems, show that in a number of cases the identical running-title or ornamental bar is used in both outer and inner formes of the same quire (compare sigs. B1/B2^{v}, B5/B6, C1/C2^{v}, C6/C6^{v}, D5/D5^{v}, F5^{v}/F6, F8/F8^{v}, G6/G8^{v}).

Such identities in both formes rule out the use of cast-off copy as a time-saver, but are consistent with the use of cast-off copy to remedy type shortage. It is unlikely, however, that a long-established printing house like Thomas Purfoot the Elder's would suffer from this type shortage. This suggests that *Sinetes* was after all probably set seriatim. If so, it is difficult to imagine a slower method of composition and imposition given the type distribution between the setting of the quire's two formes. We may, perhaps, hazard a guess that *Sinetes* was not a project on which Purfoot was willing to lavish time that could be better spent on more important and profitable books and that printing off progressed only when one of the presses was otherwise idle. It is tempting, considering the number of typographical errors in *Sinetes* noted above, to postulate a single inexperienced compositor, but whether inexperienced or not, the absence of any significant change in spelling habits or difference in page positioning suggest the work of a single compositor throughout.

The present edition of *Sinetes* (1597) may best be described as an "edited" facsimile. As such, all quotations from *Sinetes, Moderatus* (1593), Parry's Diary, etc. retain the sixteenth- and early seventeenth-century use of *V/v* for *U/u* when occurring as a word's initial letter, of *u* for *v* in any other position, and of *I/i* which is regularly used for both *I/i* and *J/j*. So-called long-*s*, however, has, as usual, been modernized, since contemporary practice was somewhat erratic. Where emendation is clearly called for, the emended readings are used in the lemmata of the Textual Notes and the Commentary, and where an emendation is open to question, it is discussed in the Commentary. The unemended reading may be consulted in the Textual Notes.

ii

Robert Parry's chivalric romance, *Moderatus, / The most delectable & famous / Historie of the Blacke Knight* (1595; sig. 2A1), is almost as rare as his *Sinetes*; only two copies are cited in *STC* (19337), one in the Bodleian Library (Douce, 212), the second in the Folger Shakespeare Library (159/29). Both lack the title-page (sig. A1) and have badly executed hand-written title-pages; the Folger copy lacks the rest of the preliminaries (sigs. A2–4). A colophon (sig. X3^{v}), however, tells us that the book was "Imprinted at London by Richard Ihones, at the signe / of the Rose and Crowne, neer to S. Andrewes / Church in Holburne. / 1595." It was entered on the Stationers' Register on 21 March 1594: "Richard Jones Entred for his copie vnder th[e h]andes of the warden, a booke in[ti]tuled *The most Delectable and famous historie of the black Knight* . . . vid"

(*A Transcript of the Registers of the Company of Stationers of London 1554–1640*, ed., Edward Arber, II [1571–1595], 1876).

Collation: 4° A4 2A–U^{4} X^{4} (quires signed throughout, except D2 (in Folger copy), D3, G3, I3, S4, X4 (lacking in both copies). Unpaged.

Irregular catchwords: sigs. B4^{v} him:/ him (E1 and/wherefore F1^{v} counterfet:/ counterfet, F4 Pandarina,/Pandarina N1^{v} him-/himself N4 in-/increased N4^{v} a braue/taking ("a braue" begins second line on O1) P3^{v} aduen-/aduentures, S1 When/What ("When" perhaps caught from line 15 of lyric No. 18) U1^{v} (no catchword) U4 Cor-/Cornelious X1^{v} per-/perswaded X2 Wor-/Worthy X3 all/all (Bodleian copy; type disturbed at the beginning of first two lines in Folger copy).

Watermarks: sigs. A, T, two-handled pot (?); sigs. A–C, F–H, K–M, O–P, R–S, U–X, hand; sigs. D, E, I, N, Q, no watermark.

Binding: Bodleian copy, late eighteenth-century polished calf, with gilt ribbon rules; red, yellow, and green swirled marbled end-papers; on the spine, in gold lettering, "THE BLACK KNIGHT." Folger copy, nineteenth-century half calf, with corners leather covered in a triangular pattern, marbled end-papers; on the spine, in gold lettering, "Parre's History of the Black Knight, 1595." Regarding Parre, see Introduction, 34, and below under Provenance.

Provenance: Folger copy, the Farmer-Heber-Britwell Court-Harmsworth copy. Richard Farmer notes on a fly-leaf: "The Author was Rich'd Parre, Gent. London printed 1595 [not mentioned by Tanner or Ames.] I have not heard of another Copy. 1782. nor had Mr. Ritson." Bodleian copy, a note by Francis Douce must refer to the Folger copy: "A very imperfect copy sold at D[r]. Farmer's sale for £0.18.0."

Press-variants: collation of the Bodleian and Folger copies has been limited to the twenty-two lyrics from *Moderatus* which are included in the present edition (see Appendix I). No substantive press variants occur, but two accidental press variants may be noticed, both of which may simply result from type failing to print or type shifting: No. 4, 2 (sig. D2v) hand,] hand *Folger*; No. 5 title (sig. G2) VEROSAES] VER OSAES *Folger*.

The evidence of the running-titles and certain idiosyncratic spellings indicates setting by a single compositor and printing by a single press. The outer and inner formes use the same set of running titles (“The strange Aduentures” [verso] “of the blacke Knight.” [recto]) with some very slight variations in quires F, S and T. Two clues in the recto running-title establish its use throughout: (1) the use of “Knight:” *vs.* “Knight.” occurs once in almost all quires in sigs. B3, C1, D1, E3, H1, I2, K2, L2, M2, N2, O2, P4, Q4, R2, T4, U2, X2 (“Knight:” appears twice in quire F and not at all in quires G and S); (2) the use of “of the” *vs.* “of the” occurs once in each quire in sigs. A3, B1, C3, D3, E1, F4, G2, H4, I3, K3, L3, M3, N1, O3, P3, Q3, R3, S4, T1, U3, X1. The verso running-title offers a single supporting clue by reading “Thestrange” *vs.* “The strange” twice in each quire (i.e., in both inner and outer formes) in sigs. A1^{v} A2^{v}, B3^{v} B4^{v}, C3^{v} C4^{v}, D1^{v} D2^{v}, E1^{v} E2^{v}, F3^{v} F4^{v}, G1^{v} G2^{v} (also G3^{v} G4^{v}), H2^{v} H3^{v}, I3^{v} I4^{v}, K1^{v} K2^{v}, L2^{v} L3^{v}, M2^{v} M3^{v}, N2^{v} N3^{v}, O4^{v} (only), P1^{v} P4^{v}, Q2^{v} Q4^{v}, R2^{v} R4^{v}, S3^{v} S4^{v}, T2^{v} T3^{v}, U2^{v} U3^{v}, X2^{v} X3^{v}.

The evidence for a single compositor is admittedly more tenuous, since I have not made a complete analysis of the volume, only of its twenty-two lyrics, which have been included in the present edition of Parry’s poems. The spelling, however, in the prose parts, printed in black letter, and the lyrics, printed in roman, is consistently the same throughout, as is the use in both of spellings like “doeth” for “doth” and “mooues” for “moues” (similarly in other *ou* words). The use of a single set of running-titles, both recto and verso, also suggests a single compositor.

In editing the *Moderatus* lyrics, substantive errors have been emended, the reading emended being recorded in the Textual Notes, but the punctuation, as in quotations from *Sinetes*, has been allowed to stand; ambiguities caused by the original pointing are discussed in the Commentary. If we may judge by the comparatively few substantive errors found in the lyrics from *Moderatus*, Richard Jones’s compositor(s) set considerably more carefully than the presumably more experienced compositor(s) in the busy print-shop of the long-established Thomas Purfoot, who served as printer for William Holme, the publisher of *Sinetes*.

FACSIMILE OF SINETES, COMMENTARY, AND TEXTUAL NOTES

SINETES

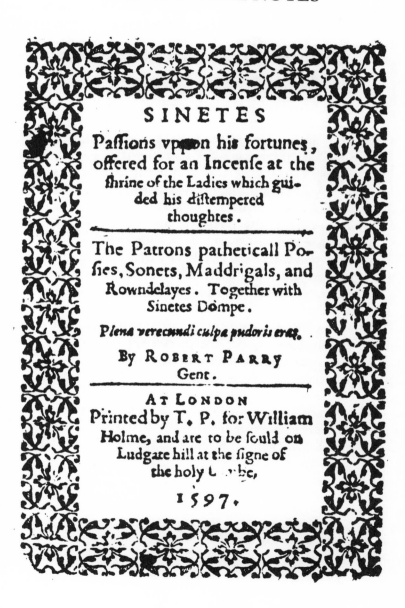

Passions vppon his fortunes, offered for an Incense at the shrine of the Ladies which guided his distempered thoughtes.

The Patrons patheticall Posies, Sonets, Maddrigals, and Rowndelayes. Together with Sinetes Dompe.

Plena verecundi culpa pudoris erat.

By ROBERT PARRY Gent.

AT LONDON
Printed by T. P. for William Holme, and are to be sould on Ludgate hill at the signe of the holy L[illegible]be,

1597.

¶ *To the right worſhipfull John* Salisburie of Lleweni Eſquier for the Bodie to the Queenes moſt excellent Maieſtie.

THe Hope of theſe, and glaſſe of future times,
O Heros which eu'n enuie itſelfe admir's,
Vouchſafe to guarde, & patronize my rimes,
My humble rime, which nothing elſe deſir's:
But to make knowne the greatnes of thy
To Honors throne that euer hath been inclyn'd. (minde,
Geue leaue a while vnto my breathing Muſe.
To pauſe vpon the accent's of her ſmarte,
From the reſpite of this ſhort-taken truce,
For to recorde the actions of my Harte:
Which vowed hath, to manifeſt thy worth,
That noble fruites to future age bringes foorth.
Eu'n thou alone, which ſtrengthn'ſt my repoſe,
And doeſt geue life vnto my dead deſire,

A 2 Which

The following textual notes for *Sinetes* (1597) and for the twenty-two lyrics from *Moderatus* (1595) offer a listing of what for the most part are compositorial typos or misreadings. In some cases, however, where the text is damaged by tears, etc. that affect the text (the copy of *Sinetes* being unique), some readings have to be reconstructed. The majority of such reconstructed readings may be determined, from what evidence remains, with relative certainty except when one or more words are missing (see sigs. A8 and A8[v]), but where a reading is uncertain and may affect meaning it will be noticed in the Commentary. The lemma preceding the square bracket gives the emended reading (the reading used in the Commentary lemmata); the reading following the square bracket gives the reading of the original text. See Introduction, 34–38, for further discussion of related textual matters.

Dedicatory Epistle (A2–A3)

For the connection between (Sir) John Salusbury and Parry, see Introduction, 5–6.

1 **glasse:** mirror (in which he is to be seen as a model).

7 **breathing:** (1) breathless; (2) living; (3) speaking.

8 **pause. . . accent's:** (1) hesitate, (2) wait upon the stressful feelings.

9 **respite . . . truce:** delay or temporary stay of this short-lived pause.

10 **actioms . . . Harte:** my heartfelt axioms (i.e., my heart's unquestioned propositions concerned with praising your worth). *O*'s "actioms," not recorded as a spelling of "axiom" by *OED*, may be only a misreading of "actions," which here can be taken to mean "feelings."

The Epistle

Which malice daunt'ste, that did thy fame oppose;
Now, with reuiuing hope, my quill inspire:
So he may write, and I may glorie singe,
That time, in time, may plucke out enui's stinge.
  Renowned Patron, my wayling verse,
To whose protect I flye for friendly ayde,
Vouchsafe to heare, while I my woes rehearse:
Then my poore muse, will neuer be dismaide,
To countenance the babling Eccho's frowne,
That future age may ring of thy renowne.
  I that ere-while with Pan his hindes did play,
And tun'd the note, that best did please my minde,
Content to sing a sheapheards Round-delay;
Now by thy might, my Muse the way did finde,
With Maddrigals, to store my homely stile,
Graced with th'applause, of thy well graced smile.
  Eu'n thou I say, whose trauaile hope doth yeilde,
That honours worth, may reape a due rewarde,
Which flyes with natiue plume vnto the fielde;
Whose paines deserues thy cuntreys iust regarde:
Time cannot dashe, nor enuie blemish those,
Whom on fam's strength, haue built their chiefest repose,
  Tis only that, which thou mayst clayme thine owne,
Deuouring time, cannot obscure the same,
In future age by this thou mayst be knowne,

VVhen

15 **Which . . . oppose:** Perhaps a reference to John Salusbury's duel with Owen Salusbury, in which Owen Salusbury was almost killed.

17 **he:** i.e., Salusbury (?); referent not clear.

19 **Renowned . . . verse:** The line is metrical only if "Patron" is treated as trisyllabic. "wayling" = bitterly lamenting.

20 **protect:** protection, patronage; "protect" is not in *OED* as a noun.

23 **countenance . . . frowne:** give heed to the foolish chattering of Echo's disapproval. In Greek mythology, Echo, in love with Narcissus, who spurned her, pined away until nothing was left but a voice, which Hera (Roman: Juno) had earlier already reduced to imitating the last word only of whatever she heard.

25 **Pan his hindes:** Pan's fellows. Pan, the Greek god of rural nature, half man, half goat, was associated with music and the dance.

27 **Round-delay:** short, simple song with a refrain. For Parry's two so-called examples, see sigs. G8^{v} and H1^{v}.

29 **Maddrigals:** short amatory lyric songs. For Parry's two examples, see sigs. G8 and H1. Parry also includes what he calls a madrigal in *Moderatus*, but with a refrain as in a roundelay (sig. 2A3^{v}).

29 **store:** fill out, build up (i.e., heighten, raise).

31 **trauaile:** painful labor.

33 **flyes . . . fielde:** rushes into combat with a large plume worn, by right of birth, in the hat or helmet as a mark of rank (i.e., he, figuratively, takes up a cause for his country).

38 **Deuouring time:** Cf. Ovid, XV, 234: "Tempus edax rerum."

39–42 Introduces the procreation theme (immortality-through-descendants); cf., for example, Shakespeare's Sonnets 1–17.

The Epiſtle.

When as poſterities renue thy fame:
Then thou being dead, ſhalt lyfe a newe poſſeſſe,
When workes nor wordes, thy worthynes expreſſe,
  Then ſhall my rime a ſort of ſtrength remaine,
To ſhielde the floriſh of thy high renowne,
That ruin's force may neu'r graces ſtain,
Which with fames ſound, ſhall through the worlde bee
Yf that th'ocean which includ's our ſtile, (blowne:
Would paſſage graunt out of this noble Iſle.
  For ſteling tyme of muſes lowe remaine.
Will from the fountaine of her chieſe conceyte,
Still out the ſame, through Lymbecke of my braine,
That glorie takes the honour to repeate:
Whoſe ſubiect though of royall accents barde,
Yet to the ſame, vouchſafe thy due rewarde,
  So ſhall my ſelfe, and Pen, bequeath their toyle,
To ſing, and write prayes, which it ſelfe ſhall prayſe,
Which time with cutting Sithe, ſhall neuer ſpoyle,
That often worthy Heros fame delayes:
And I encouraged by thy applauſe,
Shall teach my muſe on higher thinges to pauſe.

43–46 Introduces the common sonnet theme: immortality-through-the-poet's verse; cf., for example, Shakespeare's Sonnet 15.

44 **florish:** (1) perfection; (2) worthiness.

47 **includ's our stile:** confines (in an island) our works, verses.

49 **of . . . remaine:** of what is left of (1) my muse's blaze (i.e., literary brilliance); (2) my lowly muse (i.e., the product of his muse).

50 **chiefe conceyte:** loftiest thought, wit.

51 **Still out:** extract the essence of, distill.

51 **Lymbecke:** (i.e., alembic), a gourd-shaped, beak-nosed vessel used for distillation.

52 **glorie:** praise, renown.

53 **of . . . barde:** excluded from the marks (i.e., insignia) of royal blood.

56 **prayes . . . prayse:** praise that in praising (only) praises itself.

58 **That:** i.e., time.

60 **pause:** dwell.

Vpon the Authors muſe.

IF Poets with penne doe purchaſe praiſe,
Let Parrie then poſſeſſe his parte:
Whoſe Poſies rare, report doeth raiſe,
To Pernaſſe Mount of due deſarte.
In houſe of fame he ought haue place,
Yf Ouid eu'r deſerued that grace.
His pleaſaunt vaine, his phraſes fine,
Sentencious eke, in verſe and proſe:
That they include ſome grace deuine,
His former doinges doe well diſcoſe.
With his ſweete Muſe, & louely layes,
Who may compare in theſe our dayes.
But chiefiie his SINETES nowe,
Hath moued his muſe her prize to playe.
As if therein ſhe had made a vowe,
Some peerles poeſie to diſplaye.
There Cupides knacke are liuelye ſeene,
With Venus baites, that louelye Queene.
Then Momus mumme, & Zoylus ceaſe,
And foule Mouth Theon leaue to raile:
Seeing Parries penne, the beſt doth pleaſe,
What doth vour carping then auaile.
Whom valiaunt Lyon doth protect:
May well all crauing Curres reiect.

Habet ſcintilla calorem. Hu. Gry.

17 knackes] knacke

Vpon the Authors muse (A3^{v})

3 **report:** fame, repute.

4 **Pernasse . . . desarte:** Mount Parnassus, the home of the Nine (or Three) Muses, because of the merit that is their due.

5 **house of fame:** Perhaps a reference to Chaucer's "House of Fame."

8 **Sentencious . . . prose:** full of wisdom, aphoristic in both verse and prose. Here and in line 10 ("former doinges"), Gryffyth is referring to Parry's *Moderatus* (1595), a chivalric romance interspersed with a substantial number of lyrics. See Introduction, 26, and Other Poems; also 279, n23.

9 **some grace deuine:** some utterance above human endeavor.

14 **her . . . playe:** to play her part.

17 **Cupides . . . seene:** Cupid's crafty or clever tricks or dodges are vividly represented.

18 **baites:** traps, snares.

19 **Momus:** In Greek mythology, a god personifying censure and mockery.

19 **mumme:** be silent.

19 **Zoylus:** fourth-century B. C. severe critic of Homer.

20 **Theon:** notorious Greek railer.

22 **carping:** fault-finding.

23 **Lyon:** Refers to John Salusbury, Parry's patron, who bore a lion rampant in his coat-of-arms.

24 **crauing Curres:** i.e., presumably, cowardly dogs; *OED*, however, does not record "craving" as a variant form of "craven." Gryffyth (see below) employs the phrase "crauen curres" in "Posse & nolle nobile,' 15 (sig. H4^{v}).

25 **Habet scintilla calorem:** He possesses a bright spark of love's fire.

25 **Hu. Gry.:** For Hugh Gryffyth, see "Posse & nolle nobile" (sig. H4).

Vpon Sinetes Paſſions.

AH Loue, fond loue, falſe loue, deceitfu loue,
Vnkinde, vnto the kinde, to frend a foe:
A Tirant, loyall louers doe thee proue,
And faithfull hartes, thou filleſt full of woe.
Ah blind loue: bliud, but not in woũding blind,
Yea blind for why? thy frends thou doſt not ſee,
Thoſe which reſiſt, thou lika a childe doſt flee,
But they which yeilde thriſe man-like do thee finde,
Still, Still a boy, delightinge ſtill to playe,
What play? , to ſlaye, what kinde of play is this:
Soe plaies the hungrye hauke, with taken praye:
So playes the wilie Catte with captiue Miſe.
Sinetes mournfull Muſe doth this deſcrie,
His haples hapes my plaints doe iuſtifie.

The bloudie beare, which rangeth in the wood,
Doth ceaſe to rage, when that ſhee hath her fill:
The hungry woolf, which oft is bath'd in bloud,
When greedie paunch is glutted leaues to kill.
But Cupide, whom men call the god of loue,
(Vniuſtly call: nay, doe moſt iuſtly call:
For why, he loues to kill, whom? thoſe which loue)
He dayly kills, & is not ſild at all.
What thinge is rare? to ſee a Tirant olde,

A 4

1 deceitfu[ll]] deceitfu
5 blind, but] bliud, but

Vpon Sinetes Passions (A4–A4^{v})

Title. **Vpon Sinetes Passions:** Refers to the forty-six Passions which open Parry's *Sinetes.*

5 **blind loue:** i.e., Cupid, who was often thought of as blind because, as an archer, he seemed to shoot his arrows at random.

6 **Yea . . . see:** (Nevertheless) blind indeed because he does not recognize his friends (i.e., those in love with love).

8 **thrise . . . finde:** discover thee (though a boy) to have the strength of three men.

13 **descrie:** cry out against.

14 **His . . . iustifie:** Unfortunate events happening to him justify my complaints.

22 **fild:** filled, glutted.

In prayſe of the Booke.

CVupid is old, though he a Tirant bee:
What old? nay yong, wee Cupid ſtill behould,
Though young in ſight, yet Tirant old is hee.
Old may he be, and Tirants wages haue,
Which thouſands haue vntimely ſent to graue.

Happie thou art, Sinetes though vnhappie
Vnhappy were the happes, which thee befell,
Happy yet in this, that learned Parrye,
Thy happles happes, in ſugred ſonges doth tell.
Thou ſhrouded art, vnder the Lions winge,
Whoſe noble Name, all carping curres will quaile,
Now neyther Zoil. priuily backbiting,
Nor Momus barkes againſt thee ſhall preuaile.
Sing boldely then, ſing (pleaſant Nightingale)
Sweete warbling tunes, and heauenly harmonye:
Feare not filthy byrdes, which would annoy thee,
Ioues Eagle, will thee ſhend againſt them all.
Parrye thou pend'ſt, the Muſes did indite,
They ſweetely ſong, their ſweet ſongs thou did'ſt write.

H. P. gentleman.

24 CVpid] CVupid (no catchword after line 23; line 24 at the beginning of sig. A4^{v} is wrongly treated as the opening line of a new poem with the following title: "In prayse of the Booke.")

35 Zoilus] Zoil. *(the period presumably indicates an abbreviated form)*

26 **young in sight:** i.e., he appears to be young (a boy, a child).

27 **Tirants wages haue:** gain the rewards of a tyrant (ironic).

28 **Which:** i.e., a tyrant's rewards.

33 **vnder . . . winge:** i.e., under the protection of John Salusbury, whose coat-of-arms bore a lion rampant.

35–36 **Zoil . . . Momus:** See Hugh Gryffyth's "Vpon the Authors muse," 19 n.

35 **priuily backbiting:** secretly traducing, speaking ill of (behind a person's back).

40 **Ioues Eagle:** As king of birds, the eagle was naturally associated with Jove (Greek: Zeus).

40 **shend:** shield, defend.

41 **pend'st . . . indite:** wrotest down (with thy pen) what the Nine (or Three) Muses (goddesses who presided over poetry, music, dancing, and all liberal arts) composed (for you).

42 **song:** sung (variant form).

43 **H.P. gentleman:** "H. P." may tentatively be identified with one of the following: (1) H. Ph. (i.e., H. Phillips), who wrote two Welsh poems in honor of John Salusbury, Parry's patron (in CC, fols. 35^{v}, 54^{v}; (see Brown, xxix, xxx); (2) Huw Pennant, who also wrote a Welsh poem in honor of Salusbury (in CC, fol. 49^{v}; see Brown, xxx); (3) Hugh Peake of Lleweni Green, whose death on 22 March 1601 is noted in Parry's Diary.

In prayſe of the Booke.

Faire Philomele her rauiſhment hath ſong,
But Parry rauiſheth with muſefull tunes,
No ſoner hath his praiſe with floriſh ſprong,
With Daphins boſome ſtūft with ſweete perfumes,
But forth his nectar-feaſting poezie bloomes,
And eke the Delion harper doth lament,
In Paſsions poore SINETES diſcontent,

Amored ſhepheards wonder at thy wit,
And to thy piping lend their liſtning eare,
And in thy praiſe the mûſes frame a writ,
Therefore I thought my rûder lines to teare,
And ſkilleſſe riming bid my hand forbeare:
But little candles giue their glimering light,
As well as torches in the brighter ſight.

W. R. Gent.

4 Daphnis] Daphins

In prayse of the Booke (A5)

1 **Philomele:** See Sonetto 11.7n.

1 **song:** sung (variant form); cf. “sprong,” line 3.

2 **musefull tunes:** deeply meditative harmonies; “musefull” not listed in *OED*.

4 **With Daphnis:** (as) with Daphnis. *O*’s “Daphins” is an obvious error. In Greek mythology, Daphnis was a Sicilian shepherd, sometimes thought of as the father of pastoral poetry; he figures frequently in Theocritus’ *Idylls* and Virgil’s *Eclogues*.

5 **nectar-feasting poezie:** poetry that has feasted on nectar (the favorite drink of the classical gods).

6 **eke . . . lament:** moreover Apollo doth bewail. The line is parenthetical, line 5 being continued by line 7. Certainly, the “Delion harper” (i.e., Apollo, who was born on the island of Delos) does not lament “In Passions poore Sinetes discontent,” unless we are supposed to equate Parry with Apollo! If, however, we take “eke” to be a compositor’s misreading of “like,” the problem posed by line 6 disappears.

7 **Passions:** Refers to Parry’s forty-six Passions, which follow the commendatory verses in *Sinetes*.

8 **Amored shepheards:** shepherds in love. The participial “Amored,” coined from “amour,” is not found in the *OED*.

10 **in . . . writ:** See “Vpon Sinetes Passions,” 41 n.

11 **teare:** tear up, destroy.

12 **skillesse . . . forbeare:** artless, undiscriminating rhyming ordered my hand to cease (writing).

15 **W. R. Gent.:** No identifiable “W. R.” appears to be part of the Salusbury-Parry circle.

In prayse of the Booke.

THe rarest giftes neede not a Trumpe to sounde,
For fame it selfe will undertake the prayse,
The sunne needes not a light for to be founde:
But in the height of Sphere giues light alwayes:
Flye then thou worke no soile shall thee disgrace,
And why thy worthie patron is thy fort,
Thou needes not shunne t'approach into ech place,
Twy flowring bloome of wit shall thee report.
Thy wise and deepe conceytes neede not be grac'd,
For dayntie choise here found ech fancies please,
Thy mindes repose may neuer be defac'd,
Each fancie then thy fancies fame will raise.
O that my tong could duely raise thy fame,
Yet after age at large shall doe the same.

H. P. Gent.

8 Thy] Twy

In prayse of the Booke (A5^{v})

4 **Sphere:** the vault of heaven.

5 **soile:** moral stain.

6 **worthie patron:** i.e., John Salusbury; see Introduction, 8–10.

7 **place:** rank.

9 **grac'd:** embellished.

10 **dayntie . . . please:** fastidious choice here (i.e., in Parry's "deepe conceytes") discovered that each of his poetic creations pleases. Parry uses "fancie" (line 12) to describe a number of the lyrics scattered through his *Moderatus.*

15 **H. P. Gent.:** Probably a different "H. P." from the author of "Vpon Sinetes Passions" (sig. A4); see the three possible candidates there suggested.

In prayse of the Booke.

O Floue of ioy of solace sweete and pleasant vaine,
That wanted was thy sugred muse to write and sing,
Both Sonetts Maddrigals with dainty ditties playne,
What sudden chaunce hath moued to chang thy stile what
Yf Prince prelate peere and Parry discontent, (thing.
Complaynes a like gainst froward fortunes bad intent.
Compier, full many shalt thou finde with there estate;
Both discontented beare and blame their direfull fate.
When all thinges alter kinde that subiect be to change,
Then loue the ioy shal likewise turne to sorrow strange.

T. S. Esq.

In prayse of the Booke (A6)

1 **vaine:** mode of expression.

2–4 **That . . . thing:** These lines suggest that the Passions (and, perhaps, "The lamentation of a Male-content") are among Parry's most recent work. Note that "T. S." credits Parry with sonnets and madrigals, thus offering some support for assigning Sonettos 1–31 and, at least, the two "Maddrigalls" (sigs. G8 and H1) to Parry rather than to Salusbury (see Introduction, 13–23, for other attribution evidence), since no sonnets appear in *Moderatus*. However, one lyric is described as a madrigal (sig. 2A3^{v}), though in form it is more like a roundelay. Most of the lyrics in *Moderatus* are simply described as "ditties" or "fancies."

5 **discontent:** discontented, vexed. For this participial form, see Abbott, 342.

6 **froward:** adverse, refractory.

7 **Compier:** (o) fellow (sufferer).

7 **with there estate:** in their condition (i.e., discontented).

9 **alter kinde:** change their nature.

11 **T. S. Esq.:** T. S. Esq. may tentatively be identified as Thomas Salusbury, son of Sir John Salusbury, grandfather of John Salusbury, Parry's patron. He arranged for the publication of William Myddelton's Welsh translation of the Psalms (1603), who may also have contributed commendatory verses to *Sinetes* (see "In prayse of the Booke" [sig. A7] by "W. M. Esq."). Thomas Salusbury's death is noted by Parry in his Diary as occurring 27 June 1602.

In prayſe of the Booke:

SWeet is the paine which vertuous trauell brings,
High is the place which wiſedome doth commend,
Sower is the eaſe of vices root that ſprings:
Loue is the ſeate which idlenes doth lend.
None getteth wealth that puts not from the ſhore,
Paine breedeth honor, vertue winneth fame,
Glorie doth follow, courage goes before,
Though oft the vent, anſweare not the ſame.
Vertuous attempts are voide of all ſhame,
The baſe whome meanes obſcurely doth keepe,
Liues voyd of honor, dies without name,
And in eternall darknes euer he doth ſleepe.
Therefore SINETES ti's then no blot,
With mournefull Paſſions to lament thy lot.

R. S. Eſq.

8 th'event] the vent

In prayse of the Booke (A6^{v})

1 **trauell:** bodily or mental labor.

3 **ease . . . springs:** relief that springs from vice's root.

6 **Paine:** taking pains (to accomplish or produce something worthy).

7 **Glorie:** renown, fame.

8 **th'euent . . . same:** the outcome does not achieve renown or fame.

10 **The . . . keepe:** The low-minded (morally inferior), whose (1) conditions, (2) resources keep them unknown to fame.

14 **Passions:** i.e., Parry's forty-six poems called Passions.

15 **R. S. Esq.:** May probably be identified with either (1) Roger Salusbury, Esq. and D.C.L., uncle of Parry's patron, John Salusbury, who attended Jesus College, Cambridge, and composed two shield-posies for a masque presented at his nephew's wedding, on 27 December 1586 (see CC, fol. 87^{v}, and Brown, 36–37; or (2) Robert Salusbury, Esq. and D. C. L., also Salusbury's uncle, who like Parry, wrote an "Epitaph" on the death of Salusbury's mother, Catherine of Berain, in 1591 (see CC, fols. 181–82, and Brown, 42–43).

In prayſe of the Booke.

THou O too cruell guide of louers traine,
Proude in thy tyrannie on yeilded harts,
When ſhall thy thralls forget to mourne and plaine?
When wilt thou ceaſe to hurle hatefull darts?
Shall all the earth ring through her ſpatious parts,
From out the mouth of euery fordon ſwayne,
That thou in ſteed of loue, breedſt helliſh paine,
Thou dire Vſurper of cæleſtiall arts.

Shall heauenlie Poſie be prophaned ſtill,
In woes deſcription to thy peeuiſh will,
Wilt thou in ſteed of loue, true louers kill,
Far be it from a God to doe thus ill.
No PARRY no, he doth but ſhew thee ſorrow,
That from woes darknes, ioy more light may borrow.

W. M. Eſq.

In prayse of the Booke (A7)

1 **Thou:** Cupid.

1 **traine:** deceit, trickery, guile.

3 **thralls:** slaves.

3 **plaine:** lament.

6 **fordon swayne:** (1) exhausted, (2) ruined lover.

8 **caelestiall arts:** heavenly, divine rules of conduct.

9–10 **still, . . . will:** i.e., by always being a depiction of sorrows, according to your spiteful, malicious will.

15 **W. M. Esq.:** W. M. Esquire may be tentatively identified with one of the following: (1) (more probable) William Myddelton, a recognized Welsh poet, from whom Parry bought lands in Eriviatt and Bodeliog, of which he took possession 3 January 1599, and who, together with Sir John Salusbury and Dr. William Morgan, Bishop of St. Asaph, officially proclaimed James I, King of England, France, and Ireland in the town of Denbigh on 30 March 1603 (see Parry's Diary, under these dates); (2) Bishop William Morgan (see above), who translated the Bible into Welsh.

PASSION. I.

Fine ripe cōceyts forſake the wearied miude,
And fancies faile, whē ſorowes ſurges ſwaye
My pen bath'd in the waues of griefs vnkind
Muſt write of moane, of ruine & decaye:
A tragicke note doth fit a tragick chaunce,
A heauie heart with ſorrowes pipe muſt daunce.

Like PELICAN I wander all alone,
The dezart woodes and wildernes ſo wilde,
To ſenſeleſſe groues, I crye and make my moane,
Eu'n from my thoughts all hope is quite exil'd,
Left thus to mourne the ſkriching owle keepes time,
With dolefull notes that to the heauens doe clime.

Notes that bewaile the griefes of carefull heart,
That charge my minde with heapes of deepe annoy,
Which vnto none I vowed to impart,
But vnto you my drenching dolors ioy:
Keepe ladies keepe the cloſet of my griefe,
Yeilde Ladies yeilde, for ſorrowe ſome reliefe.

No darke deſpaire may drowne my drowſie hope,
If you giue life vnto my dead deſire,
Nor ought may daunt my minde, yf you giue ſcope,
To pitties floodes to quench the kindled fire:
Fortune is blinde and will not ſee my paine,
Time hath a ſalue to cure the ſame againe.

---

2 swaye:] swaye (*line over-measure*)

Passion I (A7^{v})

Title. This is the first of forty-six Passions. Taking the initial capital letter of each "Passion," Parry, acrostically, spells out three names: FRANCIS WYLOWGHBY, ELYZABETH WOLFRESTON, and ROBERT PARRY. As Brown suggests (xxxvi), the first two names must be those of the "Ladies" to whom Parry addresses his "Passions." As here used, "passion" means an amorous poem expressing a lover's affliction and suffering because his mistress has never accepted his suit and yielded to his desires. The "Ladies" are not addressed after Passion XXXV, at which point Robert Parry's name begins as the conclusion of the acrostic series, except in the last two lines of Passion XLVI.

1 **ripe conceyts:** mature thoughts.

2 **fancies:** (1) flights of the imagination; (2) poems (like the Passions).

5 **chaunce:** state of affairs, situation.

7 **Pelican:** a type of selfless love. The pelican was reputed to stab itself with its long beak in order to feed its young.

9 **senselesse:** unresponsive, unfeeling.

11 **skriching:** screeching.

13 **carefull:** full of pain and sorrow.

14 **charge:** burden.

16 **drenching dolors:** drowning griefs.

17 **closet:** cabinet (i.e., figuratively, the heart)

21 **giue scope:** make space for, open your minds to.

23 **Fortune is blinde:** The goddess Fortuna was often depicted as blindfolded because her actions appeared to be so random.

PASSION.

Rype griefe hath graft in ſlumbring harts diſpa
What ſtill increaſe the motions of my care,
Thinke I of ſalues my ſorrowes to impaire:
Then fearefull fitts the torments racke prepare;
For him that would preſume to thinke of good,
When darke deſpaire drown'd hope in ſorrowes floo

Seas, floods, and waues, of fortunes weakefull ſcou
Ceaſe not to roare, to ſwell, to toſſe with winde,
Of bale-full hap, (which increaſe the ſurge,
Of ſharpe diſgrace) where perrils foord I finde:
For to augment the terror of my paine,
Where hope of naught but carking care remaine,

The ſtocke is dead, whereon the ympe was graft,
Which beare the fruite, that wonted ſores did cure,
The graft muſt die, ſo muſt the fruit be laft
Naked to pine, and nipping fioſtes endure:
The braunch con ſumes when periſh'd ſtock doth faile,
When ſappe is gone how can the growth preuaile.

My ſappe is gone which noriſhment did yeilde,
My wythered fruite doth fall before his time,
I am the graffe which want my wonted ſheilde
For ſtocke decayed I haue no roote to clime:
Lende ladies nowe your dolefull notes ech o
Pittie at leaſt though not aſſwage my moa

Title I[I.]] I (leaf damaged)
1 dispa[ire,]] dispa (leaf damaged)
6 floo[d.]] floo (leaf damaged)
7 wreakefull] weakefull
7 scou[rge,]] scou (leaf damaged)
16 frostes] fiostes
17 consumes] con sumes
21 sheilde [,]] sheilde (leaf damaged)
23 o[ne,]] o (leaf damaged)
24 moa[ne.]] moa (leaf damaged)

Passion [II] (A8)

Leaf (sig. A8) damaged; see Textual Notes.

1 **Rype:** full-blown.
7 **wreakefull:** vengeful. *O*'s "weakefull" is obviously an error.
9 **bale-full hap:** painful mishap, chance.
12 **carking:** burdensome, troubling.
13 **ympe:** young shoot, graft.
14 **wonted:** usual, ordinary.
15 **laft:** left (variant form).
18 **preuaile:** (1) increase in vigor; (2) be efficacious.
21 **graffe:** graft (variant form).
22 **For:** because.

PASSION. III.

.CADI's Nimphs in mournfull sables drest
With plyant pipes sound dolefull musick note,
Bewayle your sheapheards fare, that thus opprest,
ewe increase of sorrowes set a floate:
course doth scarce abide the turch of time,
e wearied heart endur'd the bale-full chime.

he sound of chime doth sound in lothed eares,
at could endure such cruell sound to heare,
hich doth encrease a heape of dreadfull feares,
Where to my soule darke horror doth appeare:
Long passed cares renewe againe their course,
Fates fatall chaunce doth change from bad to worse.

A happie man had I neu'r happie byn,
For fortunes smile did cause my greatest fall,
To purchase ease by newe encrease of sinne;
Were for to make my soule, my bodies thrall:
Hap then what may, let fortune frowne or smile,
ares cruell scourge shall not my minde defile.

ur shrines I fill with volumes of my griefe,
yde I craue to quench the burning fier,
brought to CACAs some reliefe;
forts may reuiue my dead desier:
m hope by fortunes passed change,
eames the dezarts wilde to range.

---

1 [AR]CADI'S] CADI'S (*leaf damaged*)
4 [A n]ewe] ewe (*leaf damaged*)
5 [The] course] course (*leaf damaged*)
6 [Th]e] e (*leaf damaged*)
7 [T]he] he (*leaf damaged*)
8 [Th]at] at (*leaf damaged*)
18 [C]ares] ares (*leaf damaged*)
19 [Yo]ur] ur (*leaf damaged*)

Passion III (A8^{v})

Leaf (sig. A8^{v}) damaged; see Textual Notes.

1 **Arcadi's Nimphs:** Arcadia's semi-divine maidens who inhabited the sea, rivers, fountains, hills, woods etc. Arcadia was a region in ancient Greece proverbial for its rural simplicity and domestic innocence.

1 **sables:** black garments. Cf. *Hamlet*, 3.2.130.

2 **plyant:** compliant (i.e., suiting the mourning mood).

2 **musick:** musical; but, perhaps, a compositor's misreading of "musicks"; cf. Passion IX.4.

5 **tutch:** stroke.

7 **sound . . . eares:** ears that loathe the sound (of the "chime").

11 **course:** continued movement.

21 **Cacas:** In Greek mythology, Cacas was a giant, son of Vulcan, who stole from Hercules some of the cattle of Geryon; he was slain by Hercules for his theft.

---

20 [ ]de] de (*leaf damaged*)
21 [ ] brought] brought (*leaf damaged*)
22 [ ]iorts] iorts (*leaf damaged*)
23 [ ]m] m (*leaf damaged*)
24 [ ]eames] eames (*leaf damaged*)

PASSION. IIII.

Nights rest is bard with weried thoughts controle,
The pillow moanes bath'd in my dréching teares,
The sheetes beare guilt of my distressed soule,
Wherein is wrapt a multitude of feares,
When stealing nappe doth close my drowsie eies,
Then starting, feare sayth it is time to rise.

Yf sleepe at all possesse my vytall parts,
Then dreadfull dreames with gastly sights appeare,
Which do present the cause that wrought my smarts:
And doe a fresh renewe forgotten feare;
I sleepe in paine, I watch in wretched griefe,
Lyef's in dispaire sith hope forbids reliefe.

When cursed thoughts there carefnll couch forsake,
Confused heaps of new encreasing sores.
Like wildfier tost in PHLEGETONS firie lake,
Or ship that stirrs gainst raging streame with ores
So doth my heart with sorowing sobs neere spent,
Striue with the course that cares command hath sent.

My moane I make where pities bowre is built,
Your gentle brests is mercies chaire of state,
A Butt of bane which neu'r for lacke is tilt:
Yeildes fresh supplies vnto my frowning fate,
Then fortune then cleere once this smothing aire,
With salues of hope, after this long dispaire.

B

---

1 which] with
23 smoth'ring] smothing

Passion IIII (B1)

6 **starting:** involuntary, sudden.
9 **smarts:** mental pains.
12 **Lyef's:** life's (a Parry spelling).
15 **Phlegetons firie lake:** a burning, fiery river in the classical underworld (i.e., Hades).
16 **stirrs:** moves (only a little).
18 **course:** forward movement (of fear and grief).
21 **Butt of bane:** cask of poison.
21 **tilt:** tipped up, overturned.
23 **smoth'ring:** *O*'s "smothing" is a misreading given the context.

PASSION. V.

SOund TRITON forth thy heauy dolefull knill,
That rings a peale of en'r enduring woe,
No vacant place but balefull ECCHOS fill:
My heart is made a harbour for the foe:
That yeildeth foode vnto mv curſed cares,
And poyſon ſtrong with hony ioyn'd prepares.

Heau'ns ſhew your power, earth tremb'e at mv crye,
And ſtony rockes be molyfied with moane,
The rurall Gods with mournfull melodie,
Lament my chaunce, bewaile choice ech one,
Your ſheapheard ſwaine in ſables clad with care,
Doth for the dead ſome mourning weeds prepare.

The liuing doth preſage his dying dole,
His life is death while others reape his toyle,
Who hath not power himſelfe for to controle,
Is ſure the fruite of ſome aacurſed ſoyle,
His tong too long, his wiſedome is too ſhort,
Who rues in deede the thing he ſpake iu ſport.

But Ladies yet condemne not his deſire,
Though paſſed deeds his preſent griefe procure,
And lare miſſihapps yeild fuell to his fier,
That ſcant he can the ſcorching heate endure,
Whoſe ayde he craues to mollyfie his paine,
With pleaſāt ſport of ſome conceyted vaine.

2 eu'r] en'r
16 accursed] aacursed
18 in]iu
21 late misshapps] lare missihapps

Passion V (B1^{v})

1 **Triton:** son of Neptune (or Oceanus); he served as Neptune's trumpeter.

1 **knill:** (variant of "knell") the solemn sound of a church bell at a death or funeral.

9 **rurall Gods:** the so-called "Gods of the Woods," Pan, Silvanus, Dame Flora, Pomona, nymphs, etc.

10 **chaunce:** bad fortune, mischance.

10 **choice ech one:** (1) (my) choice of each rural god; (2) each one of my choices.

13 **The liuing:** i.e., his life.

13 **presage . . . dole:** foretell (1) his death from grief, (2) the time allotted for his death.

14 **toyle:** struggle (with grief).

21 **late:** O's "lare" is a compositional error.

23 **Whose ayde:** i.e., help from the "Ladies" in line 19.

24 **conceyted vaine:** witty strain.

PASSION. VI.

IN tract of time is perſ'd the hardeſt fliut,
Not by the force but by the droppinges fall,
My greefes from raging rigor neuer ſtint:
And can I then endure ſuch curſed thrall?
Yt were a hell to thinke of ſuch a paine,
Which naught but cares doth wreſt from gored vaine.

Vaine is my vaine, yet voyde of vaine delight,
Curſt is the chaunce that chayngeth to extreame,
Vnhappie man, ſubiect to Fortunes might,
Can nought but greefe my fatall greefe redeeme,
Then welcom griefe though death more welcom weare
Whoſe force at once might end tormenting feare.

Feare, which doth frett the wearie craſed heart,
More then the paine, that torment can procure,
The heau'ns I call for to record my ſmart.
That thus long did ſuch agonies endure;
Leaue to ſtraye, loue to be iuſt yee ſkies,
And martyre thoſe that doe your power deſpiſe.

Skies fild with flame, of fierie fretting ire,
That kindled wrath vnto my penſiue ſoule,
In LVCANS forge which frameth deepe deſire,
To ſell my life for Fortunes bleſſed dole:
Your dole, I craue ſweete Ladies to aſſwage,
The diſmalle doome of IANVS daughters rage.

1 flint] fliut
21 VVLCANS] LUCANS
24 DANAUS] IANUS

Passion VI (B2)

1 **tract:** course, process.

1 **pers'd:** pierced.

4 **thrall:** (1) bondage; (2) oppression.

6 **gored vaine:** bloody vein.

7 **Vaine . . . vaine . . . vaine:** useless, futile . . . course of thought . . . foolish.

17 **inuaye:** denounce vehemently.

19 **fretting ire:** destructive anger.

21 **Vulcans forge:** See Sonetto 21.11n. *O*'s "LUCANS" has no classical identity.

22 **dole:** lot, portion.

23 **dole:** charitable gift.

24 **Danaus daughters rage:** violence of Danaus' daughters. *O*'s "IANUS" is an obvious compositor's misreading of "DANAUS," which fits the context perfectly. Danaus, according to Greek legend, king of the Argives, had fifty daughters and his brother, Aegyptus, had fifty sons. Aegyptus forced Danaus to arrange a mass marriage with Aegyptus' sons, but, because an oracle had told Danaus that he would be killed by one of his daughters' husbands, he ordered his daughters to slay their husbands on their wedding night. All but Hypermestra did so, sparing her husband, Lynceus, who did indeed kill Danaus in revenge, as the oracle had foretold. Danaus' other daughters, as punishment ("dismale doome") were condemned, in Hades, to try, fruitlessly and forever, to fill a leaky jar with water.

PASSION. VII.

SCarce warme I burne, yet freeze in fierie flame,
Diſpleaſed ſtill, I reſt content withall,
Yet male-content againe, eu'n with the ſame:
What freedom wrought, eft-ſoones hath made me thrall,
Thus contrarie theſe coutraries I taſte,
Thus borne to beare I liue my life to waſte.

Life is a death, when dolors taſte doth ſway.
And death a life to ſuch as croſſes beare,
My thred is ſpoon to be the VVLTVRSpray,
That Tiger-like, my cruell death doth ſweare:
Thoughts, force my lingring life, to weare and pine,
Conceyt will kill the ſtouteſt heart in fine.

Diſtreſſed thus, my light-ſome hope is paſt,
And darknes doth with horror now appeare,
Maiſter the ſhippe that hath a broken Maſt:
Through darkeſt clouds Sonns goulden beams are cleere.
So let the beams and beautie of your grace,
Shine through the miſt that doth my ioy deface.

Hlde not the glaſſe with any wooden caſe,
Let vertues mindes ſome vertues workes bring foorth,
Doe not ſweete Nimphs your noble mindes imbaſe,
With any act that ſhall not be of worth,
But let your ſonne ſhine to your ſheapheards caſe,
The praiſe is yours, if you his griefe appeaſe.

5 contraries] coutraries
9 VVLTVRS pray] VVLTVRSpray
19 Hide] Hlde
23 ease] case (?)

Passion VII (B2^{v})

1 **burne, yet freeze:** A conventional oxymoron derived from Petrarch; cf. Passion XV.6; *Moderatus*, sig. G4^{v}, lines 29–30, and Robert Greene, *1 Mamillia* (1583), II.77: "fry in frost, & freese in fire."

4 **eft-soones:** soon afterward.

5 **contrarie:** with opposite reactions, of two minds. Cf. Passion VIII.23–24.

5 **these contraries:** i.e., burn / freeze, displease / content.

7 **dolors . . . sway:** the feeling of grief rules.

9 **My . . . spoon:** i.e., I have reached the end of my thread of life, which, my destiny having been set by Lachesis and my thread spun by Clotho, is about to be cut by Atropos, the third of the Roman Parcae or Fates (see Passion XXIII.2); "spoon" is a variant of "spun."

11 **weare and pine:** wear out and waste away.

12 **Conceyt:** sad melancholy thought.

12 **in fine:** finally.

13 **light-some . . . past:** bright, clear hope is gone.

19 **Hide . . . case:** Do not cover over any part of the mirror with any wooden frame (i.e., don't decrease or narrow the reflection of your grace).

20 **vertues . . . foorth:** virtuous minds produce virtuous actions. The form "vertues" is a recognized variant of "virtuous."

21 **imbase:** degrade.

PASSION. VIII.

VVay-faring thus in wildernes of care,
My woefull minde, with thornes of discontent,
Doth yeild new thoughts, which torments new (prepare
Then I begyn againe for to lament:
Where first began the Period of my fall,
There first I pause, and rue the summe of all.

Thus doe I mourne, thus doe I moane my daies,
And itt'terate still my heapes of deepe annoy,
Thus doe I liue, and liuing loue to prayse:
The thing which doth my comforts hope destroy,
How can I liue and lead this wearie life?
When life encrease, and death might end the strife.

O blessed death, would death but heare my crie,
And succour lend, to such as succour want,
O happie man yf lingering miserie:
Had once an end my dolors to supplante,
Yet would I feare least death would me forsake,
And lothed life my carcas dead awake.

Whom heau'ns doe spite & earthes disdaine dispise,
He whylome liu'd in pleasures pleasant bower,
With patience the low againe may rise,
The fretting horse is spent within an houre:
For all extreames doe worke extreame effectes,
And contrarie yeilde contrarie aspectes.

Passion VIII (B3)

6 **There . . . all:** Looking back to the beginning of my fall, I pause and lament the sum of all my cares.

8 **itt'terate:** (1) repeat; (2) renew.

12 **life encrease:** the act of living (will) increase (the "strife"). Perhaps "encrease" should be emended to "encreases."

19 **spite:** regard with contempt.

20 **whylome:** formerly, before.

22 **fretting:** chafing, restive.

24 **aspectes:** looks, appearances.

PASSION. IX.

YF wayling may appease the wrathfull Gods,
And pittie moue the tyranized heart,
My scourged minde with firie burning rods,
Maye paye the tribute of my restles smart,
With sacrifice of salt and brinish teares,
Which yeilde newe life to late departed feares.

No floode so heigh but hath as low an ebb,
No storme so great but hath a caulme ensuies,
No man so mad to weaue his sorrowes webb,
And being condemnd his pardon will refuse:
Floods, stormes, and webbs, of griefe, of care, of paiue,
Mayfall, may cease, may be vndone againe.

Floods, stormes, nor webs, of my new budding woe,
Will fall, or cease, or be vndone at all,
The more I striue, the stronger is the bowe,
Which will not bend but to my greater fall:
And still doth shoote the arrowes of disdaine,
My hope being dead to wound, to kill againe.

Dead hope except my froward fortnne change,
Which bends her browe, and yeildes no hope to me,
But that I must in wildest dezartes rainge,
With sauage rude and Tigers to agree;
No force, for there the Driads I shall finde
With musickes note for to refresh my minde.

11 paine] paiue

Passion IX (B3^{v})

3 **rods:** sticks (metaphorically used for instruments for mental self-torture).

9 **webb:** entanglement, snare.

12 **vndone:** reversed, uneffected.

14 **or . . . all:** i.e., or in any way reversed.

15 **stronger . . . bowe:** less pliant is the bough.

16 **but . . . fall:** except to my greater ruin.

19 **froward:** adverse.

22 **sauage rude:** violent, unnurtured savage.

23 **Driads:** mythological wood-nymphs.

PASSION. X.

LEaue soule to mourne for that which hath no cure
Yt is in vaine to striue against the winde,
Set vp thy rest; that nothing can endure,
In such extreames, except it be assignd,
By th'mperiall powers that guide the starrs,
To trie thee here that sende such deadly warrs.

These mistries vn-thought approch'd the place,
Where first I ken'd the perrill which ensu'd,
But all to late: for then did hope deface,
My passed ioyes which heauenly I view,d:
Looking astance on that which came behinde,
My heart pen'd vp in sorrowes fould I finde.

You Ladies then the Nurses of my hope,
Which may asswage the swelling of my minde,
Affoorde vnto my captiue soule some scope;
Whome to your wills is willingly inclin'd,
With firme repose of vncontrouled thought,
Whoe, but your dome, accounteth all for nought.

By PHEBVS beames, is cherished ech wight,
By PHEBVS beames, the dead obtaineth life,
When ATROP cutts (which is our ioyes delight)
The twisted twine with stroke of fatall kniffe:
Can you not then helpe dead to life againe,
And comfort yeild that PHEBVS beames retaine.

B 4

---

5 th'imperiall] th'mperiall
10 view'd] view,d
11 ascance] astance

Passion X (B4)

3 **Set . . . rest:** Make up thy mind (literally, "decide to play the limit," a term taken from the card game of primero).

6 **seade:** give birth to.

8 **ken'd:** knew, understood.

11 **ascance:** sideways (the meaning "back" seems to be called for).

11 **came behinde:** followed, ensued.

15 **scope:** free mental range (cf. "vncontrouled thought" in line 17).

18 **but . . . dome:** aside from your opinion.

20 **Phebus:** Phoebus, the sun god, here appears to take on the role of God.

21 **Atrop:** Atropos (see "Passion VII," 9 n.).

22 **twine:** thread (of life).

24 **retaine:** possess (giving "You Ladies" a kind of godlike power).

PASSION. XI.

O lampe that guides the circle of the globe,
Yf pitties fruite doth nestle in thy brest,
Scorne not in pride, the humble to disroabe,
With nakednes from his enioved rest;
That willing yeildes vnto thy sacred doome,
Thoughe web of care be knit in sorrowes loome.

You scoffing ECCHOS that repeat my crie,
And answere make when to the woods I moane,
Yf anie say I faine, you may replie ,
And witnes that vnder this curse I groane,
Who better knowes, if that the priest did ken,
All that he ought? then clark that said Amen.

You are the Sextons of my haplesse plaints,
That say amen vnto my dolefull songes,
And you doe knowe, my Ladies are the saints·
(With sweete conceyts) that may redresse my wrongs,
Applaude their praise, record my deepe despaire,
With shrill, short sound, of new abrupted ayer,

Nay praring sound cease for to brag my paine,
Thou hast no skill to itterat my smart,
Let such repeate that hath a copious vaine,
Th'xtreamest panges and langor of my heart;
My Ladies may expresse my inward griefe,
Whose changed note may sound me some reliefe.

Passion XI (B4^{v})

1 **lampe . . . globe:** i.e., the sun in the Ptolemaic system, which, as the King planet, might be said to act as guide to the other planets and stars in their circular motion around the earth ("globe") as the fixed center of the universe.

2 **pitties fruite:** outcome, issue of pity.

7 **scoffing Ecchos:** On the nymph, Echo, see the dedicatory Epistle, 23n.

11–12 **Who . . . Amen:** Who knows better than the clerk or sexton, who leads the congregation in its responses, often without knowing what the prayers he is responding to mean, whether the priest himself understands as much as he should of the Latin prayers he is repeating.

13 **You . . . Sextons:** You (the echoes) are the sextons (here used for clerks) who say "Amen." Note the close parallel in Shakespeare's Sonnet 85.

16 **conceyts:** thoughts.

18 **new abrupted ayre:** newly shattered or broken air. Earliest citations of "abrupted" in *OED* are 1633 and 1643.

19 **prating sound:** chattering (to little or no purpose) noise.

21 **Let . . . vaine:** Let only those who have an abounding, copious strain (of speaking) "itterat" (my mental pains).

24 **changed note:** altered tone (now musical because repeated by my "Ladies").

PASSION. XII.

VVaſte is the ſoile where naught but thiſtles grow
And barrē ground will nothing yeild but wee
Vnhappie is ſuch that ſoweth not to mowe ,
When hope is loſt in care, then comfort bleeds ;
Waſte ſoyle, voyde hope, thiſtles and weedes encreaſe,
In my mindes waſte, that waſte for want of peace .

Peace with my ſoule (although my bodie warrs)
Would qualifie the rigor of my paine,
But that I want and muſt endure the ſcarrs ,
To ranckle, which doe now begin againe,
When vlcers bleed, then daungers doe enſue ,
And carefull thoughts my bleeding ſores renew .

Renewed thus I count the clocke of care ,
No minute paſt without the taſt of ſmart ,
Not as the diall, which doth oft declare :
The time to paſſe, yet not perceau'd to ſtart ;
Poets faine, time ſwiftly to flie away ,
Yet time is ſlow, when ſorrowe ſurges ſway .

As rotten ragges being dipt, the water drawes ,
By ſoaking fits out of the veſſell cleane ,
Eu'n ſo from me doth ſorrowes droth (which thawes ,
My congeal'd heart, with cruell curſed ſpeene)
Soake out the ioyce and moyſture of my braine ,
For dropping eies can not from teares refraine .

---

22 spleene] speene

Passion XII (B5)

8 **qualifie:** modify.
9 **that I want:** i.e., peace of mind.
12 **carefull:** full of grief.
15 **diall:** sundial.
16 **not . . . start:** not seen to move. Cf. Shakespeare's Sonnet 104.9–10.
20 **fits:** is forced.
20 **cleane:** completely.
21 **droth:** thirst.
22 **spleene:** ill-temper, anger.
23 **Soake . . . ioyce:** draw out, drain the juice, sap.

PASSION. XIII.

GVyded by fitts, with malencholy looke,
I laie me downe vpon the winding banke,
To heare the musicke of the running brooke,
And smelt the grasse that was both fresh and ranke:
There I complaine, there lament my state,
That thus am crost with fortunes deadly hate.

Then to the brooke, I thus begyn to moane,
Thou warbling streame that doest refresh my care,
To my distilled griefe, and doest alone,
Giue place, and passage free prepare:
The same to bring vnto the boundles Seas,
Which there attend Sir NEPTVNS minde to please.

Thou searchiug scowrer of the grossest mould,
And element most subtile, fresh, and pure,
That windest about dame TERRA thowsand fould;
Behould the martirdome which I endure:
That passeth through the Limbecke of my heart,
And fetts my minde, with force of gauled smart.

Say to thy selfe in still and silent sorte,
Doth fortune thus SINETES true confound?
Ah Goddesse blind that loues such cruell sport,
To thy dishonour this will sure redownde,
Leaue of, knit thy bended browes on him,
That daylie doth in seas of sorrowes swimme.

13 searching] searchiug
18 fretts] fetts

Passion XIII (B5v)

1 **fitts:** (mental) crises.

4 **ranke:** luxuriant, thick.

9 **To . . . griefe:** resulting in the distillation or essentialization of my grief.

12 **Neptune:** (Greek: Poseidon) god of the seas.

13 **scowrer:** i.e., water.

13 **grossest mould:** most massive body of earth (i.e., Terra; see line 15).

14 **element:** i.e., air. Parry thus accounts for three of the four so-called elements (water, earth, air), omitting only fire.

17 **Limbecke:** alembic, apparatus for distilling.

18 **fretts:** gnaws at.

18 **gauled:** fretted, chafed.

PASSION. XIIII.

HArpies, and hagges, torment my fearefull goſt,
No part is freed, from horror, and deſpaire,
My carcas thus in CARONS boate is toſt,
MEDVSA doth with curſed ſnakie hayre,
Tranſ-natue quite, the vertue of my minde,
Vnto a ſtone, that is deaffe, dumme, and blinde.

Might but my ſoule enioye the fruite of reſt,
And purge the ſting, that wrought my bitter bane,
That hope mihht once my deſp'rat minde inueſt,
And ſtrenngth encreaſe, to bannish thoughts profane:
Then would I ioy to ſee ſuch happie day,
That once I might be freed from decay.

Sure I beleeue, thongh ioy could bannish care,
And that I might poſſeſſe a quiet minde,
And ſhould winde out my ſelfe from ſorrowes ſnare,
To cleanſe my thoughts from fruites of errors blinde
Yet would remembraunce of my paſſed paine,
Where griefe I left, force to begyn againe.

Then were my caſe far worſer then before,
For vlcers cut yeilde coroſiues extreame,
Salues hardly can, the former health reſtore,
And naught but death can tortur'd mindes redeeme:
Then muſt I reſt contented with my lot,
Sith ſorrowes now can not diſſolue the knot.

5 Trans-nature] Trans-natue
9 might] mihht

Passion XIIII (B6)

1 **Harpies:** rapacious, winged daughters of Oceanus and Terra.

1 **gost:** spirit or soul.

3 **Carons:** Charon was the ferryman of Hades, who, for an obolus (Greek coin: one-sixth of a drachma), ferried the souls of the dead over the rivers of the underworld to be judged by Rhadamanthus.

4 **Medusa:** one of the snake-haired Gorgons, who could turn an observer to stone from sheer terror; see line 6.

5 **Trans-nature:** change the nature of.

8 **bane:** destruction.

9 **inuest:** endow.

15 **winde out:** disentangle.

18 **force:** i.e., force me.

19 **far worser then:** much more unfortunate than.

20 **corosiues extreame:** most destructive acids.

PASSION. XV.

BEnighted thus with clouds of new-ſprong charge,
My ſwelling heart (puff'd vp by force of heate,
Supreſt) did burne, till teares did fier enlarge:
Then water quench'd the flame, and froſt the ſweate;
A dolefull choiſe of two euills one to name,
To frie in froſt or freeſe in firie flame.

The time was come, that all my ioyes ſhould end,
Then ſtraying to me was this vn-wonted care,
And ſo much more my ſcalding ſighes I ſpend:
For as I could I did my minde prepare;
For to endure theſe floods of deepe annoy,
That drown'd my hope, and rob'd me of my ioy.

O time accurſ'd that eu'r I knewe that day,
Which hath diſ-roabde my minde of ſweete content,
For then were hatch'd the birdes of my decay:
When vn-awares my liſtning eare I lent,
To SIRENS ſong, and CIRCES curſed charmes,
That train'd my minde, to worke his maiſters harmes.

No muſick then could better pleaſe mine eare,
Nor obiect ſeeme more precious to mine eye,
Then that which did my cruell torments reare.
Where but content I nothing could eſpie,
Yet faireſt flowers haue filthie Adders neſt,
And I haue found in pleaſures vaine vnreſt.

Passion XV (B6^{v})

1 **charge:** accusation.

3 **till . . . enlarge:** until tears made the burning (of my heart) to increase.

8 **Then . . . me:** then to my wandering (mind).

14 **dis-roabde:** stripped.

17 **Sirens song:** In Greek mythology, Sirens were marine monsters with women's faces and fishlike bodies, who, with their sweet singing, lured sailors to wreck their ships on promontory rocks.

17 **Circes cursed charmes:** Circe was an enchantress who possessed the power to change men into swine after they had succumbed to her "cursed charmes."

18 **train'd:** allured, enticed.

22 **Where . . . espie:** Where I could see nothing but contentment (in what I was feeling).

24 **pleasures vaine:** i.e., vain pleasures.

PASSION. XVI.

Yeilding consent hauing vnlocked the gate,
The garde which kept my minde in reasons folde,
Then fond desire wrought in my Minde debate,
How of my friends I might liue vn-controulde:
To follie then the restrained raines I lent,
Of libertie, which now I doe repent.

What toyes so vaine which then I did not taste,
What acte so badde I would not seeme to proue,
I thought that time could neuer my ioyes waste:
Nor checke the pride of mine vntamed loue,
Till on a heape my ioyes and follies toule,
The Bell of care, my louing ioyes controule.

Then gan I sighe, euen with a sad lament,
And pause vppon the remnent of my life,
Then that seemed greate which lest did discontent:
When as repentance sharpened sorrowes Knife,
To execute the Iudgement of the lawe,
On him, thereof that neuer stoode in awe.

When frendes forsooke, and enemies did prie,
To worke reuenge for some vn-modest parte,
Then gan my soule with sorrowes to discrie:
The guilte of sinne, that lodged in my hearte,
Whose memory did racke my senses soe;
That strech't they were beyond the bonds of woe.

Passion XVI (B7)

3 **fond:** foolish.
4 **of:** among.
5–6 **To . . . libertie:** I gave over then to folly the restraining reins controlling licentiousness.
7 **toyes:** frivolities.
12 **my . . . controule:** (thus) reprehending the pleasures which I then loved.
14 **pause:** stop to deliberate.
15 **Then . . . discontent:** That then seemed important (i.e., out of proportion) that least gave rise to vexation.
20 **parte:** action (on his part).
21 **gan:** began.
23 **racke:** torture (as on a rack; see "strech't" in line 24).

PASSION. XVII.

ENgendred griefe from ſeede of pleaſures vaine,
Inforcing ſtill the agents of my ſmart,
From ſinnes aſpect, my minde could not refraine,
For fretting luſt did cynge my broyled heart,
Till loth to yeilde, yet could not choiſe but yeild,
When as remorce perforce did win the field.

Then of two harmes making a choiſe of one,
To ſalue my ſoule, I paunde my life a thrall,
And gaue conſent to that which makes me moane,
Whereof proceedes the fruite of bitter gall,
Which pen'd my minde that ſoared in the ſkies,
In baſeſt ſould, where in diſpaire it lies.

An abiect throwne before the face of wrath,
That dare not view what I of late enioyed,
Of new-cut graſſe naught but a rotten ſwath,
After the raine the vertue hath deſtroyed,
My drooping thoughts forſake their wonted ſeate,
And back decline their ſorrowes to repeate.

Thus feeling ſmart opens the new ſear'd vaine,
That bled ſo faſt till lifes blood neere is ſpent,
And now incloſ'd .n Laborinth of paine,
I ſtill expect the MIMOTAVRE to rent,
The bondes which doe reſtraine my libertie,
Cloſ'd in the caue of woefull miſerie.

---

21 in] .n
22 MINOTAVRE] MIMOTAVRE

Passion XVII (B7^{v})

2 **inforcing:** strengthening.
4 **For fretting:** because gnawing, consuming.
5 **choise:** choose.
6 **as . . . perforce:** of necessity.
8 **paunde:** pawned.
11 **pen'd:** fenced in, confined.
12 **basest fould:** meanest enclosure, pen.
13 **abiect:** castaway.
19 **feeling smart:** deeply felt (mental) pain.
22 **Minotaure:** a monster, half man, half bull, offspring of Pasiphaë, the wife of King Minos of Crete, who fell in love with a bull; Minos imprisoned the Minotaur in a labyrinth or maze constructed by Daedalus.

PASSION. XVIII.

LOng loathed lookes, of my forepassed life,
Are glutted with the sense of fond desire,
And discontent did agrauate my strife,
When hope did staie, my stamring steps t'aspire:
Being tyed by fayth my fatall fortunes woe,
To this base chaunce; I must embrace my foe.

Lo he which sometimes thought great scorne to see,
Stamp made of purest mould to frowne on him,
And thought the Queene of loue might well agree,
To taste his skill that in conceyte did swimme,
And deem'd a toy, for to deserue a smile,
Of coyest she that eu'r did man beguile.

Whose ouer-weening wits and eake aspiring though
Like finest lawne which wanteth not his bracke,
By fortun's spite was sodenly ou'r-raught,
And swelling sayle endur'd the greater wracke:
The greatar oake the lowder is his fall,
The higher minde th'uneasier is the thrall:

The sillie flie in spyders web inthrauld,
The more he striues the more entangled lies,
Euen so my minde that with conceyte is gauld,
No way to scape the Laborinth he spies,
The more he seekes his follies to avoyde,
The more he loues the fruite himselfe auuoyde;

13 thought,] though (*line over-measure and worked up space prints after* though)
24 annoyde] auuoyde

Passion XVIII (B8)

2 **glutted . . . desire:** sickened with the excessive feeling of doting desire.

4 **staie . . . t'aspire:** cease to raise up (i.e., support) my staggering steps.

5 **fatall fortunes woe:** the affliction of my fated lot (in life).

6 **base chaunce:** servile lot or fortune. (It is difficult to wring much sense out of the first stanza.)

8 **stamp:** physical appearance.

8 **mould:** earth (regarded as the material of the human body). Cf. Tobit 8:6: "Thou madest Adam of the mould of the earth and gaveth him Eva for an help" (Bishops' Bible).

9 **Queene of loue:** Venus.

10 **conceyte:** fanciful thought, imagination.

11 **deem'd a toy:** judged it (i.e., imaginative thought) to be a trifling toy or sport.

13 **eake:** also.

14 **lawne . . . bracke:** fine linen, resembling cambric, never lacks its flaw.

16 **wracke:** wreck (variant form).

18 **higher . . . thrall:** higher the mind the more disquieting is the bondage.

19 **inthrauld:** caught, trapped.

21 **gauld:** vexed, harassed.

24 **fruite himselfe annoyde:** consequences of his actions which (as a result) troubled him.

PASSION. XIX.

YF fortunes crosse be bitter to endure,
That frets the minde which tasteth her despite,
The same being past, when changes new procure,
Some offer which might wearied mind delight,
But that fore-chance, his latter fate preuent,
Then will he rue the fruite of fond intent.

The freeman thinkes it small for to be bound,
Not knowing then, the daunger which ensues,
But freedome lost dispaire doth straight confound,
Confused thoughts, which bring vntimely newes,
For bondage come, and libertie being lost,
What is the the thing whereof we then can boast.

Who would not seeme for to condemne his eye,
That first did lust, and heart that gaue consent,
When fruite thereof proues seede of miserie,
But more when as some kindly glaunces lent,
Yeilde constant hope if that his minde were free,
Some better happe in time obtain'd might bee.

You iudges of my heauie dolefull song,
To whose graue doomes my selfe I doe submit,
Yf worth, may not obtaine his worth; tis wrong,
Such is the fate of those which dayly flit:
Such was my chaunce to make my primer choise,
That to be free I onely might reioyce.

12 the] the the
18 obtain'd] obtaiu'd

Passion XIX (B8^{v})

1 **crosse:** trial, affliction.
2 **frets:** gnaws at.
3 **same:** i.e., Fortune's "despite."
4 **offer:** i.e., some kind of relief (from Fortune's "despite").
5 **But . . . preuent:** Unless that earlier, previous fortune should anticipate his later lot.
11 **For:** because.
12 **thing:** special quality (of mind and life).
20 **graue doomes:** weighty judgments.
22 **flit:** change, alter.
23 **primer:** premier, first.

PASSION. XX.

ZEale is but cold, where loue-lesse law restraines,
The soaring Hawke, to cease vpon his pray,
Which from the fruite of his intent refraines,
Expecting once for to behould the day:
Which being expir'd may yeilde some hope of rest,
Yf future happs may be foretould iest.

So SIBILL sayd, SINETES doubted thoe,
She did affyrme, he still did feare the worse,
She prophesied a freedome of his woe,
And he did doubt that fate would alter course:
For though on him that Fortune false did smile,
Yet sure he thought it was but to beguile.

MEDEA did make AESON young againe,
She thought to gaine a daughters name therefore,
But she that doth a daughters name obtaine,
With art can not her fathers weale restore:
For bound he is, and freedome cannot sway,
Excepte that he whoe gaue doe take away.

Sweete ladies then what helpe is to be had,
That time decreede may once be expir'd,
But that meane time you doe with comforts glad,
And dayne a smile where no more is desir'd,
Yeilde poore SINETES hope though in his graue,
That in your mindes his worthes you will ingraue.

C

Passion XX (C1)

1 **loue-lesse law:** Meaning unclear in context; perhaps it may mean "law which is above humane feeling."

3 **Which . . . refraines:** Which refrains from acting in such a way as to gain the results of its intention.

6 **iest:** justly, correctly.

7 **Sibill:** Classical myth produced several Sibyllae (Cumean, Delphic, Erithean), all of whom were believed to possess the gift of prophecy.

7 **thoe:** however.

13 **Medea . . . againe:** In Greek myth, Medea is generally thought of as a sorceress, who restored Aeson, her husband's (Jason's) father to youth by cutting his throat and boiling him in healing herbs. Under pressure from Pelias' daughters, she pretended to use her art to restore Pelias to youth, intentionally failing to do so. Parry seems to suggest that Medea restored Aeson to youth in the hope that his son, Jason, would marry her (line 14), but Ovid (VII, 164–68) describes Medea as his wife before she treats Aeson.

16 **art . . . restore:** magic art cannot restore her father's well-being. But Medea does restore Aeson's youth; perhaps, Parry is here confusing what happened to another father, Pelias.

17 **bound . . . sway:** i.e., Aeson is bound up (in age) and being unbound (in itself) cannot order or control such an age-change.

18 **he:** i.e., God (?); the referent is unclear—like most of this stanza.

20 **decreede:** (trisyllabic) ordained.

23 **though . . . graue:** i.e., even though he is dead (with play on "ingraue" in line 24).

PASSION. XXI.

AGreeu'd in graue, of mindes dispayting crosse,
Not in the graue, which cancelleth annoy,
Yf fate will not againe, restore his losse,
The fatall graue, he craueth to enioy:
For fortune doth but spite, to smile againe,
When former frownes, did cut the attire vaine.

Suppose you came vnto a garden fine,
And might there choose one of the fairest flowers,
So choise being made as fancie did incline,
Yet walking there to view the fruitfull bowers,
Amongst those groues, a thowsand flowers you finde,
Then former choise better to please your minde.

Where sight is free, but handling, is deni'd,
And if you touch, you may not taste the fruit,
Though neu'r so faine, least Garden-keeper spi'd,
And would ympeach your crime with blazing bruite,
How much agreeu'd would you be then in heart,
That better choise befell not to your part.

Would you not curse the rashnes of your braine,
That moued speach which could not be vnsaide,
And Fortune bad which laide this subtill traine,
When you did finde how much you were betraide:
No doubt you would thinke this a heauie crosse,
Exept you myght in chosing, change your choise.

1 dispayring] dispayting
24 Except] Exept

Passion XXI (C1^v)

Linked with Passion XX by the "grave" metaphor.

1 **graue:** i.e., a mental grave vs. the "fatall graue" of lines 2 and 4.
6 **former . . . vaine:** its (Fortune's) former frowns had (already) cut the arterial vein (=pulmonary artery).
15 **faine:** eager.
16 **ympeach . . . bruite:** give a fiery report of the crime with which you are charged.
21 **band:** cursed.
24 **Except:** unless.

PASSION. XXII.

BEtrayed thus with lust of luring sight,
The flower is cropt which now I may not change,
The garden's free to view what might delight.
But passed choice restraines my minde to range:
So that beholding still what I desire:
It fuell yeilds vnto the kindled fier.

The memorie of what I might obtaine!
If I were free, extenuates my ioy,
This is the roote of mine endured paine,
Though this be great, yet not my chiefe annoy;
With dayly showers, new weedes spring, and increase
Which fruite out-growes, and future hope decrease.

Enuying fortune thrise be thou accurst,
Who not content to make me what I am,
Amongst the meane to be accounted worst,
That from one bad, vnto a worser came,
And heaped coales a new vpon my head,
To bring me home vnto my loathed bed.

Bed of disgrace, when stealing time gaue light,
Discouering the messages of fame,
Which witnes bare how deere I bought delight;
That for good will enioyed nought but blame:
And payde therefore eu'n at the deerest rate,
For had I wist doth alwaies come to late.

Passion XXII (C2)

Continues the theme of Passion XXI.

3 **free to view:** open to be looked at for.
8 **extenuates:** lessens.
15 **meane:** inferior fellows.
16 **one . . . came:** (made me) who was already bad to become worse.
17 **heaped . . . head:** gave rise to remorse by requiting evil with good. Gentrup (privately) compares Romans 12:20–21 (Bishops' Bible).
19 **Bed . . . light:** When time, passing unobserved (like a thief), revealed the bed of ignominy to the light of day.
20 **Discouering . . . fame:** laying bare the reports of (my) reputation.
22 **for good will:** in place of being credited with a virtuous intention.
24 **had I wist:** if only I had known.

PASSION. XXIII.

ECclipsed with the blemish of disgrace,
Coms ATROPOS the messenger of night,
And sayth I must, newe sorrowes now embrace,
Who hath in charge to cancell my delight:
A cruell doome thus to ou'rcharge my minde
Where hope dispaires true comforts fruit to finde.

Yf former cause did formall griefe applie,
And formall griefe in time encreased more,
This treb'e cause of woefull miserie,
Will make me yeilde to cruell fortunes lore:
That doth deuise newe tortures to encrease,
My martyrdome, the wrath-full Gods to please.

Might carcas cras'd with battring engyns noyde,
Content (the strength being scaled and defac'd,)
The cruell executioner deuoyd,
Of pitties fruite, which Iustice neu'r embrac'd:
Then Fortune would be wearied to torment,
My wracked minde, thus cloth'd with sad lament.

But sith I must endure these paines extreame,
Now let me sigh and breath this fatall doome,
For death I craue this thraldome to redeame.
If death would heare the crie of such a groome;
If not, you Gods heare now my mournfull verse,
Wherein my cares with teares I doe rehearse.

1 *E*Clipsed] *E*Cclipsed

Passion XXIII (C2^{v})

2 **Atropos . . . night:** See Passion VII.9n. In this context "night"=death.

7 **former . . . applie:** The result of earlier action activated the very essence of grief.

10 **lore:** command.

13 **cras'd:** shattered.

13 **noyde:** (=annoyed) injured.

14 **Content:** satisfy.

15 **executioner:** i.e., Atropos or Fate.

PASSION. XXIIII.

TRembling with feare my thread-bare comfort left,
To feede vppon the obiect of my smart,
And to repeat the cause which thus bereft,
The hope, the ioy, and comfort of my hart:
Sing then with me such as will mourne and moane,
Else I must sing with mourning teares alone.

For Fortunes clouded-brow doth threatnings send,
And scorning bandes a smile from stormie face,
Disdayning comforts of my cares to lend,
Intending still to keepe me in disgrace:
As seruile drudge to her commaunding will,
In cruell spights that hath a tried skill.

O sacred muse with melodie deplore,
And decke the hearse with mournfull ornaments,
Which doth to me renewed griefe restore,
And fil'd my face with sorrowes sad laments:
Whose life was deere, whose death must be my dole,
Which wringes my thoughtes, and racks my vexed soule.

You louely sweetes to whom I doe appeale,
Attire your selues in Sables with the rest,
For to assist with mone my burning zeale,
The smoke whereof hath neere my minde supprest:
In cloudie stormes it yeildeth much reliefe,
To haue a friende for to impart our griefe:

Passion XXIIII (C3)

1 **left:** stopped.

3 **cause . . . bereft:** reason which in this way took away or robbed.

8 **bandes:** bounds.

14 **decke . . . ornaments:** Elegiac verses, flowers, etc. at this time often decorated a bier.

17 **dole:** grief, sorrow.

19 **sweetes:** sweet ones (i.e., Parry's "Ladies").

20 **Sables:** black mourning garments.

PASSION. XXV.

Hector in time did scoure the greekish hoast,
And made them flee like Bees vnto the hiue,
Yet in the end his valiant minde did cost,
The price of life, when rashly he did striue.
Against such power, that rather time would yeilde;
Then force should want to vanquish him in fielde.

Braue Hercvles whome Cerbrvs might not (tame,
Could not withstand the dame of destinie,
And rash attempts to gaine a worthy name,
Bringes loftie mindes to woefull miserie;
Ou'r-weening thought of a self-willed minde,
Hath made me loose, what more I cannot finde.

Braue man, braue minde, and fitte to feare the foe,
But wordes or deedes, with fate can not preuaile,
Pittie it were, life should be prised so,
For passed deedes, wordes cannot nowe auaile:
So it befell, so destinie assign'd,
They went before, and we must come behinde.

Againe I call where ayde I hope to haue,
To you I call that may my call commaunde,
Come tune your trebled notes of care I craue,
And sooth the humor of a fonde demaunde:
Yf you doe salue with comfort mine annoy,
The prayse is yours, though I the case enioy.

---

7 CERBERVS] CERBRVS (*perhaps the intended reading is* CER'BRVS)
24 ease] case (?)

Passion XXV (C3^{v})

1 **Hector:** Trojan hero and son of Priam, king of Troy; he was finally treacherously slain by the Greek hero Achilles.

1 **scoure:** scourge.

7 **Hercules . . . tame:** In the last of his labors Hercules bound in chains Pluto's three-headed dog, Cerberus, which guarded the gates of Pluto's palace in Hades, in an unsuccessful attempt to rescue his friend, Pirithous, who, however, had already been torn to pieces by Cerberus. After being poisoned and driven mad by unwisely donning a shirt of a centaur, Nessus, whom he had slain with a poisoned arrow and whose shirt was thus rendered deadly, Hercules immolated himself on a funeral pyre on Mount Oeta.

13 **feare:** frighten.

18 **They:** i.e., Hector and Hercules.

18 **behinde:** after (like them the victims of Fate).

20 **my call:** my summons.

24 **ease:** easing (of my [mental] torment).

PASSION. XXVI.

VVEaried with cloudes of tempest-beaten sense,
Whole armies of reproches fill my sayle,
Marching with life, that hath but weake defence,
But in dispaire I looke not to preuaile:
For vnto me befell a worser spite,
Then any thing that yet my pen could write.

Far worse it is then what is worst of all,
Mine eye bewrayes the care I take therefore,
Th'annotomie of my accursed thrall,
The more I striue the paine encreaseth more.,
For that doth make the new heal'd scar to bleede,
And woundes againe; ô would it kild with speede.

Twise launced sore the thirde time now is search'd,
The first was paine, which scant I could endure,
The second hath my crased carcas pearch'd,
The third and last did latest harme procure.
And by as much the second past the first,
Eu'n by so much, or more, the last is worst:

Three harmes in one, conspired to berray,
The guiltles thought, scant wayned from dispaire,
Scarce first had end, before the next did sway,
Third came too soone his ioyes to ympaire;
But last it was that most did vexe my minde,
Though former twayne did not come much behinde.

Passion XXVI (C4)

1 **sense:** (1) mental apprehension; (2) emotional consciousness.

2 **reproches:** (1) censures; (2) shames.

3 **weake defence:** i.e., against the "cloudes" and "armies."

9 **annotomie:** anatomized body (i.e., a kind of detailed map). Presumably refers to the "worser spite" in line 5.

15 **crased carcas pearch'd:** shattered body pierced; "pearch" is a variant form of "pierce."

20 **scant wayned:** scarcely weaned or dissuaded.

22 **ympaire:** spoil, damage.

23 **last:** i.e., the third "harme" (line 19).

PASSION. XXVII.

O Pale death inexorable monster,
That seis'd vpon the remnant of my hope,
Who can thy spites with grauest wisedome conster?
That to thy selfe doest only giue a scope,
To choose the same that worst might be spared,
And doest refuse those that are prepared.

With cutting sythe why hast thou rack'd together,
The future hope of my declyning state,
And left me cut behind alone to wither,
For to bewaile the rigor of their fate?
O gentle death now let me beg and craue,
To follow them that now be clos'd in graue.

Else if I liue, let him that ruleth all,
Ioue sole commaunder both of thee, and thine,
Giue thee in charge, remembrance for to fall,
That racketh still this wracked heart of mine:
Then may I hope some rest for to enioy,
Though loaden now with burthens of annoy.

Faire choysest dames that patronize my ioy,
Now ioyne with me, in prayer to IVPITER,
That I may die, if dying may destroy,
The liuing griefe which leades me thus to erre:
Or if I liue, let life be cloathed soe,
That new attire may banish former woe.

Passion XXVII (C4^{v})

3 **conster:** (=construe, variant form) interpret, understand.

4–5 **That . . . spared:** That to thyself alone dost give the liberty of choosing the moment when you (Death) claim those who most should be allowed to live (i.e., those who "worst might be spared").

7 **rack'd:** gathered (in a sheaf).

9 **left . . . wither:** left only me (alive) of those cut down (by Death's "cutting sythe," line 7) to wither away.

10 **For . . . fate:** In order to bewail the severity of their (i.e., those who should have been spared) fate. "For to" here may mean only "to."

15 **Giue . . . fall :** Order thee (Death) to destroy the memory (of all the sorrows and injuries that life has dealt me).

19 **patronize:** (1) protect; (2) countenance.

PASSION. XXVIII.

LITIGIOUS thoughts will graunt no quiet reſt,
For care is cloſe intombed in my minde,
And memorie of paſſed woes mole t,
Such as in vaine expect ſome eaſe to finde:
When ripping of the cares long paſt and gone,
Will make a freſh the ſtouteſt heart to grone.

Ymprouident proſperitie is caught,
Within the net of new confuſed ſhame:
For ſtill the vn-reſpectiue mindes are fraught
With heape of toye·, that bring vntimely blame;
My follies firſt did leade me to this caſe,
When I began to treade the louers maze.

Vn-warie peace on fat-fed pleaſures ſtall,
Whoſe wanton thought, made weake with luſt & eaſe
Did guide my ſteps to this vntimely thrall,
And deſtinie my ſorrowes did encreaſe:
Being tangled thus in Labrinth of diſpaire,
New-ſprong effects my ioyed hope impaire.

Sing Muſes, ſing, the ruines of my time,
Reade in my face the Kalender of care,
With tragick notes repeate my paſſed crime.
My wrinckled browe records how hard I fare;
All muſt conſume ſo ſhall my care haue ende,
When as no ſap is left for life to ſpende,

---

3 molest] molest (s *barely prints*)
10 toyes] toyes (s *barely prints*)

Passion XXVIII (C5)

Compare Shakespeare's Sonnet 30.

1 **Litigious:** contentious.

3 **molest:** trouble (by recalling)

7 **Ymprouident:** unthinking, heedless.

9 **vn-respectiue:** undiscriminating.

10 **toyes:** frivolous trifles (connected with love sports).

13 **stall:** surfeit.

17 **Labrinth of dispaire:** i.e., "louers maze," line 12.

19 **Muses:** nine Greek goddesses that presided over poetry, music, dancing, and all the liberal arts: Clio, Euterpe, Thalia, Melpomene, Terpsichore, Erato, Polyhymnia, Calliope, and Urania.

24 **When . . . spende:** When no vital life-blood remains for life to consume.

PASSION. XXIX.

FOrc'd to endure the burthen of my charge,
Which loades my minde with more then I can beare,
Drench'd in dispaire, rowing 'n cares curſed barge,
I trie the foordes which dangers new doe reare:
Wherein I wade too farre for to returne,
For all in vaine against the pricke I ſpurne.

Against the pricke I ſpurne, the more I ſtriue,
The deeper wou d it makes within my minde,
For of true ioye it doth my poore heart ſhriue,
When feare doth leade and hope doth come behinde,
Thus like the Mer-maide pain'd, I watch deaths dome,
And recreat my ſelfe with glaſſe and come.

With glaſſe and combe I trifle thus the time,
Fit bables for thoſe which are children twiſe,
The flood of care, late fild with mud and ſlime,
My ſwelling heart, which nowe beginns to riſe,
Against her banke, and often doth rebell,
When paines extreame do pleaſures ſappe expell.

You handmaides which doe waite on beauties Queene,
Or rather peeres to beauties excellence,
In my diſtreſſe you which ſo well are ſeene,
For future harmes now lende your prouidence:
That though I paine, and pine eu'n to my graue,
Yet after I may hope ſome reſt to haue.

Passion XXIX (C5^{v}*)*

1 **burthen:** burden (variant form).

1 **charge:** load (of troubles, sorrows).

5 **Wherein . . . returne:** Cf. Shakespeare's *Macbeth* 3.4.135–37.

6 **against . . . spurne:** kick against the thornes; cf. Acts, 9:5.

9 **shriue:** rob.

11 **Thus . . . dome:** In medieval times, mermaids were identified with the Greek mythological Sirens, who lured sailors to their deaths by their sweet singing. According to some accounts, if they failed to entrap a sailor, they were themselves doomed; hence "pain'd" (mourning), like the poet, the "Mer-maide" awaits her death sentence.

12 **recreat . . . come:** relieve or comfort myself by using a mirror and comb (as mermaids were often pictured doing).

14 **bables:** showy trinkets, toys.

16–17 **rise . . . banke:** i.e., threatening to overflow or break bounds. One of Parry's favorite metaphors.

18 **sappe:** vital fluid or essence.

19 **handmaides . . . Queene:** i.e., the "Ladies" to whom the Passions are addressed; here imagined as ladies-in-waiting to either (1) Helen of Troy (=Helena Owen, to whom Sonettos 1 and 15–31 and "The lamentation of a Male-content" are addressed) or (2) Venus.

21 **seene:** versed (in my love's "distresse").

PASSION. XXX.

Replie and ſay my fortune is ſo baſe,
That you diſdaine to lend me any ayde,
Say it is ſoe, ſuch croſſes to embrace,
(Amidſt thoſe ſtormes) I muſt not be afrayde,
But rather ſcorne, proude fortune to her face,
Which thus with ſpite doth worke my deepe diſgrace.

Shall I now mourne for what cannot be had,
Great follie were my labour ſo to looſe,
Nay rather ſeeke ſome comfort for to glad,
The drooping hart that knowes not what to chooſe.
For chaunces whoſe euent be deſperate,
Redreſſe craues ſpeede, or elſe it coms too late.

Too late the ſuccour coms the fort being ſackt,
And comfort, when no comfort can preuaile,
Is torture to the minde alreadle rackt,
When in th'effect true comforts fruite doth faile;
Then lend your ayde before my wracke be ſuch,
That paſt recal the paines encreaſe too much.

Now muſt I ſturre to catch a liuely hould,
While fortune bends her frowning brow on me,
Who cannot ſhift being young will neu'r be ould,
And he that ſtriues with froward deſtinie:
In fortunes front muſt ſeeke a hould to finde,
Elſe 'twill not be: for ſhe is balde behinde.

15 alreadie] alreadle
19 liuely] liuely (y *barely prints*)

Passion XXX (C6)

1 **Replie:** i.e., in answer to Sinetes' plea at the end of Passion XXIX.
1 **fortune:** (1) lot in life; (2) social status.
15 **rackt:** tortured.
17 **wracke:** ruin, destruction.
19 **sturre . . . hould:** bestir myself to seize a living grasp.
21 **shift:** manage (1) matters, (2) himself.
23 **front:** forehead (to which the forelock was attached; see next note).
24 **balde behinde:** a regular attribute of Occasion (Latin: *occasio*) personified. Occasion was often associated with Fortune in the Renaissance, suggesting that, unlike the medieval view, Fortune was to some extent within man's control.

PASSION. XXXI.

Eyes weepe no more, hart breath no sighing sobs,
Ceast to repeate ô quill thy maisters griefe,
The theefe is knowne which hope of quiet robs:
And courage must (not weaknes) gaine reliefe;
Leaue of to moane, with Fortune be content,
No ease is found by this thy sad lament.

Teares cannot quench the heate of kindled fier,
Nor sighing sobs restore thy former state,
Pen cannot write the accents of desire,
Nor courage quaile the force of frowning fate:
Yeilding cannot helpe, force cannot preuaile,
Against the stormie windes no ship can saile.

Enuye not Death, he claymeth but his due,
Fortune cannot her crabbed nature leaue,
Why doest thou then these sighing sobs renewe,
And fate reuile that did thy hope deceaue?
Now debts are payde, call home thy wits againe,
Desire not that which thou shalt wish in vaine.

Thus rest content with this thy fatall chaunce,
For that will checke thy angry fortunes pride,
With enuies pipe that leades a scornefull daunce,
And with disdaine thy sorrowes doth deride:
With patience thou mayst ou'rcome at length,
And more then this repose no trust in strength.

Passion XXXI (C6v)

2 **quill:** pen.

5 **with . . . content:** be satisfied with the lot Fortune (has given thee); cf. line 19.

9 **accents:** emotional stresses.

10 **quaile:** fail.

19 **fatall chaunce:** fated lot.

21 **enuies pipe:** the piping (i.e., the attraction) of (1) deceit, (2) emulation, (3) malice.

PASSION. XXXII.

SVppose deere Dames you giue me such aduise,
This cannot please the humor of my minde,
For flesh is fraile, and cannot thus dispise,
The thinge whereto our nature is inclin'd:
Nurture may striue, but nature must preuaile;
Well may I trie, yet shall, not misse to faile.

What if I should endeauour to intreat,
Fortune no doubt would heare my carefull crie,
Sweete Fortune then giue eare I will repeate,
The totall some of this my miserie:
I want my will, I would what may not be,
Vnlesse thou doest yeilde some reliefe to me.

I seeke no more but quiet to enioy,
Yeilde me my right, and that is all I craue,
Not to dispease I doe my minde imploy,
(With chastest thought) but comforts fruite to haue
I seeke and sue not to a Goddesse blinde,
But vnto thee in hope some ease to finde.

Some one will reade that knoweth mine intent,
Let such but pause and canuas my desart,
And pittie him which thus his youth hath spent:
Then zealous thought of honour set apart:
Giue all their due and staine not vertues name,
With trifling trash that bringeth but defame.

---

15 displease] dispease

Passion XXXII (C7)

1 **such aduise:** i.e., the advice the poet gives himself in the last stanza of Passion XXXI.

2 **humor:** temper, mood.

5 **Nurture . . . nature:** moral training or discipline . . . inherent character or disposition of mankind.

6 **misse to faile:** be able to avoid failure.

8 **carefull:** full of grief.

15 **displease:** offend.

16 **but:** only, solely.

17 **Goddesse blinde:** Fortune.

18 **thee:** i.e., a Fortune that is clear-sighted, not blind.

20 **canuas my desart:** examine closely my deserving.

22 **zealous . . . apart:** considering (not only) those who fervently believe in what is honorable.

23 **all:** i.e., all others (who have some degree of honor and virtue).

PASSION. XXXIII.

THe fit is come, my trembling flesh doth feare,
These idle toyes fore-runners of my griefe,
Prognosticate what torment I must beare,
I see me thinkes the agents of reliefe,
Repulst by force of the tormentors hand,
Seeking in vaine his strength for to withstand.

Yeild then I must vnto the cursed stroke,
That shall weare out the remnant of my dayes,
And be content to beare the seruile yoke,
Which sorrowes charge from sorrowes store defrayes:
For being enroul'd within the booke of woe,
I must not scorne for to embrace my foe.

And for my follies which sometimes yeild ease,
To cleere the smoke of cloudie ATHOS fier,
Their force cannot my fettered thoughts release,
But rather doe encerease my fond desire:
And as ACTEONS dogs, spar'd not their Lord,
To hunt me from my rest, so they accord.

O harsh accord of woefull harmonie,
That naught can tune but solemne notes of care,
Wherein is crost the fruite of charitie,
Whereof I want (to salue my griefes) a share,
Then past redresse, I must remaine content,
To cherish that which frowning fortune sent.

16 encrease] encerease

Passion XXXIII (C7^{v})

1 **fit:** (1) seizure; (2) crisis.

2 **toyes:** i.e., the Passions.

7 **stroke:** blow (of the "fit").

10 **sorrowes charge . . . defrayes:** sorrow's (1) burden, (2) expense is paid out from sorrow's stock, storehouse.

13 **And . . . ease:** And as far as my follies, which sometimes afford relief, are concerned.

14 **smoke . . . fier:** Mount Athos is in Macedonia. According to *The excellent and pleasant worke of Iulius Solinus* (1587; trans. Arthur Golding), sig. M1: "Surely *Athos* is of such a height, that it is supposed to bee higher then from whence the rayne falleth . . . that the ashes which are left vpon the Altars that stande on the toppe of it, are neuer washt awaie, nor doo in anie wise diminish." Solinus' description may, perhaps, explain Parry's use of "cloudie" and "fier," but his description of Mount Atlas (sig. Q3) fits Parry's line more closely: "[it] lifteth his head aboue the cloudes," and (sig. Q3^{v}) "but in the night he glystreth with fires." If so, either Parry has confused the two mountains or "Athos" is a compositorial misreading of "Atlas."

15 **Their force:** i.e., the power of his "follies."

17 **Acteons dogs:** In Greek myth, Acteon, while hunting, spied upon Diana bathing with her nymphs; as punishment, Diana turned Acteon into a stag, in which form he was torn to pieces by his own hunting dogs.

18 **To . . . accord:** Thus my follies concur, like Acteon's hounds, in hunting me out of my repose (metaphorically tearing me to pieces).

21 **crost . . . charitie:** thwarted the issue or outcome of love.

PASSION, XXXIIII.

O Heau'ns recorde the somme of my request,
Confesse I seeke nothing but what is iust,
Some ease of that which doth my minde molest,
Eare all my hope be buried in the dust:
Ye angrie stars let my submission pay,
The ransome of my captiue hartes decay.

Tis not obscure that I long pennance bore,
To purge the guilt of my fore-passed crime,
Let tribute paide, make euen with the score,
Which in Fates booke care crost of auntient times:
Then doubtles I some comfort shall obtaine,
Though Fortune doe my sacrifice disdaine.

Yet let me yeild, it booteth not to striue,
Of force I must giue place to higher powers,
Too weake I am, for such as me corriue,
Without I might raine downe some Golden showers:
So DANAE no doubt I might enioye,
To beare a sonne his Graund-sier to destroy.

Haue I forgot my Ladies yet to moue,
Whose sole applause may pleade their sheapheards woe,
Tis you alone that shall my deedes approue,
For like the weedes, that fairest flowers out-grow,
My cares ou'r-spread the relique of my ioye,
And fatall feare did fadeing hope destroye.

Passion XXXIIII (C8)

4 **Eare:** ere.

5 **angrie stars:** malignant stars. Stars were thought by many to influence, for good or ill, an individual's destiny. Cf. "star-cross'd lovers," in Shakespeare's *Romeo and Juliet*, Prologue, 6.

9 **Let . . . score:** Let the tax paid settle my indebtedness.

10 **crost of:** marked off (as paid).

13 **booteth:** availeth.

14 **Of force:** of necessity.

15 **me corriue:** vie with me.

16 **Without I might:** unless I am able to.

16–17 **Golden . . . Danaë:** Danaë was the daughter of Acrisius, king of Argos, who, being warned by an oracle that his grandchild would kill him, shut Danaë up in a brazen tower. Jupiter, however, in the form of a shower of gold penetrated the tower and got Danaë with child, later named Perseus. After many years Perseus accidentally killed his grandfather.

19 **moue:** affect with tender emotion.

20 **Whose . . . woe:** Whose applause alone may extenuate their shepherd's (i.e., Sinetes') sorrow.

PASSION. XXXV.

NEPTVNE the wrathfull EOLVS appease,
Call TRITON foorth to summon a retreyte,
Of raging stormes, which doe my rest disease,
How they beyond their limmits past repeate:
And though EOLVS may the windes encrease,
Yet tell them this, thou canst commaund the seas.

IOVE prince of all, stop greedie fortunes iawees,
Send MERCVRIE for to edict thy will,
And let her knowe she hath transgres'd thy lawes:
Which all the Gods are subiect to fulfill:
For though she spite and spend her bitter gall,
Giue her to knowe, that thou commaundest all.

What though she may wring poore SINETES minde,
The same to heale thou hast a salue in store,
Send patience to checke this Goddesse is blinde,
For all in vaine these sorrowes I deplore:
When hope is drown'd in slymie sudds of care,
And patient lies fast in furies snare.

The raging force of agues burning fits,
(With potions cold) doth yeilde at last to cure,
Eche thing extreame in time decreasing flits;
And patient may best my ease procure:
The sound (though weake) by foode recouer'th strength,
So may my sores obtaine some salue at length.

7 iawes] iawees
15 Goddesse] Goddesse is

Passion XXXV (C8^{v})

1 **Neptune . . . Eolus:** i.e., Aeolus, god of storms and winds, which were said to be under his control; for Neptune, see Passion XIII.12n.

2 **Triton:** son of Neptune, his companion and trumpeter.

2 **retreyte:** military trumpet call ordering a retreat.

3 **disease:** deprive of ease (i.e., comfort).

4 **they . . . repeate:** They (i.e., the "stormes") seek to go beyond their former bounds.

8 **Mercurie . . . will:** Mercury, messenger of the gods, to proclaim by sovereign authority thy will.

10 **subiect to fulfill:** under (Jove's) authority to carry out.

11 **spite:** be angry.

12 **Giue . . . knowe:** make her to understand.

14 **salue in store:** remedy in reserve.

15 **patience . . . blinde:** the capacity to accept suffering in order to curb this blind goddess (i.e., Fortune). *O*'s "is" following "Goddesse" is syntactically and metrically superfluous.

18 **patient:** the one suffering.

21 **Eche thing extreame:** everything excessive.

22 **patient:** being patient (under suffering).

PASSION. XXXVI.

REpyning fretts and ſturs the angrie minde,
That patience (which is the nurſing foode,)
In ſuch extreames, can no diſgeſtion finde;
No more then meate encreaſeth ſick-mens blood:
The one by cou ſe to choller altereth faſte,
The other turn'd to excrements doth waſte.

Who ſo by art would cure infected mindes,
Muſt mildely firſt prepare the ſickly thought,
When faulkner good a ſorrie feather findes,
He firſt beginns to pare and prune the naught:
And better graffes; then keepes his hauke on fiſte,
My troubled minde of ſuch a ſalue hath miſte.

For firſt we ſhould learne to forget the cauſe,
Before a ſalue may be thereto applyed,
Then may the gulfe which waytes with open iawes
For to deuoure therewith be ſatisfied:
And this obſeru'd, roote periſheth in time,
Which fed the cauſe the ſubiects of my rime.

Who hath ſuch ſtrength to moderate extreames,
That without change his countenance may beare,
When that doth periſh which he well eſteemes;
Which ſodenly procures a dreadfull feare:
No heart ſo hard for to endure the ſame,
Who then is he that can my weaknes blame.

D

5 course] course (r *barely prints*)

Passion XXXVI (D1)

1 **Repyning fretts:** lamenting gnaws at.
2 **nursing:** nourishing.
3 **disgestion:** digestion (variant form).
4 **encreaseth:** enricheth.
5 **by . . . faste:** by force of nature changeth quickly to anger.
9 **sorrie:** bad, poor.
10 **the naught:** i.e., the offending bad feather.
11 **better graffes:** implants a better (feather).
17 **this . . . time:** This being done, the basic cause in time is obviated.
18 **cause . . . rime:** reason that gave rise to the subjects of my verse.
20 **That . . . beare:** So that he may carry on, showing no change in his outward appearance.

PASSION. XXXVII.

OFt haue I sighthe, and to my selfe thus sayde,
O poore vnhappie relique left to paine,
Thus wrong'd by death which hath my death delayed
Whose eares thou filst, with prayers though in vaine:
Leaue to intreate the fiend that forst to fall,
And doth triumph thus glutted with thy thrall.

Seest not, that time cannot so long endure,
But that thou must needes haue some speedy end,
Of that which doth thy sorrowes thus procure,
What needeth then thy breath in vaine to spend:
For date of time which shortly wastes away,
Being once expir'd, thy sorrowes must decay.

The greatest fier PIRACKMON sendeth forth,
Will soone be quench'd, when matter none is left,
And here we see that men of greatest worth,
When sap is gone, will soone of breath bereft:
Why should I thinke death would my time delay,
Syth that which feedeth life doth fade away.

Nothing so hard but time at last doth weare,
Naught wanteth rest but will consume in fine,
How can my heart which doth my sorrowes beare;
Chuse but with speede consume away and pine,
Death will at last stretch out his angrie arme,
Inforst by time, to end my endlesse harme.

16 be reft] bereft

Passion XXXVII (D1^{v})

1 **sightht:** sighed. (“sightht” is a past tense of “sithe”=sigh).

4 **filst:** fillest.

5 **Leaue . . . fall:** Cease pleading with Death (or, perhaps, the Devil) that forced (thee) to fall.

6 **glutted . . . thrall:** gorged with thy bondage.

11 **date of time:** last day of one’s life.

13 **Pirackmon:** one of the three Cyclopes who made the shield of Aeneas. See Virgil, *Aeneid*, viii, 424–25. The name is compounded from the Greek words for “fire” and “anvil.”

16 **sap:** vital fluid, i.e., animal spirits.

16 **reft:** robbed.

20 **Naught . . . fine:** Nothing that lacks repose but will waste away in the end.

PASSION. XXXVIII.

BOwes not my body with the force of age,
Ys not the skyn far wyder then my face,
And flesh consum'd by force of wrathfull age,
What doe not siluer hayres yeilde goodly grace:
And be not these the kalendars of time,
Which witnes that in cares I spend my prime.

Were none of these my blood still waxeth could,
And I doe feele a weakenes in my minde,
Feare dispossest my wonted courage bould.
Dimnes of thought doth make my senses blinde:
Benomn'd I am in euerie part at length,
That cleane I lost the force of former strength.

These tokens shew my paine not long shall last,
Nor I (thoughe steele) be able to endure,
These torments, which encrease the surging blast,
Then let me not my greater harmes procure:
By fearing paine more then the force of paine,
Which feeble strength could not in me refraine.

Should I suppose I could exceede the dayes,
Which are layde downe to finish all my cares,
And doth encrease the cause which hope delayes,
Then let me yeilde, to him that still prepares:
A salue, to such as call to him for ayde,
And to abide the brunt are neu'r dismayde:

D 2

8 weaknes] weakenes
9 dispossest] disposlest (?)

Passion XXXVIII (D2)

1 **force:** debilitating effect.
2 **far . . . face:** i.e., wrinkled.
5 **these . . . time:** Silver hairs are the register of time (signaling its passing).
7 **Were . . . these:** if none of these (defects of age) existed.
7 **still:** continually.
13 **tokens:** omens.
15 **surging blast:** increasing curse (of age).
18 **refraine:** restrain, check.
21 **cause:** mental grounds for (unhappy) action.
22 **him:** i.e., God.

PASSION. XXXIX.

EStranged from the fruite of quiete reſt,
How can I choose but waſte, and weare away,
Whoſe accents new with feeling force moleſt
The troubled thonghts which carefull minde diſmay:
Who would the ſome of ſorrowes all diſplay,
Within my life let him the ſame ſuruay.

Some one repeates, he roules the reſtles ſtone
With SISIPHVS: an other Tantals payne
Doth beare: the third is rack;d with IXION:
And others do like TITIVS complayne:
But yet the worſt of their accurſt annoyes,
Eu'n is the beſt and chiefeſt of my ioyes.

Walke I abroad to meete ſome companie,
For to remoue theſe curſed cares away,
Eche man I meet, a mappe of miſerie
Preſents, to worke my ruine and decay:
His humor ſtor'd with pleaſure and delight,
Vnto my minde new cares effect inuite.

And as in ſtormes copartners yeild content,
And maketh leſſe the burthen of the minde,
Eu'n ſo a man in ſeas of ſorowes ſpent,
And knowes not where a mate therein to finde,
Muſt needs endure the torment all alone,
When to the winde he makes his ruthles moane:

4 thoughts] thonghts
9 rack'd] rack;d

Passion XXXIX (D2^{v})

3 **Whose . . . molest:** the new stressful feelings which vex with deeply felt force.

4 **carefull:** full of grief, anxiety.

7 **Some one repeates:** Some one (like Sisyphus, line 8) is doomed to repeat.

8 **Sisiphus:** Sisyphus was condemned, in Hades, continually to roll a stone up a hill, which when it reached the top always rolled down again.

8 **Tantals payne:** Tantalus was condemned, in Hades, to stand in water up to his chin under a fruit tree, the water and fruit retreating whenever he was thirsty or hungry.

9 **rack'd with Ixion:** Ixion was tortured (i.e., racked), in Hades, by being chained to an ever-revolving wheel.

10 **Titius:** Titius was punished, in Hades, by being stretched out on the ground while vultures gnawed on his liver.

11–12 **But . . . ioyes:** i.e., the worst of their punishments is less of a torture than the greatest of my delights.

18 **new . . . inuite:** induce new griefs as a result.

19 **And . . . content:** And as in times of (mental) unrest having fellow sufferers affords some sense of satisfaction (i.e., misery loves company).

22 **a mate . . . finde:** to find a partner (i.e., fellow sufferer) to act as a curb (i.e., palliative). The syntax in line 22 seems confused.

24 **ruthles:** pitiless. Did Parry mean to write "ruthful" perhaps?

PASSION. XL.

REst I at home, remembrance rackes my minde,
The obiect which doth feede my hungrie thought,
For nothing there remaynes for me to finde,
But euen the sound which I haue deerely bought,
Repentance, purchas'd with hastie brayne,
Which stores my mind with heapes of loath,d disdayne;

For idle heads build castles in the ayre,
And being alone am I there where I am?
No sure I view full many a countrey fayre,
And forren thoughts doe feede my fancies flame,
Eu'n thus I weare and waste away the time,
Declining when I haue most minde to clime.

The day expir'd, the nights approch supplies,
Where dreames with feare preuert my quiet rest,
And MORPHEVS a sopor sweete denies,
Which after toyle should be my mornings feast.
Sometimes I bathe my carefull couch with teares,
From soundest sleepe, a wak'd with starting feares.

Iturne and tosse: for Bodies ease is scant
When minde is fraught with burthens of annoy,
And cares my ioyes with spreding bows supplant,
Dispayre doth hopewith vglie face destroy.
Thus discontents plant accentes of my griefe,
Which do suppresse the agents of reliefe.

D 3

---

6 loath'd] loath,d
19 I turne] Iturne
22 hope with] hopewith

Passion XL (D3)

2 **obiect:** i.e., what he remembers.
3 **there:** i.e., in my mind.
4 **But . . . sound:** except the auditory vibrations (of my laments).
5 **hastie:** rash.
7 **castles . . . ayre:** (proverbial) figments of the imagination.
8 **am . . . am:** am I in such airy castles even now?
9 **view . . . fayre:** see (in my mind's eye) many a fair country.
13 **nights approch supplies:** (1) replaces, (2) duplicates the troubles of the day with night troubles.
14 **preuert:** outstrip. *OED* gives only a single example (1513); probably a compositorial misreading of "peruert"=ruin.
15 **Morpheus . . . denies:** Morpheus, the god of sleep, denies a sweet, deep sleep. The earliest example of "sopor" in *OED* is 1658.
18 **starting:** frightening.
21 **cares . . . supplant:** sorrows supplant my happiness with overlaying (i.e., overshadowing) boughs.
23 **plant . . . griefe:** give rise to the (vocal) expressions of my grief.

PASSION. XLI.

TIme draweth on to frustrate my desires,
Which vent will giue to my abortiue cares,
For to burst foorth to cruell flaming fiers,
Which wastes my life, fast fettred in the snares:
Of discontents, and then shall cease to moane,
When matter wantes for griefe to feede vpon.

Yeilde then content till sorrowes wearied be,
Let them complaine what toyle they doe endure,
Both day and night in persecuting thee,
Then they will cease thy torments to procure:
And for to reape vnto themselues some ease,
Thy will consent thy bondage to release.

Then shall the heau'ns confesse they did thee wrong,
And earth possest with such a tyrannie,
Shall curse the seedes, whereof thy woes are sprong,
All moaning thus thy woefull miserie:
O man thus borne in spite of angrie starrs,
Whose selfe-conceyte worke to him deadly warrs.

Could all the Gods being ioin'd in one consent,
Frame such a one which art no time could cure,
Though SATVRNE had some crooked nature lent,
Thinges of such force but sieldome are in vre:
And though they be yet cannot much preuaile,
Yf fate giue place vnto our swelling sayle.

---

12 They] Thy

Passion XLI ($D3^{v}$)

7 **Yeilde then content:** Then put aside contentment.
8 **them:** sorrows.
15 **sprong:** sprung (variant form).
17 **borne:** (1) born; (2) sustained, upheld.
18 **selfe-conceyte worke:** exaggerated opinion of himself (will) bring.
20 **art . . . cure:** skill could never, over time, remedy (i.e., make good).
21 **Saturne:** Of dubious reputation among the classical gods; Saturn displaced his brother, Titan, and devoured all his own sons (born to him by his sister, Rhea) so that Titan's issue would succeed him. These actions and his association with the melancholy humour gave rise to the adjective "crooked," which Parry applies to him.
22 **in vre:** put to any (good) use.
24 **giue . . . sayle:** give way to our increasing good fortune.

PASSION. XLII.

Plant ſeated in a looſe vnſtable ſoyle,
Know'ſt not the ſtate of this deceiuing time,
Howe cruell FATE returne with world of ſpoyle,
After the ſacke of a moſt fertile clime:
What doth earth hould? or ſea or ayre contayne,
But a congealed heape or errors vaine.

Our dayes doe moue like ſhadowes on the wall,
What doth not moue like ſhadowes light effect?
Howers flie full faſt to bring vs vnto thrall,
What doth not flie like ſhorteſt howers aſpect:
Waues dos ou'r-flowe the ſandes that be ſo wide,
What doth not ſwell as doth the flowing tyde.

The fruites made ripe by force of haſtie time,
Doe ſooneſt fade the bloſſome being decayed,
And as the flowing waues ſwell in their prime,
So flies it faſt like ſhadowes forme diſplay'd,
The day is full of labors paynefull toyle,
The day is full of dolors deadly ſpoyle.

Pale death doth knocke eu'n at thy princely gate:
With like demaunde, as at the cottage poore,
Doth pale death knocke with iuſt demaund; no hate,
Ingraf'd with wrong, to theſe extreames do ſture:
For he deſtroyes as well Captayne boulde,
As pooreſt wretch fram'd of this earthly moulde.

D 4

3 returnes] returne
11 doe] dos
14 decay'd] decayed

Passion XLII (D4)

4 **sacke:** looting, despoiling.

5–6 **earth . . . errors:** Parry is recalling Ovid's description of Chaos before form and order were imposed on the Earth (I, 5–20). In line 6 "or" is, perhaps, a misreading of "of," influenced by "or" just above in line 5.

7 **shadowes . . . wall:** Is Parry thinking in terms of Plato's "Cave" metaphor? See *The Republic*, vii, i–ii.

8 **light effect:** seek the light ("effect" here used to carry the sense of "affect").

13 **hastie time:** i.e., "hastie" because time is reputed to fly. See lines 9–10 and cf. the Latin tag "Tempus fugit."

15 **in their prime:** at their highest point.

16 **like . . . display'd:** i.e., like the formation of shadows made manifest.

18 **dolors deadly spoyle:** injury caused by mortal griefs.

19 **thy:** Probably should be emended to "the."

21 **iust:** even-handed (i.e., distinguishing between rich and poor, etc.).

21–22 **no . . . sture:** no hatred or malice, incorporated with prejudice, incites (Death) to these extremes (i.e., distinctions between high and low, good and bad, rich and poor; Death retains his even-handedness). "Sture": stir.

PASSION. XLIII.

ARm'd to offend death maketh choyſe of none,
Nor difference to worke his ſauage will,
But all alike none by hi ſel e is gone,
Vnto the pot, his hungrie mawe t fiill:
One houſe of death is common vnto all,
One lawe of death doeth goueine great and ſmall.

Flowers, graſſe, miſt: doth fall, doth wither, doth fade,
With winde in time, to th'aire: flowers, graſſe, & miſt we (be,
For here being ſent to dig, and delue with ſpades
Our workes bring foorth the fruite of miſerie:
As flowers fall, graſſe wither, miſt fades away,
So doth our daies, fall, wither and decay.

What thinge ſo ſure but falleth at the laſt,
Or what ſo firme but ruinates in time,
Who is ſo wiſe that can endure the blaſt?
Which doth forbid the haſtie for to clime:
Of thinges that ſhalbe duſt let no man ſtore,
Duſt we ſhalbe, and duſt we weare before.

Yf choyſe be made, or difference take place,
Eu'n with that choyce death waxeth more vnmil'd,
The faireſt flowers fall ſooneſt to diſgrace;
And worſer thinges ſcape often vndefil'd.
So many bad doe daies enioye,
When dint of death doe better ſort deſtroye.

---

3 himselfe] hi sel e
4 to fill] t fiill
7 mist] mist:
20 vnmild] vnmil'd
23 doe [many]] doe

Passion XLIII (D4^{v})

1 **death . . . none:** i.e., Death's choice is at random and without distinction between rich and poor, high and low, good and bad.

2 **difference:** i.e., the difference between rich and poor, etc.

3–4 **But . . . fill:** But by the same token none chooses to kill himself just to furnish a tasty morsel to fill Death's hungry belly.

14 **Or . . . time:** Cf. Ovid's "Tempus edax rerum" (XV, 234–61).

15 **blast:** i.e., the destructive winds of life (cf. line 8).

16 **hastie for to:** rash, over-precipitate to.

17 **store:** hoard, store up.

19 **Yf . . . place:** See lines 1–2.

23 **doe [many]:** Metrical considerations call for the insertion of some two syllable word. The occurrence of "many" earlier in the line may account for its omission here.

24 **dint:** stroke.

PASSION. XLIIII.

REsted by choyse our dayes we finish here,
And IOVE himselfe the hoyse thereof hath made
Being lou'd we die, IOVE lou's as doth appeere:
By motions which errors doe inuade,
So those whom IOVE with princely care doth loue,
Them he doth chase his Godhead to approue.

O happie man of whom IOVE made a choyse,
O happie man whom IVPITER doth loue,
Whom IOVE accepts he onely may reioyce,
Whom IOVE takes to himselfe he doth reproue:
Yf chosen thus, and loued so by IOVE,
Or though reprou'd, why should we fafnt in loue.

He onely shall the flaming wals enioy,
That gardes the thorne of IOVES imperiall seate,
And shall behould that prince which may destroy,
PHEBVS bright beams which feedeth vs with heate:
No sorrowes then, nor griefe shall him molest,
Being lath'd by IOVE vnto his heau'nly feast,

So shall he rest amongst the chiefest starrs,
There a new star plac'd for to yeilde vs light,
And by his death shall end these terren warrs,
And life a newe begyn to leade vpright:
And shall no more behould the theater,
Where tragick euill leade mortall men to erre.

---

6 chasen] chase
12 faint] fafnt
14 throne] thorne

Passion XLIIII (D5)

1 **Rested by choyse:** Meaning unclear; perhaps means "Governed by what we believe to be our choice" (i.e., by free will). But, possibly, "Rested" may mean "put at ease." (Gentrup, privately, suggests "[ar]rested".)

2 **Ioue . . . made:** i.e., our choice is only ratified because it is Jove's (i.e., God's).

3–4 **Ioue . . . inuade:** Meaning again unclear; perhaps means "Jove [i.e., God] loves us, it would appear, by promptings or impulses which overcome the errors or sins to which [mortal] love is subject."

6 **chasen:** *O*'s "chase" may be right, meaning to "hunt after" or "pursue" (for our good), but considering a well-known passage in Hebrews, 12:6: "For whom the Lord loveth, he chasteneth" (Bishops' Bible), it seems probable that Parry intended "chasen" (chasten). *O*'s "chase" may be explained by the compositor's failure to notice a tilde over the *e*, a convention that asks the reader to supply an *n* or *m*.

6 **approue:** attest.

7 **Ioue:**=Jupiter=(here) God. The use of different titles for the same mythological figure (see line 8) within a few lines occurs elsewhere in Parry's work as in some other writers of this period.

12 **Or:** even.

12 **faint in:** lose heart about, fall off from.

15 **prince:** Jove/Jupiter=God.

18 **lath'd:** invited. *OED* records no use of "lathe" between 1450 and 1854. The "feast" to which Jove invites him is a veiled reference to Holy Communion; Cf. George Herbert's "Love III."

21 **terren:** earthly.

23 **theater:** i.e., the world as a stage; cf. the Latin tag: "Totus mundus agit histrionem."

PASSION. XLV.

REstes any thing more lighter then a haire,
No haire but doth IOVES godhead high reproue.
What is more light then birds which sparrowes rere,
Yet sparrowes witnes that there is a IOVE:
Is any thing of greater weight then life,
And shall life passe in mistie cloudes of strife?

Yt may not be that I should so beleeue,
Life comes to vs eu'n by the heau'ns decree,
To such conceyt I may no credit giue,
Life flies away by dynt of destinye,
Life we possesse by force of IOVES commaund,
Life we must yeild, if IVPITER demaund.

For borne we are, and die we stalbe sure,
Because we are of purpose borne to die,
But not content with our estates vnsure,
Nor pleased yet death should our patience trie:
IOVE did commaund, and death obayes his will,
So let it rest IOVES doome for to fulfill.

IOVE did commaund, which must not be gain-said,
He spake the word, and all did yeild consent,
He made a beck, and roaring seas obayed,
Then with our states why are we not content?
He wills vs from these worldly cares refrayne,
And his edict must eu'r and eu'r remayne.

13 shalbe] stalbe

Passion XLV (D5^{v})

2 **reproue:** prove again. The first stanza claims that Jove (=God) is responsible for or governs the lightest (i.e., smallest, most seemingly unimportant) and heaviest (i.e., greatest and most important) of all created things. Cf. Matthew 10:29–30.

3 **then . . . rere:** than sparrows which are nurtured by sparrows.

9 **conceyt:** belief, thought.

10 **dynt of destinye:** stroke of fate.

21 **beck:** nod (thus giving a silent command).

24 **his edict:** God's law. Stress falls on the second syllable of "edict."

PASSION. XLVI.

YF this be thus? then farewell all my ioy,
Which I possest before these cares encroc'hd,
IOVE made a choyse, death did his choise destroy,
O would that death had vnto me approch'd:
More welcome sure had been his deadly dart,
Then these annoyes which breede encreasing smart.

Farewell my ioy, I doe renounce thy smile,
I hate the thing which cause of ioy may yeild,
Least fayned hope should certaine FATE beguyle,
Despaire hath wonne the honor of the field,
My loue, my life, my ioy is gone before,
Death may alone my hope of ease restore.

Then as the faithfull which embrace the toole,
And kisse the same, which life doth take away,
Who well were taught in high IEHOVAS schoole,
That beares the bag of simple truth alway:
So will I clippe and kisse this world of paine,
Which Ioue hath sent to coole my wandring braine.

Embracing death and loathing lifes repose,
I rest content and watch the happie time,
I seeke not now to triumphe ou'r my foes,
Yet heere would faine end both my life and time:
But that I vowed ou'r as your sheapheard true,
With hand and hart to serue and honour you.

FINIS.

---

2 encroch'd] encroc'hd

Passion XLVI (D6)

1 **Yf . . . thus:** i.e., if God's law (that we must refrain from worldly concerns or fears) will forever continue to exist (see Passion XLV.23–24).

3 **Ioue . . . choyse:** See Passion XLIIII.2, 7–24.

3 **death . . . destroy:** See Passion XLIII.24.

6 **annoyes:** cares, fears.

9 **certaine Fate beguyle:** foil or cheat inevitable Fate.

13 **the faithfull:** religious martyrs.

13 **toole:** instrument (of death).

16 **alway:** always, ever.

17 **clippe:** embrace.

20 **watch . . . time:** watch vigilantly for the happy moment (of death).

23 **But:** except.

THE
Patrone his pa-
thetical Posies,
Sonets, Maddri-
galls, & Rown-
delayes.
Together
With, SINETES
Dompe.
Plena verecũ-
di culpa pu-
doris eras

Posie I (D7–D7^{v})

Title. **The patrones conceyte:** i.e., what Parry's patron, John Salusbury, may think or feel about his presumably desired mistress, Dorothy Halsall, the wife of Cuthbert Halsall and sister-in-law of John Salusbury. Her name, DOROTHY HALSAL, is spelled out in Posie I by taking the initial letter of the first seven stanzas and the initial letter of each line of the eighth stanza, except of line 7, which makes use of the first two words ("A Lampe"). The nature of the personal relations between John and Dorothy is unknown (see Introduction, 2, 17–18). For questions concerning the authorship of the Posies, see Introduction, 13–20.

POSIE. I

The patrones conceyte:

Domestick Goddes of the Sea-whal'd Isle,
Heau'ns erected trophies of thy prayes,
AVRORA'S blush, that beautifies thy smile,
Sh'nes far more bright then Phoebus goulden rayes,
Natures chiefe pride, the map of beauties grace,
Loues louely sweete, which vertue doth embrace.
Of-spring of Gudds, borne of the salt-sea foame,
Thoughts mate that doth to Pallas bower incline,
A Commet, that in starrie night doth gloame.
And doth presage of misteries diuine:
An ornament, bedeck'd with goulden tyres,
A pearle in camp'd in strength of chaste desires.
Reposed rest of ADON's ardent looke.
Thy Christall-pointed eies (like Saphyres blue,
Set in the snowe) doe hide a bayted hooke:
Which doth intrap by force of Goulden hue:
Were ADON here to viewe thy VENVS eye,
Could ADON such a VENVS suite denye.
Olympus Queene, that doth commaunde the skyes,
Whose shining beam's doe light the westerne Isle,
No base aspect in thy sweete bodie lies,
Thy fauours doe the stealing time beguile:
For precious breath so doth perfume the ayre,
That all applaude thou onl' art sweete and faire.

The

---

12 incamp'd] in camp'd

24 *Following this last line of sig. D7, the compositor indents the first three lines to accommodate a large capital "T" in italics, thus treating lines 25–48 as a separate poem.*

1 **Domesticke Goddes:** indigenous goddess (with reference to Dorothy Halsall).

1 **Sea-whal'd Isle:** This epithet is almost certainly a compositor's misreading for "Sea-wal'd"; cf. Shakespeare's *Richard II*, 3.4.43.

2 **Heau'ns erected trophies:** The heavens have raised monuments.

3 **Auroras blush:** having the appearance or look of Aurora. She was the Greek goddess of the morning, often referred to as the paramour of Phoebus Apollo, god of the sun.

5 **Natures chiefe pride:** "Natures pride," a phrase used at least four times by Parry, may have been picked up from Lodge's *Rosalynde* (1590), 385, a work from which John Simons notes borrowings in *Moderatus*.

7 **Of-spring . . . foame:** An implied comparison with Aphrodite (Roman: Venus), goddess of love, who according to some accounts was born of the sea-foam. Cf. Sonetto 6, epigraph.

8 **Thoughts-maze . . . incline:** Thought's labyrinth that is disposed to bow to the abode of Pallas Athene (Roman: Minerva), goddess of wisdom and war.

9 **gloame:** makes dusky.

11 **tyres:** adornments.

12 **incamp'd:** inset (as in a ring or broach). Cf. Samuel Daniel, *Rosamond* (1592), 205: "So well incamp'd in strength of chaste desires."

13 **Reposed rest:** settled, quiet tranquility.

13 **Adon's:** Adonis's. In Roman mythology, Adonis, a youth courted by Venus and much lamented by her when he was slain by a boar while hunting.

14–15 **Christall . . . snowe:** Borrowed from Samuel Daniel, *Rosamond* (1592), 170: "Transpearcing rayes of Christall-pointed eyes"; and Thomas Lodge, *Rosalynde* (1590), 423: "Her eyes are Saphires set in snow."

16 **by force:** through the power of.

18 **Could . . . denye:** Perhaps, as in Posie IIII.15n., a passing reference to Shakespeare's *Venus and Adonis* (1593).

19 **Olympus Queene:** Hera (Roman: Juno), queen of Mt. Olympus, the reputed home of the Greek gods.

20 **westerne Isle:** i.e., Britain.

21 **aspect:** appearance.

22 **fauours:** features.

22 **stealing time:** thieving time. Cf. Daniel, *Rosamond* (1592), 462: "Or doubting time his stealth."

POSIE. I

The Patrones Conceyte.

THe Radian beam's of natur's pureſt die,
With honours Equipage long liue thy fame,
Whoſe ſiluer arkes, ſurpaſsing Chriſtall skie,
Doth force loue Queene to reuerence thy name:
Starrs doe inuay, that earth retaineth thee,
From making Fourth amongſt the graces Three.
Heau'ns newe ioy, earth's poſſeſſed wonder,
The welkins pride, if they might thee embracce,
As they did IOVES loue that kills with thunder,
Thy memorie her beautie doth deface.
Liue long thou ſtar, which in the North doth ſhine,
That noble worth's may fill thy ſacred ſhrine.
Ympe graft with vertue in her tender yeeres,
Deriuing honour from her noble ſtocke,
Which Needles weare? for honour ſtill appeer's,
Within her browe, which doth fames cradle rocke:
Whoſe ſearching wit, dipt in MINERVAS vaine,
Fraught with content, doth Pallas prayſes ſtaine,
HIBBLA hath Bees, ſtor'd with a ſweete encreaſe,
And ſhee hath beautie, furniſhed with grace,
Liue ſtinges doe pricke, though hony's taſte to pleaſe,
So woundes her beautie thoſe which it embrace:
A Lampe of glorie ſhines in thee alone,
Liue long in earth thou match-leſſe Paragone.

25 Radiant] Radian
28 loues] loue
32 embrace] embracce
45 do please] to please

25 **Radiant:** *O* reads "Radian"; "Radiant" is probably a necessary emendation, but "Radian," although not in the *OED*, may be one of Parry's "new" words.

26 **With honours Equipage:** with all the attributes that belong to honor. Cf. Thomas Nashe, *Works*, III, 320: Thomas Watson, whose "*Amintas* . . . may march in equippage of honour with any of our Poets." See also Sonetto 11.12n., Sonetto 27.12n., and Shakespeare's Sonnet 32.12.

27 **arkes:** arches (=eyebrows).

28 **loues Queene:** Aphrodite (Roman: Venus).

29–30 **earth . . .Three:** Earth by keeping thee prevents thee from becoming a fourth among the three Graces (Aglaia, Thalia, Euphrosyne, Greek sister goddesses, who bestowed beauty and charm upon mankind).

31 **possessed wonder:** wonderful possession.

32 **welkins:** sky's

33 **Ioues . . . thunder:** Semele, daughter of Cadmus and Harmonia, was impregnated by Jove (Greek: Zeus) thus arousing Juno's (Greek: Hera's) wrath, who disguised herself as Semele's nurse and advised her that she must see Jove in his full majesty in order to be sure that her lover was indeed Jove. Jove, having promised to give Semele anything she desired, when she asks to see, and be embraced by, him in all his refulgent majesty, has to keep his promise with the result Semele is thunder-struck and devoured by fire.

34 **Thy . . . deface:** (Just) the memory of her would still, by comparison, efface Semele's beauty.

37 **Ympe . . . vertue:** child engrafted with virtue.

38 **stocke:** (1) ancestors, line of descent; (2) trunk (to which, as a sapling [="Ympe"], she is a graft or branch).

39 **weare?:** the question mark here, as not infrequently in this period, functions as an exclamation mark.

41 **Minervas vaine:** Minerva's vein or manner of discourse. Minerva was the Roman equivalent of the Greek Athene, goddess of wisdom and war. The reference to Pallas in line 42 seems merely redundant since Pallas is a Greek name for Minerva (i.e., Pallas Athene).

42 **content:** (1) satisfaction; (2) substance (of thought).

43 **Hibbla:** Hybla Minor, a city in Sicily, renowned for its honey.

43 **encrease:** harvest, crop.

47 **Lampe of glorie:** Cf. Joshua Sylvester, *Du Bartas his Divine Weekes and Workes* (1641), 639, "An Elegie [for] Master Henry Parvis": "Else had not *London* lost her lamp of glory" (written 1593).

POSIE. II

The Patrone's affection.

LAunterne of loue the patrone due of lore,
Light some beame my affection to guide,
Amongst the drerie throbbes encreasing sore,
Sore in the vaile of heart where I them shide:
Languishing in delight I doe delight to pine,
And can I pine a more contented paine,
Hart once mine-owne, is nowe possession thine,
Yeilde then to yeilde this hearts due entertaine.
Honour is the guest, let bounty be my prize,
Truth be the page of my admired light,
Occasion be thou prest at my aduize,
Regarding hand, and hart, t'attend her fight.
Or else my heart and minde I hould in hand:
Doe then my hope confirme that hope may stand.

4 *Worked up space prints after* them

Posie II (D8)

The opening lines appear to link with the conclusion of Posie I. The initial letter of each line, read from the bottom up, spells DOROTHY HALSALL.

Title. **The Patrone's affection:** i.e., the Patron's affection for Dorothy Halsall.

1–2 **Launterne . . . guide :** Cf. Spenser, *Epithalamion* (1595), 288–90: "glorious lampe of loue / . . .[that] guydest louers thorough the nights dread."

1 **patrone . . . lore:** the pattern or model of learning that has been earned (taking "patrone" as a variant form of "pattern"). Perhaps "patrone" should be emended to "patrones," meaning then something like "by right of the patron's learning." Neither gloss gives a very satisfactory meaning in the context.

3 **drerie . . . sore:** dangerously increasing doleful heartbeats.

4 **Sore . . . heart:** Painful in the valley of the heart. Perhaps, however, "vaile" should be read as "veil" (i.e., something one hides something under).

6 **pine . . . paine:** afflict myself with a more satisfying pain.

8 **due entertaine:** merited acceptance.

10 **my admired light:** i.e., the light which I admire. Looks back to lines 1–2.

11 **Occasion . . . aduize:** Opportunity be thou prepared (to follow) my determination.

13 **I . . . hand:** I keep in suspense.

POSIE. III.

The patrones phantasie.

TOrmented heart in thrall, Yea thrall to loue,
Respecting will, Heart-breaking gaine doth grow,
Euer DOLOBELLA, Time so will proue,
Binding distresse. O gem wilt tLou allowe,
This fortune my will Repose-lesse of ease,
Vnlesse thou LEDA, Ouer-spread my heart,
Cutting all my ruth, dayne, Disdaine to cease,
I yealde to fate, and welcome endles Smart.

4 thou] tLou (?)

Posie III (D8)

A multiple acrostic: contains the name DOROTHY (taking the capital letter following the caesura in the first seven lines and reading from line seven up), CVTBERT (taking the initial letter of the first seven lines and reading from line seven up), and hAlsAll (taking the final letter preceding the caesura of the first seven lines and reading from line seven up, ignoring, however, the final *e* in "distresse" in line four. The last and eighth line, taking the line's initial letter and the initial letter of the line's last word, gives IS (i.e., John Salusbury). See Brown, xxxviii–ix, xlv. Loaded as Posie III is with acrostic lumber, it is not surprising that it is difficult to make coherent sense of it or to decide because of the uncertain pointing what lines or part-lines contextually belong together.

Title. **The patrones phantasie:** i.e., the patron's dream or vision. It is difficult to see the relevance of the title.

2 **Respecting will:** taking one's desires into account.

2 **gaine:** increase.

3 **Euer Dolobella:** always fair or happy grief or pain. "Dolobella" seems to be a misformation from the Italian *duolo* (masculine) and the feminine of *bello*—an oxymoron. Any reference to Publius Cornelius Dolabella, an ally of Octavius Caesar, seems unlikely.

3–4 **Time . . . distresse:** Time will thus prove it to be an enslaving anguish (of mind). Perhaps "prove" = test it as being.

5 **This . . . ease:** This destiny (is) to leave my desires without the repose given by freedom from pain (of mind).

6 **Leda:** There are variant versions of the Leda story. According to Thomas Cooper (*Thesaurus Linguae Romanae et Britannicae*, 1565), Zeus, in the form of a swan impregnated Leda, wife of Tyndareos, king of Lacedaemon; she gave birth to two eggs, from one of which were born Pollux and Helena (wife of Menelaus, who was ravished by Paris), from the other Castor and Clytemnestra (wife of Agamemnon). The connection of the Leda myth with the present context is not clear.

7 **ruth:** pity.

POSIE. IIII.

The Patrons pauze in ode.

DImpl's florish, beauties grace,
Fortune smileth in thy face,
Eye bewrayeth honours flower.
Loue is norish'd in thy bower,
In thy bedded brow doth lye,
Zeale imprest with chastitie.
IOVE's darling deere,
Opale lippes of corall hue,
Rarer die then cheries newe,
Arkes where reason cannot trie,
Beauties riches which doth lye,
Entomb'd in that fayrest frame,
Touch of breath perfumes the same:
O rubie cleere:
Ripe ADON fled VENVS bower,
Ayming at thy sweetest flower,
His ardent loue forst the same,
Wonted agents of his flame:
Orbe to whose enflamed fier,
Loue inforc'd him to aspire.
Hope of our time;
Oriad's of the hills drawe neere,
Nayad's come before your peere:
Flower of nature shining shoes,

Rip

Posie IIII (D8v–E2)

Posie IIII is an extraordinary example of acrostic ingenuity with occasional flashes of poetry. As Brown has shown (xlv–xlvi), it contains five encrypted names: (1) IOHN SALESBVRYE (taking the first letter of the seventh line of each stanza); (2) DOROTHI HALSALL (taking the first letter of the first line of each stanza); (3) FRANSIS WILOWBI (taking the first letter of the second line of each stanza); (4) ELIZ ABET HWOL FRES TONE ROBE RTPA RRYE (i.e., Elizabeth Wolfrestone and Robert Parrye; taking the first letter of lines three to six in the first eight stanzas). Two of the ladies named ("Fransis Wilowbi" and "Elizabeth Wolfrestone") are the same as those named in the acrostic arrangement of Parry's "Passions" and, as here, they are followed by the name Robert Parry. See Brown, xlii–xliv, and Introduction, 2–3, for the possible significance of these five names and the relationships they seem to suggest. In this period, the English stanzaic ode form was strongly influenced by the French Marot/Pléiade school and employed a six or eight syllable line (here combined by Parry). See Sidney Lee, *The French Renaissance in England* (1920), 241–43.

Title. **The Patrons pauze in ode:** i.e., The patron's (musical) rest in the form of an ode.

1 **florish:** perfection.

2 **Fortune:** good luck, happiness.

2 **thy:** It is not clear to which of the three ladies "thy," here and elsewhere in Posie IIII, refers. Since the poem is addressed to John Salusbury, however, it is likely that Dorothy Halsall is intended; of the women named she seems most often associated with Salusbury, and she is given pride of place in the acrostic game.

3 **bewrayeth:** revealeth.

5 **bended:** frowning (in deep thought).

6 **imprest:** imprinted.

7 **Ioue's:** Presumably a politic way of referring to God.

8 **Opale:** irridescent. Earliest citation in *OED* as an adjective is 1649.

10 **Arkes:** eyebrows (literally, arches).

10 **trie:** determine the extent of.

15 **Ripe Adon:** Adonis fit for love (i.e., Venus). For the best-known story of Adonis, see Ovid, X.298–559, 731–39. The incestuous offspring of Cinyras and his daughter, Myrrha, and greatly beloved by Venus, he was slain by a wild boar and his body and blood turned into an anemone, blood-red and checkered white (see below, lines 24–29).

POSIE. IIII.

The Patrones pauze in ode.

Riper then the falling rose,
Entermingled with white flower,
Stayn'd with vermilion's power,
Nest'ld in our clime.
The siluer swans sing in poe,
Silent notes of newe-spronge woe,
Tuned notes of cares I sing,
Organ of the muses springe,
Natures pride inforceth me,
Eu'n to rue my destinie.
Starre shew thy might,
Helens beautie is defac'd,
Io's graces are disgrac'd,
Reaching not the twentith part,
Of thy gloases true desart,
But no maruaile thou alone,
Eu'n art VENYS paragone.
Arm'd with delight.
Iris coulors are to base,
She would make APELLES gaze,
Resting by the siluer streame,
Tossing nature seame by seame,
Pointing at the Christall skie,
Arguing her maiestie,

E Loue

29 Poe] poe
41 VENVS] VENYS
42 Arm'd] *Arm'd*

15 **fled Venus bower:** Perhaps a recollection of Shakespeare's *Venus and Adonis* (1593), in which, unlike Ovid's Adonis, he is described as being unresponsive to Venus's overtures of love.

16–20 **Ayming . . . aspires:** The relation of these lines to the Adonis myth is unclear; presumably "thy sweetest flower" may be connected with "flower of nature" (line 24), i.e., the anemone. Cf. Shakespeare's *Venus and Adonis*, 1177–78: " 'Poor flow'r,' quoth she [Venus], 'this was thy father's guise [i.e., red and white, like the anemone]—/ Sweet issue of a more sweet-smelling sire—.' "

22 **Oriad's :** nymphs that presided over mountains.

23 **Nayad's:** nymphs that presided over fountains.

28 **in our clime:** The type of anemone described in the note on line 15 flourished in England.

29 **Poe:** Po, the largest river in Italy. The "siluer swans" may have been suggested by the white swans that bore Venus's car through the sky (see Ovid, X, 708–9, 719–20). The swans' notes are "silent" (line 30) because swans were believed to sing only at their deaths. Cf. Daniel, *Rosamond* (1593), 72: "And Thames had Swannes as well as ever Po."

32 **muses springe:** Aganippe or Hippocrene, the fountains of the Three (or Nine) Muses near Mount Helicon.

36 **Helens . . . defac'd:** Helen of Troy's beauty may here be "defac'd" (i.e., destroyed) in reference to Christopher Marlowe's *Doctor Faustus* (5.2.99–100): "Was this the face that launched a thousand ships / And burnt the topless towers of Ilium?"

37 **Io:** See Sonetto 23.4n.

38 **twentith:** twentieth (variant form).

41 **paragone:** match, equal.

43 **Iris:** the rainbow, personified as a goddess in Greek mythology.

44 **Apelles:** famous early Greek painter.

46 **Tossing . . . seame:** throwing nature about furrow by furrow.

POSIE. 4

The patrones pauze in ode.

Loues rampire ſtronge.
Hayre of Amber, freſh of hue,
Wau'd with goulden wyers newe,
Riches of the fineſt mould,
Rareſt glorie to behould,
Ympe with natures vertue graft,
Engines newe for dolors fraught,
Eu'n there are ſpronge,
A Iem fram'd with Diamounds,
In whoſe voice true concord ſounds,
Ioy to all that ken thy ſmile,
In thee doth vertue fame beguile,
In whoſe beautie burneth fier,
Which diſgraceth Queene deſier:
Saunce all compare,
Loue it ſelfe being brought to gaze,
Learnes to treade the louers maze:
Lying vncou'red in thy looke,
Left for to vnclaſpe the Booke:
Where enroul'd thy fame remaiues,
That IVNOs bluſh of glory ſtaines:
Blot out my care.
Spheare containing all in all,
Onely fram'd to make men thrall:
Onix deck,d with honours worth,

O

Running heads: IIII] 4 (sigs. E1v, E2)

68 remaines] remaiues

73 deck'd] deck,d

52 **mould:** mode, pattern.

54 **Ympe . . . graft:** offspring, scion (of a noble house) implanted with nature's (1) strength, (2) worth.

55 **Engines . . . fraught:** Laden with new snares (which are) stored with pains or sorrows.

60 **beguile:** (1) charm; (2) cheat; (3) entrap.

62 **Queene desier:** This personification was probably suggested by Greene's *Greenes Never too late* (1590), 18: "Came the God . . . / Hand in hand with Queene Desire." Parry had already used this image four times in *Moderatus*.

63 **Saunce all compare:** beyond all comparison.

65 **louers maze:** Probably borrowed from Sidney's *Arcadia* (1590), lyric 62 (in *Poems*, ed. Ringler), line 33: "Your eyes may tread a Lover's maze." Love is frequently described as a "maze" in which the lover wanders without any sense of direction. See a poem by Giles Fletcher the Elder called "The Lover's maze" (Lloyd E. Berry, ed., *The English Works of Giles Fletcher the Edler* [1964]).

69 **That . . . staines:** which eclipses the splendor of Juno's glance.

POSIE. 4

The patrones pauze in ode.

On whoſe beautie bringeth foorth:
Smiles ou'r-clouded with diſdaine,
Which loyall heart doth paine:
    Voyde of diſgrace,
AVRORA's bluſh that decks thy ſmile,
Wayting louers to begnile:
Where curious thoughts built the neſt,
Which neu'r yeildes to louers reſt:
Waſting ſtill the yeilding eye,
Whilſt he doth the beautie ſpie.
    Rea'd in her face.
Lampe enric'hd with honours flowers,
Bloſſome gracing VENVS bower:
Bearing plumes of feathers white,
Wherein Tnrtles doe delighte,
Senſe would ſeeme to weake to finde,
Reaſon's depth in modeſt minde:
    Yeilding deſire.
Lode-ſtarre of my happie choyſe,
In thee alone I doe reioyce:
O happie man whoſe hap is ſuch,
To be made happie by thy tutch:
Thy worth and worthynes could moue,
The ſtouteſt to incline to loue,
    Enflam'd with fier.

F 2

79 beguile] begnile
85 enrich'd] enric'hd
88 Turtles] Tnrtles

78 **Aurora's:** For Aurora, see Posie I.3n.
80 **curious . . . nest:** (1) solicitous, (2) curious thoughts built the (love) nest.
82 **Wasting . . . eye:** Ever gradually destroying the (lover's) surrendering eye.
84 **Rea'd:** (which is to be) read. The spelling "Rea'd" may be an attempt to distinguish the past from the present tense.
85 **Lampe:** Cf. Posie I.47–48 and Posie II.1–2.
88 **Turtles:** turtle doves, types of constancy, faith.
91 **Yeilding:** (1) giving rise to; (2) surrendering.
92 **Lode-starre:** guiding star, especially the pole-star.

POSIE. V.

The dittie to Soſpiros.

THe wound of hart doth cauſe my ſighes to ſpring
And ſighes doe oft report my hartie ſore,
This ſore of heart doth woefull tidings bring,
That loue is lacke and I doe grieue therefore:
O ſighes why doe you riſe and take no reſt,
O heart why art thou thus with them poſſeſt.
My heart in ſelfe it ſelfe would pine away,
if that ſometimes ſighes muſicke I ſhoulde miſſe,
This bitter ioy and pleaſant paine muſt ſtaie,
The greateſt griefe is now my greateſt bliſſe:
The night I grone the day I teare my heart,
I loue theſe ſighes I triumph in their ſmart.
When minde and thought are clogged with their cares,
And that my heart is readie for to breake,
Then eu'rie ſigh doth queſtion how it fares,
nd heart to them replies that it is weake.
et after ſighes the heart is ſome-what glad,
us without ſower the ſweete is neuer had.

My

8 If] if
16 [A]nd] nd (*leaf damaged*)
17 [Y]et] et (*leaf damaged*); [er] *Brown*
18 [Th]us] us (*leaf damaged*)

Posie V (E2^{v}–E3)

Title. **The . . . Sospiros:** The verses (or the song) to the Sigher. The name derives from Latin *suspirare*= to sigh. See lines 1–2.

2 **report . . . sore:** express my heartfelt wound (i.e., grief, pain); "hartie" anticipates play on "heart" in line 3.

4 **loue is lacke:** love is lacking, absent. Cf. the proverb "In love is no lack" (Tilley, L485).

11 **teare:** wound, lacerate (as in line 1).

12 **smart:** pain.

POSIE. V.

The dittie to Soſpiros.

My wiſh and will for ſuccour doe aſpire ,
Vnto the ſeate of my endeered truſt ,
But want and woe enſuing my deſire,
My heart doth quaile and after ſigh it muſt :
  Yet wiſh I muſt and well I may delight ,
  Though ſighe for wants and woes doe me affright.
Theſe ſighes Ile entertertaine though they me noy ,
For they doe like the cauſe from where they riſe ,
They bring in poſt newes of my mynded ioy ,
And as they paſſe they meſſage me no lies :
  And yet they leaue behinde them ſuch a want ,
  That minde and ioy I finde to be but ſcant ,
O will you neuer ceaſe me ſighes to grieue ,
And maye not hope keepe you in calme repoſe ,
Let me ſome reſpite haue, hart to relieue ,
Leſt that your ſelues and you fullie loſe :
  Sighes doe aſpire till they obtaine their will ,
  Sighes will not ceaſe they ſeeke my heart to kill .

E 3

24 sighes] sighe

20 **seate:** throne (perhaps with sexual suggestion); cf. Shakespeare's *Othello*, 2.1.295–96 and Sonnet 41.9.

20 **my endeered trust:** i.e., the one who is held dear and trusted by me.

25 **noy:** annoy, disturb.

27 **in post:** with express speed.

27 **mynded:** remembered.

28 **message . . . lies:** i.e., send a true message to me.

31 **cease . . . grieue:** cease to grieve me, O sighs.

34 **Lest . . . lose:** The line limps metrically; read perhaps, "Lest that your selues and you [do] fullie lose." This reading of the line omits "do" because "your selues and you" seems merely tautologous.

POSIE. 6

The patrones Dilemma.

OF ſtately ſtones the Diamound is kinge,
Whoſe ſplendor doth dazell the gazing eye,
The Onix gloze, is tyed to honors winge.
Whoſe vertu's gouern'd by th'mperiall ſkie:
Theſe graces all in thee combin'd remaine,
For glorie thine their glories ſtill doth ſtaine.

Shall I not ſpeake of Rubies glorious blaze,
That blazeth ſtill, like blazing ſtar that ſhoes,
Or ceaſe to write how men at th,Opale gaze,
Whoſe beaűtie ſhines like perles of dewe on roſe:
Theſe vertues all (compar'd with thine) are baſe,
For nature gaue thee excellent of grace.

The Topas chaſt thou doeſt in kind excell,
The Hyacinth that ſtrangers loue procures,
Hath not ſuch force, nor can not worke ſo well,
As honors beautie ſtill in thee alures;
Yris ſheews not more coulors in her kind,
Then vertues be with in thy noble mind.

Th

Running head VI] 6
9 th'Opale] th,Opale
12 excellence] excellent
17 shewes] sheews
18 within] with in

Posie VI (E3^{v}–E4)

An acrostic: each of the "stones" (and two of the herbs) is capitalized (e.g., "Diamond," "Onix," etc.); the capitals, when read from line 1 down, they spell "DOROTHY HALSAL," Salusbury's sister-in-law. See Introduction, 2, 17–18. Unless otherwise noted, the authority cited for the "vertues" associated with the "stones" and herbs here referred to is Albertus Magnus, *The Boke of Secretes* (1565?); *STC* 260.

Title. **The patrones Dilemma:** The dilemma is between hope and despair. Cf. *Moderatus* (1595), sig. F4: "euerie sigh ministring a thousand doubtfull Dilemmas . . . thus bathing him selfe in a sea of confused thoughtes, betweene hope and despaire he rested speechlesse," and sig. R2^{v}: "Here *Moderatus* with volleyes of sighes, . . . made a full period, resting in a *Dilemma* betweene feare and hope. . . ."

3 **Onix . . . winge:** The special virtue of the onyx is again associated with "honor" in Posie IV.73: "Onix deck'd with honours worth."

4 **vertu's gouern'd:** power (moral or medicinal) is controlled.

9 **men . . . gaze:** " . . . and it is of suche vertu, that it blyndeth the sightes of them that stande about" (*Secretes*, sig. C1^{v}).

13 **Topas chast:** Cf. *Moderatus*, sig. E2^{v}: " . . . and if you haue not the vertue to be chaste, carrie about you the hearbe *Lupinor*, or the *Topaze* stone, which cooleth desire." Cf. Greene, *1 Mamillia* (1583), 31: "yet thou shouldest take the hearbe *Lupinar* to coole desire."

14 **Hyacinth . . . procures:** " . . . it beyng borne on the finger, or necke, maketh straungers sure, & acceptable, to theyr ghestes" (*Secretes*, sig. D7).

17 **Yris . . . kind:** "If this stone be put in the beame of the Sunne, by turning backe it maketh a rayne bowe soone to appere in the walle" (*Secretes*, sig. D4^{v}).

POSIE, 6

The patrones Dilemma.

The windie Hiſtmos ſhews, and bright aſpects,
Comes far behind this faire Angragos worth,
The Lupinar hath not more chaſt affects.
Then glorie of th' vnſpotted minde brings foorth.
My paines encreaſe thy graces to repeate,
For cold deſpaire driues out of hope the heate.

Yf Saunus fort which doth expell deceate,
Or Agathes which happie bouldnes yeild's,
And eke Luperius whoſe vertues greate,
Doth glad the minde: all which are found in fields:
Yf theſe I had to comfort my deſpaire,
Hope yet might hope to win & weare thy faire.

E 4

19 **The windie Histmos:** "This stone bloweth like a payre of bellowes, by reason of the windinesse in it, . . . if this stone be set in a garment it can be burned in no wyse, but it shyneth lyke fyre" (*Secretes*, sig. D2).

19 **shews . . . aspects:** eye-catching displays . . . appearances.

20 **Angragos:** As Simons points out, Parry presumably means to refer to *anagyros* (also known as *acopos*) a plant, the leaves of which were used to alleviate difficult childbirth, asthma, boils, etc.; used also as an emetic (see Pliny, *Naturalis Historia* [Loeb ed.], Book XXVII, 13).

21 **Lupinar:** a herb; see line 13 n.

25 **Saunus . . . deceate:** "It doth make firme or consolidate the mynd of the bearer of it" (*Secretes*, sig. D8).

25 **fort:** strong.

26 **Agathes:** i.e., agate; ". . . & that maketh to ouercome peryls, & geue strength to ye hart, & maketh a man myghtye, pleausante, delectable, & helpeth agaynst aduersities" (*Secretes*, sig. C5).

27–28 **Luperius . . . fields:** " . . . all beastes runne to it, as to their defender. It letteth that neyther dogges, nor Hunters maye hurte them" (*Secretes*, sig. D3^{v}).

30 **win . . . faire:** possess and enjoy thy beauty. Cf. lines 29–30 with Posie VIII.7.

POSIE. VII.

The Palmers Dittie vppon his Almes.

FAyre Dole the flower of beawties glorious ſhine,
Whoſe ſweete ſweet grace true guerdon doth deſerue,
My Oriſons I offer to thy ſhrine,
That beauties name in glories ſtate preſerue:
My hap (ô hapleſſe hap) that gaue th'applauſe,
Thy beautie view'd when trembling hart did pauſe.
Were I a King, I would reſigne my Crowne,
To gaine the name of Palmers happie kinde,
I would not craue to liue in high renowne,
If Do'e I had to ſatisfie my minde:
Then I for Dole a Palmers name would craue,
If Palmer might be ſure his dole to haue.

POSIE. VIII.

The Patrones Adiew.

YF loue deſerues the fruit of loues deſire,
Hope loathes my loue to ltue in hope of right:
Time after triall once may quench my fire,
Oh ſalue the ſore and cheriſh my delight:
Rue lawles force, which feruent zeale procures,
Obtaine a hart like to the Emerauld pure:
Dayne hope to graunt where feare diſpaire allures,
In deepe diſtreſſe naught but true faith is ſure.

2 liue] ltue

Posie VII (E4^{v})

Title. **The Palmers . . . Almes:** A palmer was distinguished from a pilgrim by the fact that a pilgrim journeyed on his own charges, while a palmer, a pilgrim returning from the Holy Land, was entirely dependent upon charity ("dole"=alms, and here equals some share in his mistress's love). The first stanza in its address to "Fayre Dole" uses the terms of a lover to his mistress. This palmer/pilgrim wooing metaphor is reminiscent, perhaps, of Shakespeare's *Romeo and Juliet*, 1.5.93–110.

2 **guerdon:** reward.

7–12 **Were . . . haue:** i.e., If I might only have my "dole" (alms, charity, your love), I would willingly, if I were a king, give up my crown and kingdom and become a mere palmer.

Posie VIII (E4^{v})

Title. **The Patrones Adiew:** i.e., The Farewell to the Patron. A double acrostic and the last Dorothy Halsall acrostic: read, from line 7 up, the first letter of each line (DOROTHY) and , again, from line 7 up, read the first letter of the second word of each line (h a l s a l l); in line 8, the first letter of the first word (I) and the first letter of the last word (s) gives I s (i.e., John Salusbury). It is, however, unclear how a "farewell" relates to the following poem. Possibly, the title of Posie VIII properly belongs to Posie III (both eight line poems), where it is more suitable to a farewell, just as the title of Posie III ("The patrones phantisie") is more suitable for Posie VIII, thus upsetting the proper order of the Patron-series.

2 **Hope . . . right:** Expectation (of happiness) makes my love loath to live in anticipation of justice.

3 **Time . . . once:** Time, after testing, may finally quench my love's ardor.

7 **Dayne . . . allures:** Think it worthy in you to allow for the possibility of hope where fear makes despair attractive. Cf. Posie VI, headnote.

POSIE. IX.

Fides in Fortunam.

Moſt ſacred is the ſweete where fortune ſwayes,
Deuine the ſound of her enchaunting voice,
Noe hope of reſt, wher hope, true hope delayes,
Thongh I diſpaire I may not change me choiſe:
For liue I well, though fortune me diſpiſe,
To honour her, that ſcornes my enterpriſe.
To bandie lookes will eaſe my thrauled heart,
With lookes, my life ſhalbe at her commaunde,
Yf ſo much grace to faith ſhe will impart:
With lookes againe, to anſwere my demaunde;
And that I may ſtill loue her to my graue,
With pureſt faith, is all that I doe craue.
Let Phœbus drawe his ſhining beam's away,
Let heau'ns forſake to graunt me any light,
Let foode me faile; let hope, my hope delay;
Let eares not heare; let watch-full eies want ſight:
Let ſenſe, my ſenſe, with furie fell confound,
Before that farth, to fortune falſe be found.
Thy eu'r ſworne friende, and ſeruant to thy end,
Hath made a vowe and promiſe with his ſonle,
His fortun's right with courage to defend,
Againſt proudeſt he, this offer dare controle;
My match is ſure if Fortune grace her ſwayne,
And coullors giue her quarrell to maintaine.

Coulors

4 Though] Thongh
4 my] me
18 faith] farth (?)
20 soule] sonle

Posie IX (E5–E5^{v})

Title. **Fides in Fortunam:** Faith, trust, belief, security, fidelity, promise in Fortune (i.e., in one's fate or lot in life). Both "fides" and "fortune" are difficult terms to apply with an exact or even consistent meaning.

4 **my choise:** i.e., my choice of mistress (as assigned to me by Fortune or Fate). *O*'s "me" for "my" was caught up, by eye-skip, from "me" in line 5.

7 **bandie:** exchange.

8 **With lookes:** in consideration of such (love) glances.

9 **grace . . . impart:** she will make (my) constancy a partaker of so much goodwill.

10 **lookes againe:** repeated (love) glances.

17 **with . . . confound:** confused by savage anger.

19 **seruant:** lover.

22 **this . . . contro'le:** (that) he dares defend this offer (i.e., his "vowe and promise").

23 **swayne:** lover (frequently figures as a shepherd in pastoral poetry and romance).

24 **coulors . . . maintaine:** the freshness of her complexion affords her grounds for defense (with play on regimental flags or ensigns as heading or leading her "quarrell"; see lines 27–29).

PCSIE. IX.

Fides in Fortunam.

Colours they are of pureſt Indian die,
For none but ſuch doth Fortune vſe to lend.
Whoſe ſight may moue the coward neu'r to flie,
And all his force againſt his foe to bend.
Then let ſweet ſoule thy colours be my guide,
And hap what maye, thy doome I will abide.
Then write thy Cenſure with thy prettie hand,
I will obay the ſentence of thy minde;
And graue the ſame in table faire to ſtand;
So that, enſuing age the ſame may finde:
For monument in goulden letters wrought,
To whet with ſight the accents of my thought.

26 **doth . . . lend:** is Fortune accustomed to bestow.
31 **Censure:** i.e., "doome."
33 **table:** stone (or wooden) tablet (as a memorial).
34–35 **finde / For:** discover as a.
36 **accents of:** things most stressed in.

POSIE. X.

My sorrow is ioy.

SOwre is the sweet that sorrow doth maintaine,
Yet sorrow's good, that yeildeth mickle ioy,
True ioy he hath, that can from ioy refrayne.
Which haruest's still the fruites of deepe annoy:
Yet I enthraulde in blind CVPIDOS snare,
With fond conceyte in sorrows ioy I fare.
Fortun's my ioy, which sorrow still doth yeild,
Her frowne I count a fauour to my soule;
Sorrow doth sway, and ioy hath lost the field,
Yet fame in minde doth often ioy enrole:
But when I thinke for whome I beare this smart,
It yeilds new ioy vnto my carefull hart.

Posie X (E6)

Title. **My sorrow is ioy:** As the title suggests this poem expresses a paradox.

2 **mickle:** great.

4 **Which . . . annoy:** Which always gathers in (like a crop) the consequences (i.e., unhappiness) arising from grave (mental) disturbance.

6 **fare:** carry on, travel.

9 **doth sway:** hath the victory.

10 **fame . . . enro'le:** the memory of past good often registers happiness (in one's mind).

11–12 **But . . . hart:** Cf. Shakespeare's Sonnet 30.13–14.

POSIE. XI.

An almon for a Parrat.

Diſdainfull dames that mountaines moue in thought,
And thinke they may Ioues thunder-bolt controule,
Who paſt compare ech oue doe ſet at naught,
With ſpuemiſh ſcorn's that nowe in rethorick roule:
Yer ſcorne that will be ſcorn'd of proude diſdaine,
I ſcorne to beare the ſcornes of fineſt braine.
Geſtures, nor lookes of ſimpring coy conceyts,
Shall make me moue for ſtately ladies mocks:
Then SIRENS ceaſe to trap with your deceyts,
Leaſt that your barkes meete vnexpected rocks;
For calmeſt ebbe may yeild the roughest tide,
And change of time, may change in time your pride.
Leaue to conuerſe if needes you muſt inuay,
Let meaner ſort feede on their meane entent,
And ſoare on ſtill, the larke is fled awaye,
Some one in time will pay what you haue lent,
Poore hungrie gnatts faile not on wormes to feede,
When goſhaukes miſſe on hoped pray to ſpeede.

3 one] oue
4 squemish] spuemish
5 Yet] Yer

Posie XI (E6v)

Title. **An almon for a Parrat:** Meaning uncertain; R. B. McKerrow (Thomas Nashe, *Works*, IV, 461) suggests that this proverbial expression seems to mean "an answer for a fool." "almon" is a common variant of "almond."

3 **Who . . . naught:** Who (thinking themselves beyond comparison) fix the value of each other (or of all others) at nothing.

4 **squemish scorn's:** coy, cold insults.

4 **in rethorick roule:** hold sway in the use of (insulting, scornful) language. "roule"=rule.

5 **scorne . . . disdaine:** contempt that will be treated with contempt by haughty disdain.

7 **of . . . conceyts:** arising from smirking, disdainful thoughts.

8 **make . . . mocks:** cause me to alter my feelings because of haughty, disdainful ladies" derision or contempt.

9 **Sirens:** a term of censure for the "Disdainfull dames" of line 1; see Passion XV.17n.

13 **Leaue . . . inuay:** If of necessity you must censure, stop talking.

14 **Let . . . entent:** Let those of lower degree (or understanding) gratify their lower inclination or desire.

16 **Some . . . lent:** Sooner or later someone will suffer for what (i.e., scorns, mocks, derision) you have dealt out.

POSIE. XII.

The authors muſe vpon his Conceyte.

FAire, faireſt, faire; if paſſing faire, be faire,
Let not your deed's obſcure your beauties faire,
The Qneene ſo faire of Fearies not more fayer,
Which doth excell with fancies chiefeſt fayer,
Fayre to the worldes faire admiring wonder,
Fayrer then I O V E S loue that kill's with thunder.
Eu'n to your ſwayne you ſeeme prides paſſing faire,
That naught deſires but fortun's faire to reape,
Yf fortune then will driue me to diſpaire,
No change can make your ſweeteſt faire ſo cheape,
But that I muſt, and will liue in exile,
Before your thoughtes with thought I will defile.
Fayre fierce to faith, when fortune bend her browes,
Yet fortune ſweete be thou reclaym'd againe:
For vnto thee I offer all my vowes,
That may appeaſe the rigor of my paine:
Yeilde wiſhed hope after this ſtormie blaſt,
That calm's repoſe may worke content at laſt,

Posie XII (E7)

Title. **The authors . . . Conceyte:** The use of "muse" is ambiguous: (1) in classical terms the goddess who inspires the poet's imaginative powers; (2) meditation; (3) "Conceyte"=thought (here fanciful or witty), idea. Posie XII runs the gamut on the various possible meanings of "fair" as noun, adjective, and verb (i.e., "fare"). Cf. a song on "fair" in George Peele's play *The Arraignment of Paris* (1584), 1.5.282–313.

1 **Faire . . . be faire:** (O) beauty, most beautiful one (=my beloved), if surpassing beauty be (1) impartial, equitable, (2) gentle, (3) auspicious.

3 **Queene so faire of Fearies:** Note the play on "fair" and "fairy."

6 **Ioues . . . thunder:** See Posie I.33n.

7 **swayne:** (pastoral) lover.

7 **prides passing faire:** i.e., an example of the arrogance of surpassing beauty.

10 **so cheape:** so great a bargain.

13 **Fayre . . . faith:** Incline ardently to constancy, faithfulness.

13 **when . . . browes:** when Fortune shall frown.

16 **That:** Thee (Fortune) that.

17 **Yeilde:** (May Fortune) vouchsafe.

Fides ad fortunam.

THe goulden Phebus (longing oft) is ſeene.
To pricke his furious ſteedes to run in haſte,
To clip and coll faire Thetis louely Queene,
In penſiue thoughts leſt he the time ſhould waſte,
So I make ſpeede thy ſelfe for to embrace,
Beinge almoſt tyr'd in purſuite of the chaſe.

For houndes vncoupled, range the forreſt wide,
The ſtance being prun'd, I watch the rowſed game,
And to the marke my ſhaftes full well I guide:
The craftie Doo takes on then to be lame:
But hauing paſt the daunger of my bowe,
She, limping leaues, and haſtes away to goe.

Thus I being ſureſt of my hoped ſport,
Still miſſe the faireſt marke that eu'r was kend,
Words doe abound of comfort to exhorte,
But deedes are ſlowe ſuie promiſes to end;
The hope theu left is game to rowſe a newe,
(Till deedes ſupplie) and feede my ſelfe with view.

Fortune hath ſayde, and I beleeued that,
Renewed hope might eaſe my heart neere ſpent:
Deſpaire in ſequell oft my hope doth ſquat;
That doubtfnll I remaine ſtill diſcontent,
Wherefore to faith if faith remaine in thee,
With faithfull wordes let deedes in one agree.

FINIS.

Running head XIII] 13
17 then] theu
22 doubtfull] doubtfnll

Posie XIII (E7^{v})

Title. **Fides ad Fortunam:** Fidelity to (or trust in) Fortune (i.e., one's lot in life). The hunting-sport metaphor on which the poem turns refers, of course, to the lover's pursuit of his mistress.

2 **pricke:** spur.

3 **clip and coll:** embrace and hug.

3 **Thetis louely Queene:** In Greek mythology, Thetis was a Nereid (i.e., sea nymph) and the mother of Achilles by Peleus. The connection with Phoebus here described (lines 1–4) is repeated by Parry in *Moderatus*, sig. D2^{v}: "By this had Phoebus clearely made escape, / And Vesperus his action did assoyne, / Of Thetis Queene then cloyed with the rape, / With Lucina in coiture doeth ioyne." The Phoebus connection does not appear in accounts of Thetis' "life." Confusion, not uncommon, between Thetis and Tethys, a sea-queen and the wife of Oceanus, may be at work here; cf. Shakespeare's *Troilus and Cressida*, 1.3.39.

4 **pensiue:** anxious.

5 **thy selfe:** i.e., his mistress.

8 **stance being prun'd:** hunting-station being prepared (i.e., by cutting back superfluous branches, etc.).

10 **takes on:** pretends.

13 **hoped sport:** hoped for game (i.e., love sport).

15 **exhorte:** earnestly to admonish (in regard to action or conduct).

16 **sure . . . end:** to fulfil promises for certain.

18 **deedes supplie:** deeds replace (hope).

18 **view:** just looking (at the new "game").

20 **neere spent:** almost exhausted.

21 **in sequell:** in the outcome.

21 **squat:** crush.

22 **That doubtfull:** so that full of fears.

23 **faith:** fidelity, trust.

Sonetto. 1

REade theſe my lines the the carrecters of care,
Sweete Nymph theſe lynes reade ou'r & on'r againe,
View in this glaſſe (that glorie doth prepare,)
The depth of worthes which in thee doth remaine,
Heare I ſet foorth the garden of thy grace,
With plentie ſtor'd of choyſe and ſweeteſt flowers,
Where I for thee abortiue thoughtes embrace;
When in conceyte hope lodgeth in thy bowers:
Heare ſhalt thou finde the Orphans of my hope,
Shad'wed with vaile en'n of thy rare deſeart,
Of all my thoughtes here ſhalt thou finde the ſcope,
Which to the worlde thy honour ſhalt ympart.
Thus will I ſay when skies aduaunce thy name,
Liue HELENS peere eternized thy fame.

---

1 the] the the
2 & ou'r] on'r
10 eu'n] en'n

Sonetto 1 (E8)

The first of a group of sonettos (1, 15–31) addressed to Helena Owen; see the note on line14. On Helena Owen and Parry's authorship of Sonettos 1, 15–31, see Introduction, 2–3, 20–23. Aside from sporadic uses of "sonetto" by Robert Greene (*OED*), Thomas Lodge, and Thomas Nashe, Parry seems to be the only contemporary to employ the Italian form of the word throughout a sonnet sequence.

3 **glasse:** i.e., this sonnet (as a mirror reflecting your "depth of worthes"); see line 4.

3 **glorie doth prepare:** provides honor, splendor.

5 **garden . . . grace:** fruitful ground of thy charm.

7 **for . . . thoughtes:** thoughts about thee which come to nought.

10 **Shad'wed with vaile:** (1) protected, (2) obscured with a veil.

11 **scope:** purpose, intention.

14 **Helens peere:** the equal of Helen of Troy (with reference to Helena Owen, Parry's wished-for mistress). Among other Helen of Troy references, see particularly "The lamentation of a Male-content," 155–56: "Paris a sheaphard I [i.e., Parry] a homely swayne, / He wanton, I chast Helen would possesse."

Sonetto. 2

FArewell my hope thy hap did thee not ſteede,
And thou my hap vnhappie come to mee,
Farewell my truſt which voide waſt of all meede,
And thou heart-ſore attend my miſerie,
Farewell my hold which waſt to ſtronge to hold,
And thou my ruine welcome to my gaine,
Farewell my life which dead are in my monld,
And life no life torment my hart with paine
Farewell my chiefe that conquerſt with thy looke,
And thraldome I appeale to riue my heart,
Farewell my thought, thy thong t ſhe w ll not brooke,
Yet thinke I will for that I feele the ſmart.
Farewell my choiſe I laſtly doe thee chuſe,
I cannot chuſe another to my will:
Farewell my comfort comfortles o muſe,
And ſorrowe weake thy wrath my ioy to ſpill.
Farewell long ſtay for winde to fill thy ſayle,
Come baniſhment. Adieu, loue muſt preuayle.

S.

7 art] are
7 mould] monld
11 thought she will] thong t she w ll
16 wreake] weake

Sonetto 2 (E8^{v})

The first of thirteen sonettos, each distinguished from the other sonettos (nos. 1 and 15–31) by a capital "S" placed below the last line, the "S" indicating that the S-Sonettos were written by Parry for John Salusbury (see Introduction, 19–20).

1 **thy . . . steede:** (1) thy good luck, (2) lot in life did not advantage or profit thee.

2 **thou . . . mee:** thou, my bad luck, unhappily (did) befall me. Throughout the poem "thou" refers to Salusbury's "mistress," presumably, (1) Dorothy Halsall, Salusbury's sister-in-law (see Introduction, 2–3), or (2) possibly Eleanor Salusbury (see Sonetto 5).

3 **which . . . meede:** which was empty of all reward. The use of "wast," here, and in line 5 is anomalous, "wast" being a second person singular form.

5 **hold . . . hold:** struggle which was too burdensome to endure.

7 **life . . . mould:** life which dead art in my body (which is made of earth). Cf. "earth to earth, ashes to ashes, dust to dust" in the Anglican burial service. *O*'s "are" has been emended to "art" on analogy with "wast" in lines 3, 5.

9 **chiefe:** chosen one, most beloved.

10 **thraldome . . . heart:** Challenge (my) bondage (to thee) that is going to split my heart.

17 **long . . . sayle:** long period of waiting for a (favorable) wind to fill my sail (i.e., put me in a position to act with success).

18 **Come banishment:** (And therefore) exile must result.

Sonetto. 3

EMerald of treasure eternall spring,
Nurst by the graces day-starre shine on hie,
Ingendring perfect blisse with valens ring:
Twisting loue and liking with constancie.
Now stanchlesse hart redres & soule-sick wound,
Enwrap the same in foldes of fresh desire,
Let loue be waking haruest hope be found,
And liuing spring to quench this flame of fier:
Vnto your excellent loue sole commaund,
Seing ės you may procure I me commend,
Into your counsels grace vourch my demaund,
Heate burning ioy sustaine in ioyfull end.
So shall my muse your name ay coronize,
I will it blaze to all posterities.

F S

Sonetto 3 (F1)

An acrostic: the initial letter of each line, read from the bottom up, spells "I[ohn] S[alusbury] HIS VALENTINE." Presumably addressed to the Elanor (or Eleanor) who figures acrostically in the next two sonettos.

1 **Emerald . . . spring:** (O) treasured emerald (i.e., his jewel of a mistress) grow or flourish forever.

2 **graces:** i.e., the Three Graces (Aglaia, Thalia, Euphrosyne), as goddesses, presided over nurture and all good services.

3 **with valens ring:** ring out with power. "Valens" is probably a variant form of "valency"; not recorded in *OED*.

5 **stanchlesse hart redres:** bleeding, weakened heart be restored to health.

6 **the same:** i.e., the "redressed" heart.

7 **Let . . . found:** Let love be found (as) a lively ingathering of hope.

8 **liuing spring:** lively well-head.

10 **Seing . . . commend:** Seeing that you are able to obtain comfort, I recommend myself. *O*'s peculiar spelling of "ease" as "ês" is, so far as I know, unique.

11 **Into . . . demaund:** (Allowing me) into the favor of your considerations, grant my request.

12 **Heate . . . end:** (Let) ardor preserve an ardent happiness for a happy conclusion, issue.

13 **ay coronize:** forever crown.

Sonetto. 4

RElieûe my minde being oûerpreſt with care,
O heare my ſorowes for I doe complaine,
Non may thẽ help ſaue you the cure being rare,
Ah put me not to death with lingring paine.
Leſt that my death;to you ſhall nothing gaine,
Enforced loûe diſlikes which is not meete,
Equalitie of loûe doth neûer paine;.
You paragon moſt pretious pure and ſweete.
Reioyce your louers hart with loûe for loûe,
Vnlace diſlike and let be far diſdaine,
Both one in one and let affection mooûe:
Since that in hart affection doth remaine.
Vntie diſtreſſe to finde my bliſfull ſport,
Let not your hart be cruell to the meeke,
Attend my harts deſire in humble ſort:
Soone grant my humble hart what it doth ſeeke.

S

5 *Worked up space prints after* death
7 *Worked up space prints after* paine

Sonetto 4 (F1ᵛ)

An acrostic: the initial letter of each line, read from the bottom up, spells "SALVSBVRYE ELANOR." The relations between John Salusbury and Elanor are unknown; nor is it clear whether her name was Elanor Salusbury or, perhaps more likely, the juxtaposition of the names in reverse order may be taken to suggest some sort of relationship between John Salusbury and an Elanor. Sonetto 5 repeats the two names in the same order, though in slightly different spelling.

3 **Non:** i.e., None.

6 **Enforced . . . meete:** i.e., Love that is forced (on a person) produces aversion, which is not (1) fitting, (2) equal (unlike "Equalitie of loue," i.e., love for love; see lines 7 and 9).

10 **Vnlace . . . disdaine:** Free yourself of aversion and let disdain be banished.

11 **Both . . . mooue:** i.e., Let lover and beloved be one person ("one soul in bodies twain") and let love be stirred up, aroused.

13 **Vntie . . . finde:** Unbind restraint in order to (1) reveal, (2) obtain my most happy (love) sport.

Sonetto. 5

REtire you thoughts vnto your wonted place,
Or let your place be where your thought are prent;
Newe ioyes approching with a kindely grace:
And hope that bloſſoms on affections dent.
Excelling worth lyeth buried in my breſt,
Loue take concealing paine in tombe of heart,
Each ioy is griefe wherewith thou art oppreſt;
Yound is thy griefe but ſudden old thy ſmart.
Rich is thy choyce deſire hath twiſe a neede,
Eu'n ſo my hope would reape hope to ſuſtaine,
Bearing in my heart the wiſh of heartie deede,
Sealing ſelfe and lore high concealed vaine.
Vnſpotted truſt and truth ty'd to the ſame,
Loue keeping awe as awefull truſt ſhall prooue,
Amongſt the ſtings where heart doth feele the flam
Such is the meauing of my fixed loue,
Such be her hart my dolors to remooue.

F 2 S

2 thoughts] thought
8 Young] Yound
12 lores] lore
16 meaning] meauing

Sonetto 5 (F2)

An acrostic: the initial letter of the first sixteen lines, read from line sixteen up, spells "SALVSBERY ELEANOR." See headnote to Sonetto 4.

2 **Or . . . prent:** Or let your (mental) point of concentration be where your thoughts are fixed.

4 **affections dent:** the force or pressure of love.

6 **eke:** also.

8 **sudden . . . smart:** quickly old thy pain (joining it with earlier remembered pains).

9 **desire . . . neede:** desire is doubly demanding.

10 **Eu'n . . . sustaine:** In a like manner my hope would harvest further hope to sustain itself.

12 **Sealing . . . vaine:** Certifying or stamping the self and learning's lofty, hidden strain or manner as true. It is possible that "concealed" is a misreading of "conceited" (i.e., "high conceited vaine" = lofty imaginative strain); cf. *Moderatus*, sig. F2: "conceited vaine." Against this, however, is the theme of concealment which has appeared earlier in lines 5–6 above.

14 **Loue . . . prooue:** Love preserving a reverent fear as the majesty of constancy or faith shall prove.

Sonetto. 6

Vppon the sandes where raging sea doth roare,
With fearefull sound, I standing with desire,
The element his billowes sendes to shoare,
And takes away my ioy to my great ire.
So water tho did seeke to quench my fire,
Whose furie (I beheld) with rash rebound,
That would furflow my life, ô rage to dire,
My hearts high rocke was rent which stood on ground:
But high commaund retreait she made him sound,
Who once immite his furie did surcease,
And way-white waues to vieū her did redoūnd,
Breaking at her sight her empire to compleasé.
And blustring windes their forces did release,
Least that their tūmult might her eares offend,
And with a calmie fawne breath'd to her ease,
Thus was my wish to port they should her send.
So waū ie seas and windes once made me sad,
So wâuie seas and windes haūe made me glad.

Amore é mare. S

Sonetto 6 (F2^{v})

2 **desire:** i.e., sexual desire (implied by "standing"). Cf. Shakespeare's Sonnet 151.12.

3 **element:** i.e., water (one of the so-called four elements: earth, water, air, fire).

5 **tho:** then.

7 **surflow:** overflow (not in *OED*).

8 **high . . . ground:** chief stone (i.e., main foundation), which had an earthy, not heavenly, base, was split.

9 **But . . . sound:** But being the commander-in-chief, she (i.e., my mistress) made him (i.e., water) sound the retreat.

10 **Who . . . surcease:** Who (i.e., water) once infused or admitted its fury ceased.

11 **way-white . . . redound:** pale white waves in order to view her swelled.

12 **Breaking . . . complease:** Disintegrating at sight of her in order to gratify (her sense) of absolute rule.

13 **release:** withdraw.

15 **calmie . . . ease:** tranquil courtesy breathed comfort to her.

16 **port:** (home) port (i.e., her lover's arms).

Epigraph. **Amore é mare:** Love arose out of the sea. According to Greek myth, Aphrodite (Roman: Venus) was born from the sea-foam. Cf. Posie I.7.

Sonetto. 7

MArching in the plaine field of my conceyte,
I might behold a tent which was at reſt,
My forces I did bend but ah deceite:
There left I freedome laſt which is now leaſt.
For when I thought to fight with Mars for beſt,
There Cupid was which brought me to diſtreſſe,
Of foe when I thought to make a conqueſt.
Loûe and deſire in tent did me oppreſſe.
Theſe captaines twaine from tormẽt may ſurceaſe,
If they did know the lore I beare in minde,
They may as Turtles one procure my eaſe,
O that to me of twaine one would be kinde.
Thou tẽt that holdſt in night ſuch turtle doûes,
Reioice, embrace the twayne of world the loûes.

F 3 S

11 once] one

Sonetto 7 (F3)

1 **plaine . . . conceyte:** open field (or country) of my dreaming thought (i.e., imagination, taking the mind as a field of battle).

2 **might . . . rest:** could imagine a military pavilion which was in a state of quiet repose (i.e., out of the area of conflict).

3 **bend:** bring to bear (against the tent).

5 **fight . . . best:** combat with Mars, aiming for victory.

7 **foe:** i.e., Mars.

9 **Captaines . . . surcease:** i.e., Mars and Cupid may cease from tormenting me. It is unclear whether line 10 should be read with line 9 or with line 11.

11 **as . . . ease:** Like turtle doves (types of constancy in love), they may once and for all bring about my relief or comfort. *O*'s "one" for "once" was caught up, by eye-skip, from "one" in line 12.

13 **in night:** in secrecy, undercover.

14 **embrace . . . loues:** eagerly accept the two (i.e., war and love), loves that are beloved by the world.

Sonetto. 8

OF all the bûddes that yeild to men delight,
Sweete eglantine that ſenteſt in the aire,
Art worthie pen of gold thy praiſe to dight:
Thy flowers of bloome make world both green &
To wearied ſence thou comfort doſt repaire, (faire,
Thy pleaſure from the eye doth neuer ſtray,
To fancies heſt thou art a ſtately chaire:
And wounded hartes deſire thou canſt allay.
More bright then ſun thou ſtand'ſt in window bay,
And to thy light the ſûnne may not come neere,
Thou laſting flower doſt euerlaſting ſtay:
O that within thy flowers I might appeere.
As I did paſſe ſweete ſent to hart did clime,
O thou ſweete branch the ſweetnes of my time.

S

Sonetto 8 (F3^{v})

2 **Sweete eglantine:** sweet-briar (which, however, is prickly). There are four sonettos on the eglantine (8, 9, 11, 12), which is, almost certainly, a metaphor for Dorothy Halsall, Salusbury's sister-in-law (see Introduction, 2–3).

3 **dight:** treat.

6 **Thy . . . stray:** i.e., the pleasure you give the eye is always there to be found.

7 **To fancies hest:** according to the demands of imaginative thought.

9 **window bay:** window opening. Cf. *Moderatus*, sig. F2: ". . . they might see the yong prince *Cornelius* standing in a Bay window, which bouaded [*sic*] vpon a very faire garden."

Sonetto. 9

As eye bewrayeth the secretes of my minde,
I did regard an Eglantine most faire,
That sprong in sight of sun that brightly shind,
And yet no sunne her springing could empayre.
I did reioyce to come within her aire,
Her sweetenes to receiue within my brest:
O that her sent in hart ay might I weare,
With griping griefe heart should not be opprest,
Heart panting sore would cease or take some rest,
And feare disloyall vanish would away,
Then ouer griefe in triumph were I blest,
To be reuiued when life went to decay,
With shadow hide me from these hart-breake showers,
And with thy sent refresh me in thy bowers.

F 4 S

Sonetto 9 (F4)

2 **Eglantine:** See Sonetto 8.2n.

7 **ay:** forever.

9 **panting sore:** sorely throbbing.

10 **feare disloyall:** i.e., fear that makes him unfaithful to his love. Cf. Sonetto 14.1.

13 **shadow:** i.e., the shade or protection offered by the eglantine (= his mistress).

Sonetto. 10

THe onely helpe that ſome diſtreſſed haue,
To keepe the life though lingring in the paine,
Is that a time ſome place will find to ſaue,
The loſſe of heart procured by diſdaine.
Nowe place is faire yet hope I doe retaine,
That diſtance neuer altereth the minde,
The height of hills doth make the lowly plaine,
The riſing ſunne in ſkie feares not the winde:
And yet I ſee place is ſomewhat vnkinde,
To offer me the lack of her ſweete face,
Which cannot ſolac'd be till I it find:
To free my heart and loue of loues diſgrace.
O place if thou didſt take her from my eye,
Bring her in place where place may remedie:

S

Sonetto 10 (F4^{v})

3 **Is . . . saue:** Is that at some time a fitting occasion or opportunity will be discovered to rescue.

5 **Nowe . . . yet:** Under such circumstances the occasion (or time) seems favorable or promising nevertheless.

11 **Which . . . find:** Which (i.e., the "lack of her sweete face") cannot be alleviated until I (again) find it (i.e., her face).

14 **in . . . remedie:** at a fitting time where the occasion may lead to some easing of the situation.

Sonetto. 11

VVHen chirping byrds did chaunt their musickeslayes,
For to salute Dame Flora with her traine,
And vesta cloth'd with chaung of fresh arayes,
For to adorne Hopes happie entertayne:
Then sweetest Bri re that shylded our repose,
Sent odours sweete, from her fresh hanging bowes,
And Philomel' oft-changed notes did close,
Which did accorde eu'n with our hallow'd vowes.
But then; ah then, our discontent began,
A barking Dog step'd foorth with scolding rage,
And Musick chang'd to notes of singing Swanne,
That March wee must with swiftest Equipage.
Loose not sweete bird thy voice, nor brier thy sent:
Wee'le meete againe when fortunes frownes be spent.

S

1 musickes layes] musickeslayes
3 Vesta] vesta
5 Brier] Bri re
7 Philomel's] Philomel'
10 A] *A*

Sonetto 11 (F5)

2 **Dame Flora:** Roman goddess of flowers and spring.

3 **Vesta:** Roman goddess of hearth and home.

5 **sweetest Brier:** i.e., eglantine or sweet briar; see Sonetto 8.2.

5 **shylded:** Cf. Sonetto 9.13n. and Sonetto 12.3–4.

6 **Sent:** Perhaps used with intentional pun on "scent."

7 **Philomel's:** In Greek myth, Philomela was ravished by her brother-in-law, Tereus; his wife, Procne, and Philomela, in revenge, killed Procne's son, Itys, and served him to Tereus for dinner. As he was about to kill the sisters, Tereus was transformed into a hawk, Procne into a swallow, and Philomela into a nightingale.

7 **did close:** melded (as she sang in the "bowes"). It is the male nightingale that "sings," a technicality usually ignored by Elizabethan-Jacobean writers (as by Keats).

10 **barking Dog:** Cf. "caytiffe dog" in Sonetto 12.12. Probably refers to some interfering busybody, a tell-tale.

11 **notes . . . Swanne:** i.e., sad notes, since swans were believed to sing only as they were dying.

12 **March . . . equipage:** We must tread deliberately with swiftest even pace. Does this mean to "walk in step with thoughtful care"? See Posie I.26n. and Sonetto 27.2n.

Sonetto. 12

Liue long ſweet byrde, that to encreaſe our ioy,
Made ſoleme pauſe, betweene thy chirping layes;
When ſtately brier ſhilded our anoye,
And ſheltred vs from peeping Phebus rayes:
Sweet Philomel' recorde not our delightes,
In Muſicks ſounde, but to the ſubtill ayre;
Leaſt any ſhould participate our ſpites,
Wrought by a ſudden Cerberus repayre.
The pleaſing ſound our ſpirites did reuiue,
The ſweet, ſweet ſent, refreſh'd our yeilding ſence,
The happy touch, moſt to delight did ſtriue,
But caytiffe dog did hynder our pretence.
Then happie Byrd farewell, that eaſ'd my paine,
Farewell ſweet brier, till fortune ſmile againe.

S

Sonetto 12 (F5^{v})

3 **shilded our anoye:** protected us from annoyance. Cf. Sonetto 9.13.

5 **Philomel. See Sonetto 11.7n.**

6 **but:** except.

7 **participate our spites:** gain knowledge of our (1) vexations, (2) lovers' quarrels.

8 **Wrought . . . repayre:** created by a sudden Cerberean haunting (=dark mood change). Cerberus was Pluto's three-headed watchdog of Hades.

11 **toutch:** (1) sensuous contact; (2) effect of Philomel's singing.

12 **caytiffe dog:** wretched dog (looking back to Sonetto 11.10 and, perhaps, to Cerberus in line 8 above).

12 **pretence:** intention, desire.

Sonetto. 13.

VVHen Lordlin Tytan lodged in the weſt,
AndE B O N darknes ou'r-ſwayde the light,
L A T O N A S beams decreaſing were ſupprect,
When ſilent ſtreames did murmur el ere delight.
Then I entrench'd neere to a noble marke,
With courage bould a ſpeare I tooke in hand,
To wyn my will fired with honours ſparke,
Or looſe my life in my commaunders band.
My ſpeare I brake vpon my gentle foe,
Which being perform'd the ſecond *I* did charge,
But honours force would not be quailed ſo:
The third I tooke my thoughts for to enlarge;
Then call'd I was for treaſon armes to take,
And wiſedome would my former charge forſake.
S

1 Lordlie] Lordlin
10 I] *I*
14 And] *And*

Sonetto 13 (F6)

1 **When Lordlie Tytan:** Titan Helios was an alternative name for Phoebus Apollo. Although the emendation from *O*'s "Lordlin" to "Lordlie" seems called for, a curiously similar form appears in Parry's *Moderatus* (sig. G3^{v}) in context with Titan: "Then Titan lordly-n his seate," where "lordly-n" = "lordly in." Parry actually begins a lyric in *Moderatus* (sig. C3^{v}) with "When lordlie Titan. . . ." For possible explanations of these coincidences, see Introduction, 26.

2 **Ebon:** black. The compositor apparently mistook "ebon" for some kind of deity and set it in capitals.

3 **Latonas:** Latona, the Roman form for the Greek Leto, who was the mother, by Zeus, of Apollo and Diana (Greek: Artemis), goddess of hunting, who was also associated with the moon. Here, however, Latona appears as a name for a moon goddess. The only authority I can find for such a designation is Michael Drayton's *Endimion and Phoebe* (1595; line 828), where she is listed as one of thirteen titles, along with Diana, belonging to Phoebe as moon goddess. Possibly, however, both writers are confusing Latona with Latonia, who is described by Thomas Cooper in his *Thesaurus Linquae Romanae et Britannicae* (1565) as "a goddess, also called Diana."

5 **entrench'd:** dug in (as for battle). The military imagery here and below is presumably used metaphorically for some kind of amorous "war."

5 **noble marke:** (1) member of a noble stock; (2) individual who may be taken as a symbol of nobility. There is also, perhaps, a play on "marke"=target (i.e., the "noble marke" or mistress is the target of amorous assault).

8 **commaunders band:** i.e., the troop that is under the command of Cupid or Love.

9–12 **gentle foe . . . enlarge:** Just who or what these three "foes" are is unclear. Although "gentle" would naturally seem to refer to a woman in line 9, the reference may possibly be to some obstacles (see Sonetto 14.7: "riualls"), which must be overcome in winning his "will" (line 7 above), i.e., the favor of his desired mistress.

12 **The third . . . enlarge:** The third (foe) I took on in order to broaden or extend the scope of my mind's desire.

13 **Then . . . take:** As a result I was summoned to take arms for treasonous actions (against the "noble marke").

Sonetto. 14

SHould feare pale feare make me forgoe my minde,
Or legions of monsters make me quaile,
No, no, I was not borne of so base kinde,
As dreadfull sighes would make my heart to faile.
Yet care commaund that honors my conceyte,
Made me forsake what my desire embrac'd,
And loth I was that rivalls should repe are:
My armes should be by humane force vnlac'd,
Which made me yeilde vnto the tyms restraynt,
And leaue the charge of that most noble fight,
Where kindnes more then force could make me faint,
To shild my fame from fortunes cancred spite.
Thus *I* did charge, thus I discharg'd my launce,
And so I rest contented with my chaunce.

S

4 sightes] sighes
5 cares] care
13 I did] *I* did

Sonetto 14 (F6^{v})

Sonetto 14, the last of the sonettos distinguished by an "S" and thus connected in some way with Salusbury (see the headnote to Sonetto 2), contains two rather close parallels with Parry's Passions: Passion IV.18: "Striue with the course that cares command hath sent" (cf. line 5); Passion XXXI.18: "Thus rest content with this thy fatall chaunce" (cf. line 14). The phrase "rest content" (or "contented") is a favorite of Parry's recurring in Passions VII, XIIII, and XLVI; and "pale feare" (line (1) occurs in *Moderatus* (sig. G4). See Introduction, 19–20, on the question of authorship of the S-series sonettos.

5 **Yet . . . conceyte:** Yet the sway of fears honors my state of mind. As it stands this line seems to mean the opposite of what the larger context calls for. Possibly, however, "honors" is a compositorial misreading of "horors" or "horrors," a rare verbal use meaning "frightens" or "terrifies" (see *OED*, s.v. Horror 6 *v*).

7 **rivalls should repeate:** foes (of whatever kind) should return to the attack. Cf. Sonetto 13.5–14.

8 **My . . . vnlac'd:** The laces of my armor should be unfastened (i.e., I should be disarmed) by the power of courtesy or humanity.

10 **leaue the charge:** (1) give up the impetuous assault; (2) leave the protective custody.

12 **cancred spite:** malignant ill-will.

13 **Thus . . . launce:** In this way, I attacked; in this way I delanced my lance (i.e., I took the "charge" or power out of my weapon).

Sonetto. 15

AS fond conceyt doth moue the wauering minde,
Of artlesse sottes that knowe not wisedoms lore,
Inconstant still to chang with eu'rie winde,
Whose base desires wants fruites of vertues store.
So doth the arte and knowledge of the wise,
Stirre vp his minde in honors foorde to wade,
With feruent zeale base changlinges to dispise,
And their weake strength, with courage to inuade.
Whose mind being arm'd with true loues strong defence,
He gyrdes his loynes with bondes of constancie,
And scornes that ought should alter his pretence,
Or stayne his name, with blot of infamie.

Thus wisedome is not giuen to manye,
And but to such for to be constant anye.

Sonetto 15 (F7)

Sonetto 15 picks up the series of sonettos begun with Sonetto 1. See Introduction, 20–23.

4 **desires wants:** desires lacks. See Abbott, 333, for use of the third person plural in *s*.

5 **arte:** skill.

7 **changlinges:** turncoats.

11 **pretence:** intention, purpose.

13 **to:** For metrical considerations we probably should emend to "vnto."

14 **but . . . anye:** only to those (few) to whom wisdom is given to render them faithful.

Sonetto. 16

NEu'r-resting chariot of the firie god
Emboss'd with beames of his eternall light,
Waytes at her beck when she but shakes her rod
Of her commaund; who is the heau'ns delight:
AVRORAs shine doth blush to see her grace,
Nymphes gather flowers to make her chaplets fine,
Engendered griefe my hoped fauour deface,
Loue hates to liue when longing makes it pine:
Euen so her faire makes longing deere to me,
HELEN the faire was not so faire as she.

Sonetto 16 (F7v)

The first of three sonettos (16, 17, 18) addressed acrostically to HELENA OWEN, whose name is spelled out by reading the initial letter of each line from the bottom up. For Helena Owen, to whom Sonettos 1 and 15–31, as well as "The lamentation of a Male-content," are addressed, see Introduction, 2–3, the headnote to Sonetto 1, and the note on line 10 below.

1 **firie god:** Phoebus Apollo (Greek: Titan Helios).

2 **Emboss'd:** sumptuously decorated.

3–4 **rod . . . commaund:** wand of authority (i.e., perhaps, magic wand) symbolizing her rule or dominion.

5 **Auroras:** See Posie I.3n.

6 **Nymphes:** In Greek myth, semi-divine maidens, who inhabited the woods, rivers, etc.

7 **Engendered . . . deface:** Grief born of grief destroys my hoped-for privilege (in her love).

9 **faire:** beauty.

10 **Helen . . . she:** Helen of Troy was less beautiful than she (i.e., Helena Owen). Cf. Sonetto 1.14: "Liue Helens peere eternized thy fame"; and "The lamentation of a Male-content," 155–56: "Paris a sheaphard I a homely swayne, / He wanton, I chast Helen would possesse."

Sonetto. 17

NO care ſo great nor thoughts ſo pining ſeeme,
Enioying hope to reape the hearts deſire;
Which makes me more your beauties grace
Oppreſt with heate of PAPHOS holy fier. (eſteeme,
Appoint ſome place to eaſe my thrauled minde,
Not freed yet from thy late lnriug looke;
Enioye thy time and ſolace ſhalt thou finde,
Let VVLCAN toyle to forge his bayted hooke:
Eyes glorious glaunce will trayne him to the lure,
Heau'ns do repine thou ſhouldſt his frownes endure

10 *No period after* endure

Sonetto 17 (F8)

Addressed acrostically (like 16 and 18) to HELENA OWEN; read the first letter of each line from the bottom up.

1 **pining:** tormenting, afflicting.

4 **Paphos holy fier:** Phaphos was a city in Cyprus, where (according to Virgil) the temple of Astarte (Roman: Venus) was located, in which three hundred priests kept sacred fires smoking on a hundred altars.

6 **late luring looke:** recent enticing glance or appearance.

8 **Vulcan:** See Sonetto 21.11n.

9 **trayne . . . lure:** decoy him into the trap or snare. The reference in "him" (and "his" in line 10) would appear to be Vulcan (meaning unclear), but, perhaps, "him" and "his" are intended, if indirectly, to refer to the "me" in line 3.

Sonetto. 18

NAmelesse the flower that workes my discontent,
Endlesse the cares for her I doe sustaine,
Waste is the soyle which shadowes my content
Once lende a salue to cure my curelesse paine.
Ah deere, how deere I purchase my delight?
Not longe when first I view'd thy sweetest fayre.
Except thy beauty lend my darknes light,
Long shall that looke my heauie lookes ympayre;
Esteeme of him that liues to honour thee,
Hopes true repose shall then be lodg'd in mee.

3 content:] content (*end of line contains no space for pointing*)

Sonetto 18 (F8^{v})

Addressed acrostically (like 16 and 17) to HELENA OWEN; read the first letter of each line from the bottom up.

1 **Namelesse:** In the dedicatory Epistle to "The lamentation of a Male-content," Parry signs himself as "Namelesse," dedicating the poem "To the Honorable minded vnknowne"; here Parry transfers "Namelesse" to refer to the "vnknowne" (i.e., Helena Owen).

5 **delight?:** The question mark, as not infrequently at this period, is here used for the exclamation mark.

6 **Not longe:** i.e., my "delight" didn't last long.

8 **looke . . . ympayre:** glance of the eye (when he first saw her) shall make my gloomy, sad appearance worse (i.e., more "heauie").

Sonetto. 19.

NO ſooner I had thy beautie eſpied,
Cleane waſhed from the dreggs of vices ſtayne,
But heart to thee with conſtant loue was tyed;
And thou perhapps wilt yeilde me but diſdayne:
Yf thou wilt not my loue with loue requite,
I ſhall weare out in paine my diſmall dayes,
But if thy heart once harbour my delight;
Then ſhall I liue thy heart to loue and praiſe:
Yeilde thy conſent to cure my fatall wounde,
And let deſert preuaile to gayue thy grace,
So ſecret truth ſhall eu'r in me abounde;
Yf we may meete in ſome conuenient place:
And then be ſure his name I will deface,
That ſhould be ſeene to ſpeake in thy diſgrace.

G

10 gayne] gayue

Sonetto 19 (G1)

1 **beautie:** accented on second syllable here.
11 **secret truth:** hidden constancy, fidelity.
12 **Yf:** providing.

Sonetto. 20

CAmpaſpe's fayre freſh-paynted forme embrac'd,
By the rare Father of the paynters art,
Could yeilde ſmall ioy except that ſhe had grac'd,
His liuely cuning by her good deſart,
Yet he reioyc'd her counterfeyte to kiſſe,
Which ſhe nev'r ſawe though he the ſame profan'd,
How infinite is then my ioyfull bliſſe,
That ſtill enioy the Id'ea of thy hande;
Thy gloue it is mine onlye comfort left,
Which thy ſweete hande made happie with her touch,
This is the Idole that my heart infeoft,
With loues ſweete hope: which I adore to much.
That *I* retayne a monument for thee,
Though without life: life it affordes to me.

---

8 Idea] Id'ea
13 I] *I*

Sonetto 20 (G1^{v})

1–2 **Campaspe's . . . art:** Campaspe was a favorite concubine of Alexander the Great. He asked Apelles, one of the most famous of Greek painters, to paint her portrait; in doing so he fell deeply in love with Campaspe, who equally reciprocated his love. Alexander magnanimously allowed them to marry.

3–4 **except . . . desart:** unless she had (1) rewarded, (2) honored his brilliant skill by being truly worthy (of it).

5 **counterfeyte:** portrait.

8 **still . . . hand:** always enjoy the mental image (i.e., in memory) of her hand.

11 **my heart infeoft:** my heart possessed.

Sonetto. 21

Sweete ladie I loue, by stelth my loue doth creepe,
Vnto the depth of my profounde conceytes,
Not daring when I wake I dreame a sleepe,
Thus stealing loue by inward signes entreate:
Though merrie gale bydes anchor vp to waye,
And canuas store swells with a puffing blaste,
Yet feare of storme doth make vs keepe the baye,
For he is safe that sitts on shoare at laste:
So loue embrac'd when others presence fear'd,
Makes sweete proue sower whẽ shadowes substance seeme,
And Mars himselfe when Vulcans net he fear'd:
Doth witnes feare doth stolen loue redeeme.
When sweete repose doth calme the troubled minde,
Feare of suspect doth leaue his sting behinde.

G 2

2 depth] *Worked up space prints after* depth

Sonetto 21 (G2)

3 **Not . . . sleepe:** Not daring openly to declare my love when awake, I dream of my love when I sleep.

4 **by . . . entreate:** (does) entreat by means of secret tokens, indications.

5 **bydes:** bids.

6 **canuas store:** sails in plenty.

8 **at laste:** in the end, finally (i.e., he never left the safety of the bay or harbor).

9 **others presence fear'd:** the presence of others is suspected.

11 **Mars . . . Vulcans:** Vulcan (Greek: Hephaestus), god of fire and metal-working and husband of Venus (Greek: Aphrodite), snared Mars (Greek: Ares), god of war, and Venus in a net as they were making love.

12 **witnes . . . redeeme:** bear witness that fear repays stolen love.

14 **Feare of suspect:** fear generated by suspicion.

Sonetto. 22

MY heart enthraul'd eu'n with mine owne deſire,
Makes me to be, more then I dare to ſeeme,
For ieloſie may kindle enuies fire,
To hazard that which ſtrength cannot redeeme:
The fayreſt roſe, on ſtatelyeſt ſtalke that growes,
Drawes a delight his odours ſweete to ſmell,
Whoſe pricke ſometime doth ſting at later cloſe,
Which makes ſuſpect the wiſhed ſent t'expell.
Loue prickes my minde to gather fayreſt flowers,
And feare forbids leſt garden keeper ſpie,
Whoſe ieloſie raines downe vntimely ſhowers,
And Argos-like doth loues repoſe diſcrie:
Thus doth thy fayre my ſecret glaunce detect,
For ieloſie doth dayly breede ſuſpect.

---

12 Argus-like] Argos-like

Sonetto 22 (G2^{v})

1 **enthraul'd:** (1) in bondage; (2) enraptured.

6 **Drawes:** breathes.

7 **sometime . . . close:** occasionally stings at some later juncture.

8 **Which . . . t'expell:** which makes the wished for scent to be regarded with suspicion and exhaled. Syntactically, the line is unclear and meaning uncertain.

9 **prickes:** stimulates.

11 **ielosie . . . showers:** mistrust, suspicion rains down ill-timed, unseasonable showers (i.e., the "garden-keeper" pours cold water on his desire to pick "fayrest flowers," i.e., make amorous advances to his mistress).

12 **Argus-like:** See Sonetto 23.4n.

12 **loues repose discrie:** cry out against love's peace of mind.

13 **Thus . . . detect:** Thus thy beauty causes me to betray my otherwise hidden oeillade (i.e., amorous glance). Cf. "stolen loue" in Sonetto 21.12 and Sonetto 23.13.

Sonetto. 23

WHen ſweete repoſe in loues fayre bower doth reſt
Enchamp'd with vaile of an vnfain'd deſire,
Then carefull thoughtes the fearefull mindes in-
Leſt ARGVS ſhould eſpie the kindled fire: (ueſt,
For where the dicte of ſuch as may commaunde,
Forbidds the ſame, which louers muſt embrace,
There feare, and care, together doe demaund;
Account of thinges which honour may deface:
So is their ioyes with fearefull paſſions mixt,
Which doth encreaſe the ardencie of loue,
On the forbidden thinges our eyes are fixt;
Whoſe accents ſtill doth loues affections moue:
Thus ſtolen loue is eu'r with feare poſſeſt,
As ſhadowes glymſe oft feares the friendly gueſt.

G 3

1 rest,] rest (*line contains no space for pointing*)

Sonetto 23 (G3)

2 **Enchamp'd with vaile:** Meaning unclear; perhaps "lodged within or fenced in with a curtain" (i.e., hidden from sight). "Enchamp'd" as a form of "encamped" is not illustrated in the *OED*. Cf. "The lamentation of a Male-content," 224: "Fenced with vaile."

3 **fearefull mindes inuest:** besiege minds full of fear.

4 **Argus:** In Greek mythology, Io was loved by Zeus, who turned her into a heifer to conceal her from Hera (Roman: Juno), his jealous wife. Being asked for the heifer by Hera, Zeus was forced to grant Hera's request and Hera placed Io under the guard of Argus, who possessed a hundred eyes. Zeus then ordered Hermes (Roman: Mercury) to kill Argus. After his death, Io, though freed, was driven out of her homeland by Hera; in Egypt, however, she regained her human form and bore Zeus a son, Epaphus.

5 **dicte:** order.

6 **the same:** i.e., the happy situation described in lines 1–2.

6 **which:** i.e., the "dicte" of line 5.

8 **Account:** accounting, estimation, consideration.

12 **accents:** characteristic signs.

14 **shadowes . . . feares:** faint suggestions of unhappiness often frightens.

Sonetto. 24

THimpatient rage of fretting Ieloſie,
Suſpectes the winde that comes from Cupids winges,
Whoſe watch preuents the oportunitie,
Whoſe louers ſeeke to cure his noyſome ſtinges:
Eche looke, a feare, infuſeth to the minde,
That gauled is with ſuch a baſe conceyte,
Which makes them proue to their hearts ioyes vnkinde
When loueſweete-ones, of ſorrowe, ſucke the teate:
Yf one but ſpeake to doe another right,
Suſpect ſayth then, of ſmoke there commeth fier
His good deſerts are houlden in deſpite:
And rancor doth his cruell fate conſpire.
So Ieloſie ſtill breedeth baſe ſuſpect,
Whoſe fruiteleſſe feare there owne good name detest

7 vnkinde,] vnkinde (*line contains no space for pointing*)
8 loues sweete-ones] louesweete-ones
14 detect.] detest (*line also contains no space for pointing*)

Sonetto 24 (G3^{v})

1 **fretting:** gnawing.

2 **Suspectes the winde:** (Jealousy) is suspicious of even the most ephemeral things (as evidence of inconstancy).

3 **Whose . . . oportunitie:** The continual watchfulness of jealousy anticipates the (supposed) opportunity (of sinning).

4 **Whose . . . stinges:** Lovers suffering from jealousy seek to remedy the harmful, sharp pains that it causes.

6 **gauled:** vexed, hurt.

8 **loues . . . teate:** love's dear-ones suck sorrow's breast. *O*'s reading "louesweete-ones" may mean "ones who are sweetened by love."

9 **but . . . right:** only should speak out in support of another person.

10 **Suspect:** suspicion.

14 **detect:** will leave open to (1) exposure, (2) accusation. *O*'s "detest" fails to rhyme with "suspect."

Sonetto. 25

IF Argus, with his hundred eyes, did watch
In vaine, when oft loue did his cunning blynde:
Who doubtes but shee that meanes to make a match
For to performe, both time, and place can finde.
And to abridge a woman of her will,
Is to powre oyle in fier, to quench the flame:
For then far more she is inclined still,
(Though once despis'd) againe to seeke the same.
Loue doth commaund, and it must be obayde;
The sacred deitie of the god is much,
Whose maiestie makes louers oft afrayde,
That to his shrine with bended knee they crutch.

This is the cause, let women beare no blame,
Who would not play if they did like the game.

G 4

Sonetto 25 (G4)

1 **Argus:** See Sonetto 23.4n.
4 **For to performe:** in order to accomplish her design.
8 **the same:** i.e., "her will" (line 5).
10 **god:** i.e., Cupid.
10 **much:** great.
12 **crutch:** bend low in submission.
13 **cause:** i.e., the reason men submit to love.
14 **Who would not:** What man would not. "Who" is here taken to refer to "lovers" (line 11) and not to "women" (line 13).

Sonetto. 26

VVHeare true desire, (in simpathie of minde)
Hath ioin'd the heartes; with APHRODITES de-
There louing zeale,(to swete aspect inclin'd)(light;
Will finde a time in spite of fortunes might.
ARGVS foresight, whose wake-full heedie eyes
Seeke to preuent the wynged Gods commaunde)
Is all to weake his charmes for to-surprise;
Gainst whose resolue his cuning could not stande:
Yet if in Delphos sleepie laye the God,
Authoritie gainst Hundreth eies had fayld,
But MERCVRIE, with his enchaunting rod;
Brought all a sleepe; when Argus Ioue assayl'd:
Then since such happs to watching is assign'd,
Nothinge is harde where willing is the minde.

5 foresight, (whose] foresight, whose

Sonetto 26 (G4^{v})

2 **Aphrodites:** Aphrodite, Greek goddess of love (Roman: Venus); here trisyllabic.

3 **aspect:** face.

5 **Argus:** See Sonetto 23.4n.

5 **foresight:** forward-looking watch (over Io); see Argus above.

6 **wynged Gods commaunde:** i.e., the order given to Hermes (Roman: Mercury) by Zeus to kill Argus, who had the oversight of Io.

7 **charmes . . . surprise:** to overpower magic spells by sudden attack.

9 **Delphos:** an erroneous, if not infrequent, Elizabethan term for Delphi; see Shakespeare's *The Winter's Tale*, 3.2.126.

9 **God:** Apparently refers to Hermes, but we would expect a reference to Apollo, whose famous temple was at Delphi, where the Delphic oracle gave its ambiguous forecasts.

10 **Authoritie . . . eies:** i.e., Zeus's order to Hermes to kill Argus (i.e., "Hundreth eies"). The form "hundreth" is a common Elizabethan variant of "hundred."

11 **enchaunting rod:** magic wand; such a "rod" (caduceus) was associated with Mercury.

12 **Argus Ioue assayl'd:** Refers presumably to Jove's (Greek: Zeus's) order to kill Argus.

13 **watching:** standing watch as guard (like Argus).

13 **is:** singular form by attraction of "watching."

Sonetto. 27
Daiungers altered delayes in loue.

THe heart inthraul'd with loues attractiue force,
(Whose hope doth martch with honours equipage,
When reason doth his true desertes remorse)
Must take his time his sorrowes to assuage:
For cheeries ripe will not so long endure,
But will in time, fade, wither, and decay,
That which this day, cou'd finest witts allure;
To morrowe, CORIDON doth cast away,
The Iron being hot who list not for to strike,
Shall sure, being colde, neu'r forge it to his minde,
And all those parties, moueth loue to like;
Doe oft (in time) make loue to proue vnkinde.

Eu'n so in time daiunger attends delaye,
For time and tide for no mans pleasures staye.

Title attend] altered

Sonetto 27 (G5)

Title. **Daungers attend delayes in loue:** To make sense of the title, it is necessary to read "attend" for *O*'s "altered" (see line 13). Cf. *Moderatus*, sig. F1: "sleepe not long in doubt, for delay breeds daunger"; and Greene, *1 Mamillia* (1583), 96: "So loue encreaseth by delay, and delayes breede daungers."

2 **martch . . . equipage:** walk in step with the followers of honor.

3 **doth . . . remorse:** feel pity (or affection) for its (i.e., the heart's) true merits.

8 **Coridon:** name for a shepherd in the pastoral tradition of Theocritus and Virgil.

11 **partes . . . like:** (1) personal qualities that stir up love to liking ("those partes"); (2) actions that affect love to the same ("partes").

Sonetto. 28

VVAs Io watch'd by Argus in the downes?
What did not then the winged god iuchaunt,
The heardmans eyes, obaying Iunos frownes:
What needes loues crosse so much to make her vaunt.
The brazen tower could not his valour quaile,
Who scorn'd that Danae should liue a maide:
Loues inward force gainst enuy will preuaile,
And hap what may: his lawes must be obayd.
What though fayre starre thy glorie is obscur'd;
And cou'rd with a thicke and foggie cloude:
Yet Titan when he hath the heau'ns invr'd,
Will cleere the stormes which fatall frowues did shrowde:

And though that fate abridgeth our delight,
Yet time I hope will cleare this cloudie spight.

11 inur'd] invr'd
12 frownes] frowues

Sonetto 28 (G5^{v})

1–3 **Io . . . Iunos:** See Sonetto 23.4n.

4 **What . . . vaunt:** Why needs must thwarted love cause her (Juno) to boast so much?

6 **Danaë:** See Passion XXXIIII.17n.

7 **inward:** spiritual.

11 **Titan:** See Sonetto 13.1n.

11 **inur'd:** put in order.

14 **cloudie spight:** darkly troubled (1) feeling, (2) affair.

Sonetto. 29

THe fluent ſtreame, whoſe ſtealing courſe being ſtayed,
Breakes out vnto a greater deluge rage,
The force of fier with violence delayed,
Makes all thinges weake his furie to aſſwage:
Deſire contrould, will agrauate deſire,
And fancie croſt will fancies force encreaſe,
When louing thoughtes will motiue loue inſpire,
Enuies oppoſe can not their bondes releaſe:
Thus currents ſmall doe 'proue the greateſt ſtreames,
Small cinders doe encreaſe, to raging flame,
The hardeſt hartes are pearc'd with beauties beames,
I hide my griefe yet loue diſcou'rs the ſame:
Sweete beautie is the ſparke of my deſire,
And ſparkes in time may breede a flaming fier.

Sonetto 29 (G6)

2 **deluge:** overflowing. Not recorded as an adjective in *OED.*

3 **with violence delayed:** held back, retarded with violent action (with reference, perhaps, to destroying houses, etc., to try to stop a fire's spread).

7 **motiue loue inspire:** animate love to take action.

8 **oppose:** opposition, antagonism. Not recorded as a noun in *OED.*

8 **their:** i.e., "louing thoughtes."

Sonetto. 30

SWeete beautie in thy face doth still appeere,
Myne onely ioye and best beloued deere:
Myne onlye deere and best belou'd content,
Reuiue my heart and dyinge spirrits spent:
The onlye agent of my thoughtes delight,
Embrace my loue and doe not me despight:
Secure my feares and solace cares content,
With hopes repast to sauour mine entent;
The fier will out if fuell doe but want,
And loue in time will die if it be scant:
Let then desire yeilde fuell to your minde,
That loue be not blowen out with euerie winde:

So shall my heart like Etnas lasting flame,
Burne with your loue and ioye still in the same.

---

4 dyinge] *O's* d *shows type disturbance*
8 sauour] *O may read* fauour

Sonetto 30 (G6^{v})

6 **doe . . . despight:** Do not scorn or disdain me.
8 **hopes . . . entent:** the food of hopes season my frame of mind.
13 **Etnas:** of (Mount) Aetna, a volcano in Sicily.

Sonetto. 31

I Loue, inforst by loues vnlouing charmes,
My loue is pure, my loue is chast, and true,
And that I loue, the greater is my harmes:
Yf loue doth purchase hate, then loue adiew.
Why should not loue be recompens'd with loue,
And true desire, obtayne his due desert,
Yf beautie stirre thee to disdayne to moue?
When mighty stormes oppresse my troubled hart:
Knowe then that truth, may beauties blaze dismay,
And loyall hartes, scorne periur'd beauties pride,
Yeilde then in time, prolonge not my delay?
Lest others should your beauties grace deride:

So shall your worthes eternished remaine,
And gaine his loue which others pride disdaine.

9 truth] truth,

Sonetto 31 (G7)

1 **charmes:** (1) magic spells, (2) charms (of female beauty) that excite love and admiration.

3 **And that:** and because.

7 **Yf . . . moue:** If (your) beauty does prompt or incline you to disdain (me).

9 **truth . . . dismay:** Honesty, truthfulness may utterly daunt or paralyze with fear beauty's splendor.

11 **prolong . . . delay:** Don't draw out the process of putting me off.

13 **eternished remaine:** remain eternally famous.

To Paris darling.

VVere I sheapheard as I am a woodman,
Thy Paris would I be if not thy goodman.
And yet might I performe to thee that dutie,
Yf thou wilt add that fauour to thy beautie.

Nowe that these feastes make other minions frolike,
Why is my loue, my doue, so melancholike:
O but I neere gesse, what the cause should be,
Which to tell, tel-tale paper, were but follie;
Ile therefore for this time conceale it wholye:
For that must counsell betwixt thee and mee,
Twixt thee and me where none may heere nor see.

Buen matina.

Sweete at this mourne I chaunced,
To peepe into the chamber; loe I glaunced:
And sawe white sheetes, thy whyter skinne disclosing;
And soft-sweete cheeke on pyllowe soft reposing:
Then sayde were I that pillowe,
Deere for thy loue I would not weare the willowe.

2 thy] che

To Paris darling (G7^{v})

Title. **To Paris darling:** i.e., Helen of Troy, who should here be taken as referring to Helena Owen, to whom Parry addresses Sonettos 1, 15–31. See "The lamentation of a Male-content," 155–56, where Parry makes the analogy explicit: "Paris a sheaphard I a homely swayne, / He wanton, I chast Helen would possesse."

1 **woodman:** hunter.

2 **goodman:** husband (with probable play on someone of gentle birth and substance).

4 **fauour:** kind indulgence, permission.

5 **minions:** darlings, lady-loves.

7 **neere guess:** can almost guess.

10 **For . . . counsell:** For counsel must be taken on that matter.

Buen matina (G7^{v})

Possibly intended as a tail-piece to "To Paris darling."

Title. **Buen matina:** Good morning (Spanish).

5 **weare the willowe:** grieve for the loss of a loved one (Tilley, W404).

Maddrigall.

MAdame, that nowe I kisse your white handes la- (ter
Then wild my louing dutie,
Retayner to thy beautie:
The water crost my wishe, to crosse the water.
Yet thinke not (sweete) those gallants helde thee deerer,
Who for thy beauties, then the sunneshine cleerer:
Eu'n seas vneu'n haue coasted,
But thou art wise and know'st it:
No; thy Leander, whose hartes firie matter,
Cannot be quench'd, by the deuyding water,
Will with his oare-like armes quite sheare a sunder
The waues that floate him vnder:
Yf when I shall so trie mee,
In thy sweete circled armes I may respire mee.

Maddrigall [I] (G8)

Title. **Maddrigall:** a lyric written to be set to music.

2 **Then . . . dutie:** than my loving duty desired.

3 **Retayner:** (1) servant (i.e., lover); (2) dependant.

6 **Who for . . . cleerer:** who (i.e., gallants) because of thy beauties which are brighter than the sunshine.

7 **Eu'n . . . coasted:** have explored even rough seas.

8 **it:** i.e., that those "gallants" had not "helde thee deerer" than I.

9 **Leander:** According to the Greek myth, Leander was a youth of Abydos, who was drowned in a storm swimming across the Hellespont to meet his mistress, Hero, a priestess of Venus, at Sestos. See Christopher Marlowe and George Chapman's poem, *Hero and Leander* (1598), based on a fifth-century Greek poem by Musaeus.

13 **trie mee:** test, prove myself.

14 **respire mee:** recover my breath.

Rounde-delay.

COuld st thou none other spite me,
When but once fortune friendly did indite me:
Thy selfe thou shouldst absent mee?
And all vnkinde, vnkinde, to those torment me:
I haue not thus deserued,
To be with tell-tale Tantulus hunger-starued:
That hauing store of dishes,
I could not feede according to my wishes?
But this he for reuealinge,
Gods counsell bide: and I for yours concealing?
In this yet doe we varie,
That desert to his, is quite contiary?
Then o most kinde and cruell,
(Except thou minde to starue thy beauties fuell)
For all my loue, fayth, dutye,
Let me but pray, I pray thee on thy beautie?
And thou my new-borne dittie,
Desire her for my second dishe but pittie.

1 COuld'st] COuld st
6 Tantalus] Tantulus
12 contrary] contiary

Rounde-delay [I] (G8^{v})

Title. **Rounde-delay:** Technically, a roundelay was a short, simple song with a refrain (*OED*), but Parry's two "Rounde-delays" contain no refrain. The same unusual hyphenated spelling (not recorded in *OED*) occurs again in Parry's dedicatory Epistle to Salusbury, line 27. Although Parry does not employ a refrain, there is noticeable and obviously intentional echoing of this "Rounde-delay" in "Rounde-delay [II]," something that possibly might be described as a kind of "delayed" refrain.

1 **thou . . . me:** you of all people treat me maliciously.

2 **but . . . me:** for once (i.e., uniquely) Fortune prescribed favorably for me.

3 **Thy . . . mee:** Thou shouldest absent thyself from me.

6 **tell-tale Tantalus hunger-starued:** According to Greek mythology, Tantalus exposed the secrets of the gods and was punished in the underworld by being set in water up to his chin below a fruit tree; when he was thirsty, the water would sink out of reach and when hungry, the fruit on the overhanging tree would be withdrawn.

7 **store of dishes:** metaphorical for a variety of "amorous wishes." Cf. Greene, *1 Mamillia* (1583), II.75, for the "first/second dish" metaphor.

10 **Gods counsell bide:** suffered the judgment of the gods.

12 **desert . . . contrary:** his (i.e., Tantalus') action (in revealing the gods' secrets) was (unlike my concealing of your secrets) without merit.

14 **(Except . . . fuell):** Unless you intend to starve your beauty by denying it what nourishes it.

18 **Desire . . . pittie:** Ask her only to give me pity as my second dish (i.e., amorous wish).

Maddrigall.

I Loue, iust loue, not luste, thus constant liue I:
My lyfes deere loue mislikes me,
Yet her sweete fayre doth like me:
Yf loue dislikes; to like and loue why should I?
Yf she be coy, why should her loue be trustie?
Yf she be slowe; why should I be so hastie?
Yet loyall hart hath vow'd it,
And constant truth performes it:
Fayre; to thy beauties fayre, firme haue I vowed,
Sound is the seede that my resolue hath sowed:
But weede is the fruite that my fate hath mowed.
Yet luste I banish, louing
True zeale, I liue, yet still dying:
Thus still to be constant eu're haue I plodded.

H

Madrigall [II] (H1)

1 **iust:** only.
3 **sweete . . . me:** i.e., I find pleasure in her sweet beauty.
5 **coy:** disdainful, distant.
7, 8 **it:** i.e., his act of loving (her).
9 **Fayre . . . fayre:** fair one to thy (1) fair beauties, (2) beauty's beauty.
11 **fate hath mowed:** lot in life hath harvested.
14 **plodded:** worked steadily.

Rounde-delay.

MVch griefe did ſtill torment me,
In this regard thou doeſt thy ſelfe abſent me;
Thy beautie (ah) delihgtes me?
And this thou know'ſt to well and therefore ſpites me.
So womens mindes doe varie,
And change of ayre doth worke quite contrarie;
Proofe tried my truth and truſt too,
Still to be thine, moſt conſtant, firme, and iuſt too:
Therefore ſhouldeſt regard me,
And loue for loue (fayre loue) thou ſhould'ſt award me,
For ſince I ſtill attend thee,
Howe canſt thou chooſe vnkinde (vnkinde) but friend me,
Fayne I alone would finde thee,
That my hearts griefe(ſwete hart)might thẽ vnbinde thee:
For were I with thee reſident,
I doubt not I, to be of thy heart preſident:
Yeilde then to loue (loue kinde is)
Elſe would I had byn blinde, eu'n as loue blinde is.

3 delightes] delihgtes

Rounde-delay [II] (H1^v)

See headnote to Rounde-delay [I]. Apparently the poet's mistress has failed to grant him the "pittie" he had asked for at the end of Rounde-delay [I]. Among other echoes of Rounde-delay [I], note that three of the rhymes in the first four lines are here repeated, but in reverse order, and that the fourth rhyme-word though different nevertheless still rhymes (i.e., "indite me" / "delightes me").

2 **In this regard:** in respect of the fact that.
7 **Proofe tried:** trial tested.
9 **regard:** value, esteem, be concerned for.
13 **alone:** (1) by myself; (2) only.
14 **vnbinde thee:** open thee up to my love.
16 **president:** (1) governor; (2) guardian.
17 **kinde:** (1) natural; (2) friendly, affectionate; (3) generous.

Sinetes Dumpe.

YE angrie ſtarrs, doe you enuie my eſtate,
Becauſe content is lodged in my minde;
And therefore will you needes repioue my fate?
That diſcontent in glorie lookes to finde:
My thonghtes were far aboue my fortunes bent,
Which was your fault to frame vnequall partes,
Except it were of purpoſe to torment.
Gloring in cloudes to ſmother my deſertes:
When I did yeilde vnto the times deſpite,
And ſtroke downe ſayle leſt ſhypracke would enſue,
Inforciug nature to ſubdue delight?
A cuning bayte within my way you threwe?
Ys't then my fault if feathered thoughtes aſpire,
Clippe not the winges, that gaue them forcc to flie,
Eythor giue ſcope vnto my wiſh'd deſire;
Or ſalue my ſores with preſent remedie.
Who ſeekes by art his nature to ſuppreſſe,
In vaine doth ſtriue againſt the raging ſtreame,
My ſoaring minde procured my diſtreſſe?
The braunch will growe vnleſſe you cut the ſteame.

H 2 Thus

Sinetes Dumpe (H2–H3^{v})

Title. **Sinetes Dumpe:** Sinetes' melancholy reverie.

3 **reproue my fate:** censure my lot.

4 **discontent . . . finde:** discontentment hopes to attain to an honorable situation (i.e., a kind of honorable unhappiness).

5 **bent:** aimed, directed.

6 **to . . . partes:** (we) being furnished with unequal personal qualities (yours being higher and better than mine).

8 **Gloring . . . desertes:** (you) being extremely dazzling in order to smother my merits under clouds.

9 **despite:** (1) injury; (2) outrage.

10 **stroke:** struck (variant form).

10 **shypracke:** shipwreck (variant form).

12 **cuning bayte:** crafty temptation.

13 **feathered:** winged.

20 **steame:** trunk, stock.

Sinetes Dumpe.

Thus if I ſhould ympugne my fantaſies,
In vaine it were my nature to oppoſe,
Then yeilde I muſt vnto theſe myſeries?
Or to the heau'ns my ſecret griefes diſcloſe.
Heau'ns then beare witnes of my ſecret ſmart,
For you alone are priuie to my paines,
Becauſe to her I dare not once ympart:
Howe loue inſculpt within my breſt remaynes.
The feruent heate of hartes repoſed zeale,
Doth vrge me ſtill for to embrace her fayre,
To whom for grace and fauour I appeale:
My only refuge for to ſalue diſpayre.
Yet all in vaine I throb my breath-leſſe playntes,
When feare doth daunte my once vn-daunted minde,
But neede-leſſe feare: for fewe of them are ſaintes.
Yet duties care deniall lookes to finde.
Thus as my thoughtes doe cope with Ioues deſire,
And ſcorne the meane ſhoulde once their riuall bee,
So fearefull loue doth burne like glowing fier,
And threates reuenge if I make ſuite to thee.

The

23 mysteries] myseries
37 loues] Ioues

21 **ympugne my fantasies:** resist my flights of imagination (i.e., his "soaring minde," line 19).

23 **mysteries:** i.e., "soaring minde" or "fantasies." *O*'s "myseries" is a possible but flat reading given the context.

28 **insculpt:** engraved.

29 **reposed zeale:** settled, undisturbed ardent love.

33 **throb:** beat out.

35 **But neede-lesse feare:** However, an unnecessary fear.

35 **fewe . . . saintes:** few of my thoughts are saintly in nature (i.e., chaste). Possibly, however, "them" may refer to rivals in love.

36 **Yet . . . finde:** Yet a concern for moral obligation expects to encounter denial. The meaning of lines 35–36 is far from clear.

38 **the meane:** moderate or ordinary thoughts (as opposed to the "feathered" [line 13] of "soaring minde" [line 19]).

Sinetes Dompe.

The one perſwades, that beauties bower is ſtor'd,
With pittie, and grace, for to requite my loue?
The other ſayth the ſubtill ſerpent (gor'd:
With pearſing darte that Ieloſies approue)
Will ſoone infect the vertue of thy ſhyne,
To giue repulſe; regarding no deſert,
Though nought I ſeeke but thou ſhould'ſt know I pyne:
And in thy minde thou wonld'ſt my worthes inſert.
Knowe ſou'raigne beautie of thy noble race,
And flower of all that beare thy parents name,
That I deſire thy preſence to embrace.
To glut mine eyes with looking on the ſame.
Which is an obiect that doth pleaſe mine eye,
Then will I arme my ſelfe againſt the ſtorme,
For to endure this curſed miſerie:
For hope will helpe mv charge for to performe.
Then will I ſay to my diſquiet minde,
Reioyce thou mayſt doe ſeruice to her lookes,
What needſt thou care although ſhe be vnkinde.
Let it ſuffice thy name is in her bookes.

Though

41 **The one:** i.e., soaring, aspiring, imaginative thoughts (see line 38n.).
43 **The other:** i.e., moderate or ordinary thoughts (see line 38n.).
43 **subtill serpent:** i.e., the Devil. See Genesis 3:1 and Revelation 12:9.
44 **approue:** (1) confirm; (2) recommend.
45 **vertue . . . shyne:** power or force of thy light, brilliance.
51 **thy . . . embrace:** to clasp thy presence (in my thoughts).
55 **For . . . miserie:** In order to endure this (storm) I curse (my) extreme unhappiness.
56 **helpe. . . performe:** help me to carry my trust, responsibility.
58 **lookes:** good looks, beauty.
60 **Let . . . bookes:** i.e., it is enough that she at least knows my name; or, perhaps, "in her bookes"= in her favor.

Sinetes Dumpe.

Though crost for follye of thy soaring minde,
Yet art thou blest her name is in thy ringes,
At last thou shalt of her some comfort finde:
Though she be now dispos'd to clippe thy winges:
Yf thou art bashfull to discou'r thy minde,
Let thy ringe tell that she thou doest adore,
Yf then thou mayst not some contentment finde:
In mourning weedes thy woefull happs deplore:
Thy habyte then will sure reueale thy care,
She will enquire thy cause of thy annoy,
Then mayst thou seighe if thou canst not declare:
Howe that her fayre hath thus obscur'd thy ioy:
She then no doubt will soone conceaue thy minde,
When in thy lookes thy ruines will appeere,
And with a smile thy thraulled chaynes un-binde;
Whose bright-beam'd sun thy cloudy stormes wil cleere:
And graunt thee that (at last) thou lou'st so deere.

FINIS.

70 the cause] thy cause

61 **crost for follye:** thwarted on account of flightiness.

62 **name . . . ringes:** It was common practice for lovers to exchange rings inscribed, on the inner surface, with what were called "love posies" (e.g., "In thee my choice I do rejoice."). Initials might be included with the "posy," but names appear to have been rare (see Joan Evans, ed., *English Posies and Posy Rings*, 1931).

69 **habyte:** clothing.

Poſſe & nolle nobile.

A worthie man deſerues a worthie motte,
As badge thereby his nature to declare,
Wherefore the fates of purpoſe did alot?
To this braue ſquire, this ſimbole ſweete and rare:
Of might to ſpoyle, but yet of mercie ſpare.
A ſimbole ſure to Saliſberie due by right,
Whoſe ſtill doth ioyne his mercy with his might.

Though lyon like his *Poſſe* might take place,
Yet like a Lambe he *Nolle* vſeth aye,
Right like himſelfe (the flower of Saliſberies race)
Who neuer as yet a poore man would diſmay:
But princockes pride he vſ'd to daunt alway:
And ſo doth ſtill: whereby is knowen full well
His noble minde and manhood to excell.

AV

Title et] *CC*; & *O*
3 alot,] *CC*; alot? *O*
6 Salsberie] *CC*; Salisberie *O*
10 Salsberies] *CC*; Salisberies *O*

Posse & nolle nobile (H4–H4^{v})

Title. **Posse . . . nobile:** "To be able [to do harm] and not to do it is noble." Proverbial; see Tilley, H170, and Shakespeare's Sonnet 94. Griffith's verses have nothing to do with Parry, except that they are addressed to John Salusbury, his patron, to whom *Sinetes* is dedicated. The verses refer to Salusbury's "worthie motte" (i.e., motto, line 1), and his coat of arms (a lion rampant with three crescents, line 20). A copy of this poem occurs in CC, fol. 83^{v}, in a collection of Welsh and English poems for the most part either by, or addressed to, Salusbury (see Brown, 32–33, who prints the manuscript copy). In the manuscript copy, a second title precedes the present title: "In Motto Mecaenatis" (with reference to the motto of a Maecenas). He was famous as the patron of Virgil and Horace, among others, and his name became a synonym for "patron." Another poem by Hugh Griffith appears among the commendatory verses at the beginning of *Sinetes* titled "Vpon the Authors muse," which concludes with a bow to John Salusbury, a bow most of the other commendatory verses don't fail to make.

5 **spoyle . . . spare:** injure, destroy, but yet out of mercy to refrain (from inflicting harm or punishment).

7 **still:** style, behavior, manner of acting.

8 **take place:** take precedence.

9–10 **aye . . . himselfe:** ever justly, as he himself is (ever) just.

11 **dismay:** discourage.

12 **princockes pride:** coxcomb's inordinate self-esteem.

All crauen curres that coms of caſtrell kinde,
Are knowne full well whē they there might would ſtraine,
The poore t' oppreſſe that would there fauour finde?
Or yeilde himſelfe their freinpſhip to attayne:
Then ſeruile ſottes triumphes in might a mayne.
But ſuch as coms from noble lyons race,
(Like this braue ſquire) who yealdes receaues to grace.

Haud ficta loquor.

Hugh Gryffyth Gent.

---

17 t'oppresse] *CC*; t oppresse *O*
18 ffrendshippe] *CC*; fre:npship *O*
19 amayne] a mayne *O*
21 squire] squire) *O*

15 **coms:** A northern third person plural in *s* (see Abbott, 333); cf. "triumphes," line 19.

15 **of castrell kinde:** of a hawklike (devouring) nature.

16 **straine:** use violently.

18 **yeilde . . . attayne:** surrender himself servilely in order to win the goodwill of "crauen curres."

19 **Then . . . amayne:** Thus slavish dolts (i.e., "crauen curres") conquer violently with (brute) force.

21 **who . . . grace:** Whoever renders service is received into (this brave squire's) favor.

22 **Haud ficta loquor:** In no way do I speak untruths.

23 **Hugh Gryffyth Gent.:** Hugh Griffith, Gentleman, may tentatively be identified with one of the following: (1) Hugh Griffith, son of Ieuan ab Llywelyn of Lleweni (Salusbury was also of Lleweni); (2) Hugh Griffith of Wrexham, Denbighshire; (3) Hugh Griffith, a tenant of Marchwiail. For the last two, see Brown, 33.

¶ *To the Honorable minded* vnknowne, the Name-leſſe wiſheth perfect health and perpetuall happines.

DEare Patroneſſe of my hapleſſe lamentations; guided by the ſterne of thy beauty, which hath the ful commaund of my hart, and wearied with tiranyzing ouer my ſelfe, in forcible ſuppresſing the agonies of my afflicted minde, by ſmothering the feruencie of my deſires, in the cloudie center of dumme ſilence: at the laſt with the raging violence of a ſtopped ſtreame, for wante of courſe in the intelligible parte of my minde; I am driuen to ouer-flowe the bankes of reaſon, and in deſpite of my ſelfe to yeilde vp the raynes to vncontrouled deſires, which inſuing Poem will fullie manyfeſt vnto you, with the obſeruation of my co[illegible]ed fancyes: Written vppon a dreame, wherein me thou[illegible] I heard a voyce from

A

12 will fullie] willfullie

Dedicatory Epistle to "The lamentation of a Male-content" (2A2–2A2^{v})

Dedicatory Epistle heading.

Name-lesse: See Sonetto 18 in which "Namelesse" is used to refer to Helena Owen, his desired mistress, whose name is there spelled out acrostically. Here, however, Parry uses "Name-lesse" to refer to himself.

9 **wante . . . minde:** lack of a way into my mind's understanding.

13 **with . . . fancyes:** by calling attention to my hidden amorous desires.

The Epiſtle.

a Cloude pronouncing theſe wordes enſuing. *Maiſter thy deſires or liue in deſpaire*, and albeit I helde dreames but phantaſies, which commonly doe fall out by contraries; my fortunes being ſo far inferior to my thoughts, maketh me to doubt the ſequell thereof. Yet noble beautie of this ſea-bound Region diſdayne not to reade ende, and pittie if you will vouchſafe to mitygate the heauines of my martyred heart, which neere ſtifled with the dampe of my diſcontentments, lamentably beggeth for comfort at your handes.

Yours euer true, ſecret, and faithfull.

Nameleſſe.

20 reade, and] reade ende, and

19 **doubt the sequell:** question the outcome (i.e., the success of this "insuing Poem" in winning your favor).

The lamentation of a Male-content.

Maiſter thy deſires , or liue in deſpaire,

DEpoſe deſires , or in deſpaire re-
maine ,
A heauy doome, what my deſire's de-
poſe ?
How can I from my chiefeſt ioyes re-
fraine?
And marchi · · inde retire frō hopes
repoſe.
Maiſter deſire; this ſeemeth ſtr. ne:
What voise is this that doth di thy muſe ?

A 2 Yf

5 stra[nge to]] stra (*leaf damaged*)
6 voise] voisc (?)
di[sturbe]] di (*leaf damaged*)

The lamentation of a Male-content (2A3–2A8v)

Title. **Male-content:** discontented, disaffected person.

1 **Depose:** give up, divest one's self of.

2 **what:** Here used as an exclamation, introducing a question.

4 **And . . . repose:** And my forward-moving mind (thinking of love's desires) retreats from the peace of mind afforded by hope.

The lamentation

If Iupiter that frõ his throne doth see,
My secret woes which ruin's cares induce.
  Then mightie Ioue impugne not my content,
For thou hast been in such an error trayn'd,
What god soeu'r, yet pittie my lament,
That cannot from my sweet desires be wayn'd.
  Yeilde me no reasons to disswade my course,
Though some obiecte, who clym's may hap to fall,
The bad is good for to avoyde a worse:
And better venter then to liue in thrall.
  Or in dispayre remayne; a cruell threate,
Ay me remaine still in despayre I muste,
Feare which forbids my languor to repeate?
Hath cou'red hope with vayle of sad distruste:
  For that her sonne which doth obscure my sight,
Shines alwayes cleere, whose beams reflecte to mee,
The greater still doth drowne the lesser light;
So I am blinde when I would faynest see:
  Opposed by the starre that lendes me hope,
I glutt mine eyes with sweete aspects content;
All are but shadowes hem'd in narrow scope:
Within the orbe of wearied mindes lament:
Lookes cannot l... mme motions cannot moue,
So eyes and gestures ...h doe play their part,
Giue,

29 [du]mme] mme (*leaf damaged*)
30 [whic]h] h (*leaf damaged*)

8 **ruin's cares induce:** the pains or sorrows brought about by ruin.

10 **in . . . trayn'd:** (1) brought up in, (2) allured by such a mistaken belief.

11 **What god soeu'r:** whatever god you may be.

14 **Though some obiecte:** though some may point out that.

16 **venter:** venture (variant form).

18 **Ay me:** alas.

20 **sad:** serious.

22 **reflecte:** turn back.

23 **The . . . light:** i.e., his mistress's light continually smothers the sun (="the lesser light").

25 **starre:** i.e., his mistress.

26 **sweete aspects content:** the satisfaction of delightful glances.

27 **Hem'd . . . scope:** imprisoned in a restricted range of mental activity.

28 **orbe:** sphere.

29 **Lookes:** (amorous) glances (from me).

of a Male-content .

Giue her no knowledge that I am in loue :
For with deſſembled myrth I hide my ſmart ,
Repugnant feare controuleth my deſire,
When I woulde ſpeake diſpayre pluckes backe the raynes,
But yet no cheokes can quench the kindled fire;
For fantaſie to be controul'de diſdaynes :
The marke is fayre, for beautie giueth ayme ,
Yet maieſtie forbids the meane to ſhoote ,
The ſame is it that gaue my heart the mayme,
With whom to ſtriue I feare it is not boote:
Could but my pen, finde out the way to write ,
The moane I make, the flint to teares would melt,
Or that I could the worthy prayſe indite;
Of that rare Iem for whom theſe paines I felt :
The world would wonder for to reade my verſe ,
That nature coulde frame ſuch a perfect ſtampe ,
Yet as I can I will the ſame reherſe :
And for to light this Iſle ſet out this lampe .
O blooming bloſſomes with the riſing ſunne ,
Cou'rd with the dewe diſtilled from the ſkies ,
You are like ſhewes that be vnſpected donne ?
And ſeeme but miſte which from the cloudes ariſe.
When this fayre Nymph ſhe[illegible] forth her golden ſhine,
She ſcales the pride eu'n of th pire ſkie ;

A Eche

54 th[e em]pire] th pire (*leaf damaged*)

33 **Repugnant:** opposing, refractory.

34 **pluckes backe:** pulls in.

37 **marke . . . ayme:** target is (1) beautiful, (2) proper because beauty shows where to aim.

38 **the meane:** persons of low degree.

39 **The same:** i.e., “beautie” (line 37).

40 **not boote:** of no avail.

43 **indite:** express.

46 **stampe:** model, type.

48 **lampe:** i.e., source of illumination (i.e., “perfect stampe”).

51 **You . . . donne:** You are like shows (pageants, masques) which when not looked at or seen are finished (i.e., in one sense no longer exist). The form “vnspected” is not recorded in *OED*; “spect” = to see, look on.

54 **She . . . skie:** She rises above the splendor of even the imperial sky.

The lamentation

Ech blossom'd flower to honour her incline,
There vertues all vpon her shrine do lye;
The Gods built vp a trophie of renowne,
Honour to add to her admired grace,
The Queene of beautie must resigne her Crowne:
To her whose fayre doth her proud fayre disgrace.
How can I then maister my sweete desire,
That takes no rest but in this heau'nly bower,
Fuell is scant to kindle reasons fire?
My minde inclosed lyes in fancies tower.
The heau'ns are sad when she is Male-content,
And Phæbus doth intome his goulden beams,
In Ebon darknes till her cares be spent:
Hyding himselfe within the Oce'n streames.
But when her frownes be turn'd to smiles againe,
He lendes his light out of a Cloudie tower,
Thus the superior bodies doe remaine,
Subiect to this Semy-goddesse power:
Can I resist what Ioue could not controule,
Who can resist the power of beauties force,
'Tis to well knowne vnto my troubled soule,
Bootelesse I striue vnlesse she take remorse:
Remorse sayd I, how can she pittie take,
On him that yet durst not for pittie craue,

she

78 yet] yer

57 **trophie of renowne:** monument of fame.
58 **Honour:** i.e., the "trophie."
59 **Queene of beautie:** Helen of Troy (=Helena Owen) or, perhaps, Venus.
64 **fancies tower:** imagination's castle.
67 **In . . . spent:** In blackest darkness until her (i.e., his mistress's) sorrows have passed away.
71 **superior bodies:** i.e., the planets, including the sun.
76 **Bootelesse:** without success.
76 **remorse:** pity.

of a Male-content.

She doth not knowe I languish for her sake:
How am I like her sweete resolue to haue.
Had she but knowne the secrets of my thought,
How her sweete fayre is shrined in my heart,
And but for hor I count my life for nought?
Yt would neu'r grieue me to abide this smart.
But she whose Orbe with Roses circled is,
Both red and white of purest die on earth,
Doth oft of course shew me a heau'n of blisse,
When modest smile is strayn'd with sudden mirth:
This is the ease that my desires enioy,
This is the cause that hath procur'd desire,
And this dosire hath sommon'd myne anoye:
Loe see the fruite of such as would aspire.
I heere a threate of this my fonde intent,
Yet cannot haue the thinge I loue so deere,
O heau'ns beare witnes how my dayes are spent?
In sighes, in sobbs, in sad and mournefull cheere:
Eche night my bed, I bath with brinish teares,
And turne me still in hope to haue some rest,
When first I sleepe my minde (incamp'd with feares)
Makes me to starte with trembing care possest:
Thẽ thoughts approch vnto my troubled braine
And nowe I thinke that she for whom I pine,

Fu'l

83 her] hor(?)
91 desire] dosire
100 trembling] trembing

80 **resolue:** decision.

88 **strayn'd:** stretched (beyond the range of a "modest smile").

90 **cause . . . desire:** action (i.e., "sudden mirth") that has given rise to desire.

93 **heere . . . threate:** i.e., hear of something that poses a threat to my desire or thought.

95 **spent?:** wasted. The question mark here, as frequently at this period, functions as an exclamation point.

99 **incamp'd with feares:** embattled by or fenced in with fears.

100 **starte:** wake suddenly.

The lamentation

Eu'n couched doth in happie bed remaines
And ſo in minde, I doe behould her ſhine,
Then I begyn for to commend the fate,
Of that ſweete bed, perfum'd by her ſweete breath,
And with my ſelfe eu'n thus I doe debate:
What rareſt beautie there appeares in death;
Her ſpirits moue with ſuch a liuely grace,
That death doth ſeeme in her an ornament,
Whoſe stately tower the pillow doth embrace;
And clipping kiſſe repoſ'd with ſweete content.
Art can not paynt how thus ſhe Nature feedes,
Or liuing death her fayre ſeemes to poſſeſſe,
Wherein no doubt the careleſſe gazer reedes;
The Calender of his accurſt diſtreſſe.
Theſe thoughes encreaſe the heate of my deſire,
Whoſe accents baniſh'd reaſon from the ſtage,
My bed beares guilt of this my burning fire:
That acceſſarie was of this my rage.
For when ech place denied me ſcope of thought,
He gaue repoſe vnto my wearied minde,
To feede vpon what to my harmes I ſought,
Which now a poyſon to infect I finde:
The night being ſpent in theſe vnhal'wed cares,
The dayes aproch doth [illegible] deſires encreaſe,

Her

---

107 debate] debate (*followed by a raised period*)
117 thoughtes] thoughes
122 She] He

108 **death:** Parry here uses the classical theme that sleep was actually a form of death. Cf. Shakespeare's *Hamlet*, 3.1.59–67.

109 **spirits:** vital power or energy. Probably used with reference to the natural spirits (made in the liver), the vital spirits (made in the heart from the natural spirits), and the animal spirits (made in the brain from the vital spirits); thought of as subtle, refined substances, which permeated the blood and chief bodily organs and were believed to "knit that subtile knot" between body and soul "which makes us man" (John Donne, "The Exstasie," 63–64).

112 **clipping kisse repos'd:** hugging caress, she being rested.

114 **Or liuing death:** or, she living, how death possesses her beauty.

115 **carelesse:** thoughtless.

116 **Calender:** record.

118 **accents:** stressful effects.

121 **scope of:** room for.

122 **She:** *O*'s "He" appears to have no referent.

of a Male-content.

Her goulden trammels which my ſenſes ſnares:
Like towring Fawlcon doth on my ſight ceaſe,
To view this ſtarre I rowle my light-leſſe eye
Aſqu'int, and then ſights force is cleane bereſt,
That ſenſe can not her ſweeteſt fayre deſcrie,
Which hath my heart in ſobbing ſorowes left.
Then like the theefe that ſhunns the Iudges face,
I flie her ſight that may iudge my deſire,
Although in heart her preſence I embrace;
For ſtill my thoughtes to her ſweete fayre aſpire.
Her noble breſt eu'n is that bowre of bliſſe,
Which in it ſelfe doth harbor my delight,
My ſtay of life therein intombed is,
Which lock'd retaynes from wiſhed hope his right:
From wiſhed hope his right, ah booteleſſe hope,
That ſoothes his maiſter in his ruins courſe,
In vaine I ſtriue, too large is honours ſcope,
That to his center hath a ſtill recourſe.
Cught Palmers come and ſit in Princes throane,
To beg for Dole to ſatisfie there want,
Shall I to her uenter to make my moane,
Whom for to ſerue I am right worthy ſcant.
No ſure, the Roe which ſwift beaſts out-ran,
Would ſcorne to ſee the bearded goate contend,

Yet

147 venter] uenter

127 **trammels:** fetters (i.e., hair). Cf. line 166.
128 **towring:** flying high in order to swoop down (as a falcon does).
128 **cease:** seize upon.
129 **eye:** Elizabethans often used the singular "eye" in contexts where we would expect "eyes."
137 **bowre of blisse:** Parry is probably recalling Spenser's "bower of bliss" in *The Faerie Queene*, II.xii.
140 **retaynes:** holds back.
141 **bootelesse:** unprofitable.
143 **scope:** (1) range; (2) outlook.
144 **still recourse:** constant return.
146 **Dole:** alms, charitable gift. See Posie VII.
147 **venter:** venture (variant form).
148 **Whom . . . scant:** To serve whom, I am very wanting in worth.

The lamentation

Yet Paris thought the go ddesse striefe to scanne,
When he did Venus beautie in Ide defrude:
Why shall not I her loue hope to obtayne,
Though Venus peere, or yet rather peerelesse,
Paris a sheaphard I a homely swayne,
He wanton, I chast Helen would possesse.
No Pherecleau barke with treason stor'd,
Loaden with heape of desembling layes,
Nor cruell darts with friendes deere blood begor'd,
Did guide my course to view thy glorious rayes.
Was't to reuenge of auncestors the wronge,
As Paris did; these passions me molest?
No, without fraude of pure affection spronge,
True loue, yea lone which robbs me of my rest.
Thy Idea ymprest is in my heart,
And gonlden trammels shrined in my minde,
That if dome signes doe not my griefe ympart,
And hope of thee my entertaynment finde.
I shall weare out the remnant of my dayes,
In cursed cares, and sorowes deepe despayre,
Diuine sweete Nymph cut off my fates delayes:
And let consent salue this thy ioyes ympayre.
For my desires, with tombling waues, are tost,
Within th'Ocean of thy sweete beautie,

And

152 defende] defrude
164 yea loue] yea lone
166 goulden] gonlden

151 **Yet . . . scanne:** Nevertheless, Paris (son of Priam), king of Troy, believed he could judge a contest between Juno, Minerva, and Venus (Greek: Hera, Athene, and Aphrodite) as to which of them was the fairest. Paris chose Venus, because she promised him, as a bribe, that he would some day win the most beautiful woman in the world (i.e., Helen of Troy), a judgment that finally led to the Trojan war when he stole Helen from the Greek Menelaus. The so-called "Judgment of Paris" took place on Mount Ida (see line 152), where he had been brought up as a shepherd.

155 **homely swayne:** simple youth, as shepherd or lover.

156 **He . . . possesse:** He (Paris) wished to possess a wanton (Helen), I a chaste Helen. This is an obvious reference to Helena Owen, to whom Parry addresses Sonettos 1, 15–31; her name appears acrostically in Sonettos 16–18.

157 **Phereclean barke:** a ship made by Phereclus, who made the ships in which Paris sailed into Greece to steal Helen.

158 **desembling layes:** deceiving songs. What connection such songs have with the rape of Helen is not clear.

161–62 **Was't . . . did:** Hesione, daughter of King Laomedon of Troy and aunt of Paris, was rescued from a sea monster by Hercules; Laomedon refused Hercules his promised reward (two magic horses), who then sacked Troy and abducted Hesione, taking her to Greece. Paris's theft of Helen was in revenge for the seizure of Hesione.

162 **molest:** vex, trouble.

163 **without . . . spronge:** without deception (unlike Paris), (but) arising out of "True loue" (see line 164).

164 **True loue:** (it is) true love (i.e., "pure affection").

165 **Idea:** essential image.

166 **goulden trammels:** blonde plaited hair braids (literally, "golden fetters"). Blonde hair was usually the ideal for a sonnet-mistress.

167 **dome:** dumb.

171 **my fates delayes:** hindrances caused by my lot in life.

172 **let . . . ympare:** allow acceptance of me to heal thy sense of impairment. This line would better fit its context if "my" is substituted for "thy."

of a Male-content.

And I in wildernes of cares am loſt,
Deuiſing ſtill how to performe my duety:
None knows my minde nor yet what I doe meane,
In vaine it is to thunder foorth my griefe,
And thus to ſpend my ſelfe on ſuch a ſpleane,
When ſure I am not to obtaine reliefe:
What though ſhe reade theſe run's of my time,
She will not thinke that ought by her is ment,
For my meane fancies are too baſe to clime:
Or once to ayme the Period of my bent.
That ſoares aloft eu'n in the racking Cloudes,
Beyonde the reach of any mortall ſight,
And in bright Phœbus beams her honour ſhrowd's,
Which doth from thence encreaſe fayre Tytans light.
So that no ſight vnleſſe the Eagle eyed,
(For feare of taynt) dare gaze on this bright ſonne,
But happie is he that peeping hath eſpyed,
The vayle that co'u'rs the fayre this thrid hath ſpunne:
Sometimes mine dye (forgetting duties charge)
Gaze on thoſe orbes that be ſo orient fayre,
Where anchor-leſſe they ſayle in fancies barge,
And feede themſelues eu'n with thy heau'nly payre:
Then while ſhe doth on other obiectes looke,
They thinke a vauntage for to ſteale a ſight,

Forget-

192 thrid] third
193 eyes] dye

179 **spleane:** peevish fit of temper.
181 **ruin's . . . time:** i.e., his verses (because "ruin" grows out of his unrequited love).
184 **Or . . . bent:** Or even to take aim at the goal of my desires (i.e., acceptance by his mistress).
185 **That:** i.e., "my bent."
185 **racking:** wind driven.
187–88 **Phœbus . . . Tytans:** Alternative titles for the god of the sun.
187 **shrowd's:** clothes.
189 **Eagle eyed:** Eagles were believed to be the only creatures (including man) that could look at the sun without blinking.
190 **taynt:** (eye) injury.
192 **The . . . sponne:** This thread hath spun the veil that shields her beauty. There seems to be no referent for "this thrid."
193 **eyes . . . charge:** eyes forgetting the responsibility that is a part of duty. *O*'s obvious misprint "dye" has been emended to "eyes" because the poet's eyes are referred to in the plural in lines 195–96, 198, 201.
194 **orbes:** i.e., his mistress' eyes.
194 **orient fayre:** brilliantly beautiful.
195 **fancies barge:** imagination's bark (which being "anchor-lesse" sails any direction imagination draws it).
198 **thinke a vauntage:** believe it an opportunity.

The lamentation

Forgetting that they snatch the bayted hooke:
But being encountred by those circlets bright,
They doe retire for to prepare excuse,
And blush for feare least that they were descried.
Or that her eyes would messuage heere the newes,
When as they had vnto my glavnces pried:
Thus would I faine that she did know my case,
And yet am loth she should my fancies knowe,
Lest that she would my little hope deface,
And being my friend begyn to be my foe.
Haue I not heard that hollow fearefull voice,
Sound in mine eares? which late pronounc'd my care,
Had she fayde so, it had byn past all choice:
For then I had byn fetered fast in snare.
Bnt sith this Eccho of abrupted ayre,
Breathes out these threates from bowels of conceyte,
Yt shall not Coward-like cyre my despayre,
But rather giue me conrage to entreate.
Then noble patronesse of my repose,
Diuine the meaning of my pure intent,
And though that feare forbids me to disclose,
My inward care, that banisheth content.
Yet haue remorse on him that liuing dyes,
Vnlesse thou take compassion on his fate,

Whose

204 glaunces] glavnces
213 But] Bnt
216 courage] conrage

203 **messuage:** transmit (variant form of "message").

204 **When . . . pried:** When they had pried into my oeillades (amorous glances).

209 **fearefull:** frightening.

213 **But . . . ayre:** But since this echo of air that has been broken off. Cf. what happened to the mythological Echo; see the volume's dedicatory Epistle, 23n.

214 **bowels of conceyte:** inmost reaches of thought.

of a Male-content.

Whose wynged thought in pensiue passion lyes,
Fenced with vaile of sorowes deepe debate.
Eu'r-during care possesseth my poore minde,
Once freede from the badge of discontent,
To be thy thrall my soaring thoughtes inclinde,
View then my playntes which do my hap lament.
Dayne to regarde the silent griefes I beare,
Hoping that signes add inward motions pleade,
True tokens of vnfained loue, yet feare,
Eclipseth still the hope I had to speede.
Bashfull I am, sweete loue speake thou for mee,
Ah well thou know'st the some of my desire,
Loue made me thrall and thou canst make me free,
Then lende me hope to quench the kindled fire.
I only craue that thou should'st knowe I loue,
And that I spend my dayes in care for thee,
Thou art the sterne which wearied barke doth moue,
Ane to the harbour of thy grace I flee.
Not for my selfe alone, these passions striue,
And torture still my neere-decayde heart,
Nor yet of malyce others to corriue,
But secret matters which the heau'ns ympart,
For to encrease thy noble beauties race:
That barren lyes for want of timely seede,
The braunch-spread Palme the blossom'd buds deface,
Note this is true when thou my Poem reede.

Yf

230 Hoping] *O inverts* H
230 and] add
240 And] Ane

223 **pensiue passion:** melancholy suffering.
224 **Fenced . . . debate:** Overshadowed with the veil of sorrow's great (inner) strife.
226 **badge:** distinguishing mark.
230 **inward motions:** inner promptings.
239 **sterne:** rudder.
243 **corriue:** vie with, rival.

The lamentation of a Male-content.

Yf barren Sara vnto Abraham gaue,
Agar her mayde, his seede to multiplie,
That She a childe by her brought foorth might haue?
For to fulfill the sacred Prophesie:
Why should not I being mou'd by loues desire,
And stir'd by motion of the heau'nly powers,
Yeilde to the furie of this hallowed fire,
Whose heate cannot be quench'd with stormie showers.
Depose the scruple of a double zeale,
For time once lost cannot be had againe,
From all the worlde to thee I doe appeale:
Though thou shouldst hate, my loue shall still remaine.
I vowe to be true vnto thee alone,
And eu'r in heart none other to embrace,
Nowe let fonde Eccho iterate my moane,
And part in Cloudes, my fates hope to deface.
I still will sing the glorie of thy name,
And glutt my selfe in praysing thy sweete fayre,
My pen is bound for to aduaunce thy fame;
Vnto the heau'nly region of the ayre:
Then Ioue will pine and fret for such a loue,
When thundering blasts, of thy renowned grace,
Shall, that great God, with thy fayre beautie, moue:
Which I in heart doe honour and embrace,

These secret griefes this loue vnknowne doth forge,
Whereof I die vnlesse thou take remorse.

FINIS.

272 embrace] *O inverts* m.

249–50 **Sara . . . Agar:** See Genesis 16–17.
251 **her:** i.e., Agar.
252 **sacred Prophesie:** See Genesis 15:18.
257 **Depose . . . zeale:** Bear witness to the propriety of a two-fold ardor (in my love for you).
259 **From . . . worlde:** putting aside all others in the world.
263 **fonde Eccho:** foolish, doting Echo.
264 **part . . . deface:** disintegrate into "abrupted ayre" (i.e., into mere echoes: see line 213n) to ruin hope of my future fortune.
273 **loue . . . force:** love, which is unknown to the beloved, effects.

Other Poems by Robert Parry

[fol. 179]

The Epitath of mistris Katheryn Theloall whoe / deceased the xxviith day of Auguste and was buried / the first of September folowinge in the yeare of / our Lord god 1591.

The blustringe blastes of sturdie storme, wyth duskie vapore covers,
the welkyn aye in rackinge cloudes, the boysterous *Boreas* hovers.
Triton beinge wett wyth raging waves the mightie whall doyth stride,
to saue hymselfe from *Neptunes* wrath in ffrothye waters glide.
The *Sirens* cease their melody, and weeping eyes appeare:
the *Neyads* stuffd wyth stormes of stryffe haue lost their wonted cheare.

Transcribed from a scribal copy in CC, fols. 179–180^{v}.

Title. **The Epitath . . . 1591**: In his Diary, 118, Parry records the death of Catherine Thelwall (i.e., Katheryn Theloall): "The 30th of August [1591] Mrs Katherin Tudir then wyef to M^{r} Ed Theloall & mother to the heyre of lleweny [i.e., John Salusbury] died & was buried at llanwyth [i.e., Llannefydd] the fyrst of September." This is the earliest reference to the Salusbury family in the Diary. Prior to her marriage to John Salusbury, Esq., the father of John Salisbury, Parry's patron, she was Catherine of Berain, famous as a great beauty, the daughter and heir of Tudor ap Robert Fychan of Berain (and Jane, daughter of Sir Rowland Velville, Governor of Beaumaris Castle) in the parish of Llannefydd, Denbighshire. On the death of John Salusbury, Catherine married successively (1) Sir Richard Clough, wealthy merchant and partner of Sir Thomas Gresham, founder of the Royal Exchange; (2) Maurice Wynn of Gwydir; (3) Edward Thelwall of Plâs y Ward (see *Powys Fadog*, vol. 4, 337–38; 4:269; 4:334, 343). Despite the lack of earlier references to the Salusbury family, it would appear that Parry was by 1591 a member of a group that may be called the "Salusbury circle," a number of whom, like Parry, wrote elegies on Catherine's death (see CC, fols. 174–82, and Brown, 38–43). In the course of this prosaic and alliteration-ridden set of verses, Parry gives details concerning Catherine's four marriages and her various off-spring.

2 **aye . . . cloudes:** continually wind-driven clouds.

2 ***Boreas***: the north-wind.

3 ***Triton***: See Passion V.1n.

5 ***Sirens***: See Passion XV.17n.

6 ***Neyads***: See Posie IIII.23n.

O cruell fate that pourd this plage over *Camber* soyle to swaye,
oh heavie happe to harmelesse wyghtes, oh dreirie dolefull daye.
You *Muses* mone, and musicke cease, no myrthe in mynd doethe rest:
eche on redubles his complaintes, wyth sorowinge sobbes oppreste.
Sicelian nymphes drawe neare, your selues attire in mourninge weed,
helpe to bewayle the losse of hir, spronge out of pryncly seed.
One thousande, and fyve hundreth more, foure score, a leven wyth all,
when god vnto his mercy great, did *Katheryn tudir* call.
August the seventh and twentith day, her soule this lyfe did passe,
wyth worshype thoughe wyth waylinges great, ye fyfte day terred was.
A braynche of *Tudir Robartes* sonne, the head of Helines race,
a worthy squier of auncient stock, wch vertue did imbrace.
gotten by hym on the sole heyre, of *Roulande Velvel* knyghte,
a ma*n* whose name is not obscure, by force of fortunes myghte.
To boeth these pearlesse paragones sole heyre shee did remaine,
whose death procures full many a wyght, to langwyshe thuse in paine.
Nowe orphanes nowe complaine your losse, which earst she usd to reare,
all hope is turned to floudes of teares, your paled faces leare.
The helplesse maydes y^{t} needie weare, she did preferre alwaye.
noe marvaill then, thoughe they bewaylle, the wante of such a staye.
All you that by her lyvinge livid, howe can you greif refraine, [fol.179^{v}]
for portiones great she franckly dealt her kynsmen to mayntaine.

---

7 ***Camber***: Cambrian (i.e., Welsh).

9 ***Muses***: See Passion XXVIII.19n.

11 **weed:** garment.

12 **spronge . . . seed:** Catherine of Berain was descended from Marchweithian, Lord of Is-Aled.

15 **twentith:** twentieth (variant form).

16 **fyfte:** fifth (variant form).

17–19 **braynche . . . knyghte:** Catherine ("A braynche") was the daughter of Tudor ap Robert Fychan and Jane, the daughter of Sir Rowland Velville, Governor of Beaumaris Castle (hence line 20).

17 **head . . . race:** the direct descendant of Heilin Gloff of Carwedd Fynydd, a descendant of Marchweithian, Lord of Is-Aled.

21 **sole heyre:** Catherine was a wealthy woman, a fact that may explain her multiple marriages.

24 **leare:** inform (us of their grief).

25 **alwaye:** always (variant form).

All tasted of her frendly turnes, non empty went her froe,
betweene her servantes and the poore, the rest she did bestowe.
Had she bein giuen to hoorde vp wealth, she myghte had coyne in store,
for to compare wyth any one, that *Camber* bred before.
What others kepte to purchase landes, and gathered in longe space,
she did distribute to the poore, in heaven to gaine a place.
Her like this countrey never hath bred, her peare in pitie wantes,
not one soe many frutfull Impes, in vertues soyle that plantes.
Of worshippe foure right worthye squieres, were coupled to this Iem
of three to her fiue buddes remaine o happie frutfull fem.
ffirst *Iohn* the sonne of *Iohn* whose sire, was knyghte of worthye fame.
the florishinge hope of *Salusburies*, and beautie of the same.
The staffe of comones comon good, and staye of kynsmen true,
this pearlesse youth his mothers losse wyth ceaselesse plaintes doth rue.
His lovinge spowse of noble bloude, associates him in mone,
her trickling teares bedewe her cheekes, her seighes to skyes are blowen.
To second feere she fostered frutes, wch now are full of paine
twixt *Clough* and her two daughters fayre as pledge of faith remaine.
Wyth whom shee lead a welthy lyfe, in many a countrey strayngе,
whose worthye coredge not dismayed through raging seas to raynge.

---

29 **froe:** from.
35 **wantes:** is lacking.
36 **not one:** i.e., no other.
36 **Impes:** off-spring, children.
37 **foure . . . squieres:** See headnote.
37 **Iem:** gem.
38 **of three . . . buddes:** from three of her husbands five off-spring (are alive).
38 **fem:** woman.
39 **ffirst . . . fame:** i.e., John Salusbury, Parry's patron, son of John Salusbury, son of Sir John Salusbury, Chancellor and Chamberlain of Denbighshire and an M. P. (*Powys Fadog*, 4:334, and Introduction, 8–10).
43 **spowse . . . bloude:** Ursula, illegitimate daughter of the fourth Earl of Derby who, like Catherine, died in 1591 (*Powys Fadog*, 4:335).
43 **associates:** joins with.
45 **second feere:** second husband (i.e., Clough; see headnote).
46 **two daughters:** Anne, married Roger Salusbury of Bach y Craig; Mary, married William Wynn of Melai; a son, Richard, was presumably already dead, hence Parry's "remaine" (*Powys Fadog*, 4:343).
47 **countrey strayngе:** foreign country.

These two lament wyth wayling cheere, their husbandes doe no lesse.
  boeth *Wynn* and *Salesburie* for her do languyshe in distresse.
Two braynches yeke of her theyrde spowse rest nowe tormented sore,
  Edwarde her sonne of *Morys Wynn*, whoe restlesse doth deplore.
And *Iane* his sister pynes wyth woe, whose pantinge harte doth paine
  to hyghest note of sorowe these their heavie harte stringes straine.
And last her latest loyall feere, thoughe not in fayth the leste,
  of foure he only doth surviue wch livinge her posseste.
And by as much as he survives, by soe much more is he [fol.180]
  enthrald wyth dartinge panges of woe, and pynching agonie.
Theloall he is wch thuse complaints, whose staye is pacient sap,
  yet mournfull countenaunc doeth bewraye his losse of later hap.
His sonne not meanly mones this chaunce, her double sonne in lawe,
  Symon wyth his lovinge spouse, doeth pills of sorowe chawe.
Her kinsmen, and her tenantes poore, ring out a dolefull knyll,
  resoundinge Echoes of their cries, ech holowed cave doeth fill.
The poore exclaime on cruell fate, wch reft ther soveraigne staye,
  in the North parte of *Camber* soyle, her death did all dismaye.
Not on but markd that day wyth stones, that blacke did seeme in sight,
  in token of disaster loocke, thuse wrourght by fatall spight.

---

50 ***Wynn* and *Salesburie*:** i.e., Roger Salusbury and Edward Wynn (see line 52), son of Maurice Wynn, Catherine's third husband (*Powys Fadog*, 3:358). Edward's sister Jane, mentioned in line 53, is not recorded in *Powys Fadog*; Parry may be confusing her with Maurice Wynn's first wife, Janet, the daughter of Sir Richard Bulkeley of Beaumaris.

55 **latest loyall feere:** Edward Thelwall (see headnote and line 59).

55 **leste:** least (in status).

59 **complaints:** complains (variant form not in *OED*).

59 **sap:** ? a colloquial form of "sapience." Cf. line 89.

60 **losse . . . hap:** loss of future good fortune or happiness.

61–62 **sonne . . . *Symon* . . . spouse:** Simon Thelwall was the son of Edward Thelwall, the fourth husband of Catherine of Berain, by his first marriage to Dorothy, daughter of John Griffith of Penrh of Kichley. Simon married Jane, sister of Edward Wynn, both children of Maurice Wynn by Catherine of Berain, her third husband. This rather tangled relationship explains why Parry described Simon as Catherine's "double sonne in lawe" (see *Powys Fadog*, 3:358; 4:308–9). At this time "son-in-law" could also mean "step-son" (see *OED*; earliest citation 1628).

62 **chawe:** chew (variant form).

63 **knyll:** knell (variant form).

67 **on:** one.

68 **in . . . loocke:** look like a symbol of disaster.

O cursed *Saturne* didest thow grudge, at many hundrethes weale,
to heighe *Iehova* for this losse our author we apeale.
Whye *Lachis* hast thow ben soe slowe, why *Clotho* didst necglect
to lengthen out her threede of lyfe wch did the poore protecte.
Howe dirst the cruell *Atrops* toutch her threede wyth bloodie hande,
that earst to heare her worthye name wyth trembleing feare did stande.
Seing Destinie would here that she, no longer tyme should haue.
loe heere behould *Natures* ou*er*mache, intombed in her graue.
Whose death if coyne could haue redeamd, or teares haue purchasd lyfe,
no wealth should want, nor weepinges lacke, to ease this mortall stryfe.
Or if that god were pleasd y^{t} one should for another payne,
full many would haue offerd lyfe, her lyfe to haue againe.
Whose corps interred thoughe yt be, all pale in concave denne,
her livelye fame shall flye abroad, throughe living mouthes of men.
Whose cheeff desire was here to lyve, by lyvinge soe to die,
that die*ing* she myght lyve againe, in Ioye eternallye.
Wherfore giue ou*er* for to lamente cease nowe to wayle & crie,
syth god alwayes ordained hath ech livinge wyghte should die.
As here we cam not all at once, soe hence we most not goe: [fol. 180^{v}]
but at our makers will: therfore leave of tormenting woe.
And vewe the chaunce wyth wysdomes eye, lett pacience rule yor mynde:
and yeld the kynge of glorie prayes, to whom is prayes assynd.
And then no doubt in tyme you shall, wyth her in heaven appeere:
for to enioye her companie, as earst you haue donne heere.

finis, *Robert Parry*—gentleman.

---

69 *Saturne*: See Passion XLI.21n.
70 **author:** i.e., God ("Iehova").
71–73 ***Lachis . . . Clotho . . . Atrops***: See Passion VII.9n and Passion X.21–22n.
83 **by . . . die:** to die while living in such a way.
86 **syth:** since.
87 **cam . . . once:** i.e., as we are not all born at the same time, so we do not all die at the same time.
88 **of:** off.
90 **prayes . . . prayes:** praise . . . praise.

MODERATVS, OR THE ADVENTURES OF THE BLACK KNIGHT,

LONDON PRINTED BY
RICHARD IHONES,
1595

[A2]

To the right Worshipfull

AND HIS SINGVLAR GOOD MASTER,
Henry Townshend, Esquire, one of her Maiesties Iustices of Assise of the countie Pallatine of Chester, and one of her Highnesse honourable Counsell, established in the marches and principality of Wales:
ROBERT PARRY wisheth all encrease of honorable vertues.

THe wisest Senators (Right worshipfull) sometimes delighted themselues as well in beholding Roscius counterfeit gestures, which recreated the wearines of their minds, as in reading of learned Orators, which prescribed vnto them precepts of maners. Tullie, notwithstanding his great grauitie *Alternis vicibus* dallied with his Terentia: And Domitianus the Emperour did vse to catch flies to auoid idlenesse. So I to passe

For Sir Henry Townshend, see Introduction, 5.

2 **Roscius:** generally referred to by the Elizabethans as the archetype of Roman actors.

4 **Tullie:** i.e., Marcus Tullius Cicero, most famous of Roman orators.

5 **Terentia:** Cicero's wife.

5–6 **Domitianus:** For this story about the Emperor Domitian, see Suetonius, *Lives of the Caesars*, Book VII, 3.

ouer the prolixitie of time, endeuoured my selfe to pen this treatise of fancie: and albeit vnworthy to the viewe of your learned and graue iudgment, yet let it serue for a Roscius to make a iest of, & for a Terentia to toy with al, therin to refresh your wearied mind continuallie exercised in the affairs of the common wealth. And notwithstanding, that I haue many times considered with my selfe, how that to publish these [A2^{v}] first fruits of my simple trauels, was wittingly to offer my selfe to the ignomie of the popular speaches, and like the Hartes in Calabria to feed vpon Dictanum, knowing it to be deadly poison: yet choose I rather so to do, though neuer so great a disparagement to my name, than that my dutiful affection (tyed to your Worship by your so many fauors vnto me) should be adnihilated by obliuion, when as the recognizing thereof was the onely meane to discouer the true meaning of a faithfull, and welwilling heart, trusting rather to the curtesie of the gentle Reader, than any way fearing the curiosity of backbiting Momus, yet being well assured that this my simple pamphlet being shrouded with the countenance of so worthy a Mecenas, may well defend it selfe notwithstanding the sharpest inuectiues that can be deuised against it. Thus beseeching your Worship to censure, that though euerie horse is not Bucephalus, yet the meanest is a horse: in like maner though this my fancie be not vested with eloquence, yet a booke, which being fauourably accepted, yeeldeth vnto his master the expected desired fruit of all his trauels.

Your Worsh. most bounden seruant
in all dutifull affection,

ROBERT PARRY.

12–13 **these first fruits:** If Parry was indeed the translator, as I have argued, of several parts of the *Mirror of Knighthood* (see Introduction, 28–34), he must be referring to *Moderatus* as his first published original work.

13 **trauels:** travails, labors.

14–15 **Hartes . . . poison:** Probably borrowed from Greene's *Greenes Never too late* (1590), 47: "Women, poor soules, are like to the harts in *Calabria*, that knowing *Dictannum* to be deadly, yet they bruse on it with greedinesse." The use of dictanum or dittany to cure wounds is attested by Pliny. In the early history of Italy, Calabria was a dukedom bordering on Naples.

21 **Momus:** See "Vpon the Authors muse" (in *Sinetes*, A3^{v}), line 20.

23 **Mecenas:** Maecenas was the patron of Horace and Virgil; his name became a synonym for "patron."

25 **Bucephalus:** a horse belonging to Alexander the Great, the head of which resembled a bull.

To the Reader.

GEntle Reader, although none but *Apelles* could drawe *Venus* counterfeit, and that no man durst presume to set foorth *Alexanders* portrature in Copper but *Lysippus*: yet *Phydias* shewed his skill in painting of pictures, and others more simple than *Lysippus* practised ingrauing in brasse. Euen so I, though none of those that are rapt up (as it were) into the second firmament, with some inspiration of heauenly furie, whose writings be as well replenished with wisdome and learning as polished with a very fine and eloquent mothod, of which sort (in this age) our English soyle yeeldeth manie that might chalenge *Cicero* (if he were liuing) to the Lystes, writing in their owne mother tongue, which language is growne nowe to be so copious, that it may compare with most of the richest tongues in all *Europe*, such is the carefull industrie of our Countrimen (who in mine opinion deserue due praises,) to amplifie the same. Euen so I say, though none of those, and that I acknowledge my self their inferiour in skill, yet I dare presume to be their equals in good will to pleasure the curteous reader. And though with *Apelles* I be not able to feed thee with curious sights, yet with *Phydias* I can present thee with pleasant delights, which if thou reade aduisedly, I doubt not, but will yeeld vnto thee some good precepts amongst a number of delectable discourses and pleasant conceits: I haue (to auoid tediousnesse, and to procure thy further delight) deuided the whole Historie into Chapters, with the seuerall Arguments therein handled, before each Chapter ensuing: vouchsafe then to accept this my *Fancie* with patience, wherby I may

---

1 ***Apelles***: famous Greek painter, who at the time of his death left a portrait of Venus unfinished, a portrait so incomparable that no other painter dared to finish it; the only painter allowed by Alexander the Great to paint his portrait.

3 ***Lysippus***: a famous metal-worker and sculptor; he alone was permitted to sculpt a statue of Alexander.

3 ***Phydias***: Phidias was another Greek sculptor specially known for his large gold and ivory statues of Athene and Jupiter Olympus. Parry mistakenly describes him as a painter.

6 **second firmament:** i.e., heaven.

10 **Lystes:** lists, spaces set apart for tilting.

be encouraged to wade further in this exercise, if the same maye yeeld mee any hope of procuring thy delight, to say trulye, good Reader,

Multa mouent tibi plurima scribere: salue
Multa vetant, vellem scribere plura, vale.

R. P.

26–27 Multa . . .vale: Simons translates as: "Many things move to write much to you; hail, / Many things forbid, though I would wish to write more: farewell." The couplet is not classical; probably composed by Parry.

Poems

[1] Moderatus (sig. 2A3^{v})

WHat Fortune so fell doeth foster my fall,
  what heapes of griefe doe grow:
The hope of my stay, is causer I say,
  to aggrauate my woe.
Sing lullabie, lullie, lullabie,
  sing lulla, lull, lullie.

Lullabie, lullie to rest thee, sweete childe,
  with sleepe deere childe rest thee:
It doubles my paine, I still doe complaine,
  if thou be reft from me.
Sing lullabie, lullie, lullabie,
  sing lulla lull lullie.

Syth fate is so fell, we can not possesse,
  the soyle which vs did reare:
Haste Atropos, haste, my twist for to waste,
  to ende tormenting feare.
Sing lullabie, lullie, lullabie,
  sing lulla, lull, lullie.

Thy daunger, sweete Infant, makes me to mone,
  and liuing thus, to die:

Described by Parry as a "Madrigale"; it should probably, with its refrain, more properly be called a "roundelay." See *Sinetes,* headnotes to Maddrigall [I] (sig. G8) and Roundedelay [I] (sig. G8^{v}). The lament is sung by Flaminea, the exiled duchess of Florence, who, lost in a forest with her child, Moderatus, is slowly perishing of hunger. Unknown to her, her husband, Lord Perduratus, has just been given sanctuary by Duke Devasco, duke of Albigena, for himself and his family. This lullaby was perhaps suggested to Parry by a lullaby in Greene's *Menaphon* (1589), 43, which also has a two-line refrain and is sung in a similar situation.

1 **doeth foster:** doth promote. The form "doeth" instead of "doth" is usual in *Moderatus.*

3 **stay:** (future) support (i.e., her starving child).

10 **reft:** taken, robbed (by death).

15 **twist . . . waste:** to cut (my) thread (of life). For Atropos, see Passion VII.9n.

If so it be prest from thy dying breast,
    my vitall breath shall flie.
Sing lullabie, lullie, lullabie,
    sing lulla, lull, lullie.

[2] Moderatus (sigs. B2v–B3v)

CAliope assist my quill,
With Sisters three lend me the skill,
Your ayde I craue, I want the same,
For to describe this pearelesse Dame:
Who is the flower of beautyes trayne,
Which Nature made her selfe to stayne.
Her azure veynes on forehead hie,
Doe shine so bright as Christall skie.
Her Amber hayres with wyers of golde,
Trim'd in good order to beholde.
Her eyes beneath her browes doe shyne,
Which doe intrap the gazers eyne.
Her Visage shewes like Roses cleere,
Where redde on white seemes to appeare.
Her nose so comely set betweene,
Where excellencie may well be seene.
Her cherry lippes so soft and sweete,
Her teeth within so whyte and meete.
Her dimpled chinne so round and bryght,
Might well entice a mort-fied wyght.
Her necke the piller of this Peere,
With skinne so whyte, and veynes so cleere,
Vpholdes a wonder to the eye,

An ode written by a courtier in praise of Florida, Duke Devasco's daughter, here however, sung by a shepherd. On the ode form, see Posie IIII, headnote. Cf. a similar "catalogue of beauty" in Greene's *Menaphon* (1589), 122–25. Parry's ode, at several points, suggests the influence of Sidney's *Arcadia* (1590), lyric 62 (ed. Ringler); see the examples cited below in lines 41, 47–48, 50, 58, 67–72.

1–2 **Caliope . . . three:** One of the Nine Muses, the inspirer of eloquence and heroic poetry; "Sisters three" seems to suggest that Parry is confusing the tradition of the Nine Muses with another tradition that reduced nine to four, but the name "Caliope" is associated only with the Nine Muses.

6 **her . . . stayne:** to obscure her own lustre (by comparison). Lines 5–6 are influenced perhaps by Shakespeare's *Venus and Adonis,* 8–9.

12 **eyne:** eyes (archaic plural).

20 **mort-fied wyght:** dead man. "mort-fied" is either a Parry coinage or a misreading of "mortified."

Excelling natures puritie. [B3]
Her Armes, two branches of the vine,
Where nothing els but beautie shine.
Her shoulders bene the roote, I trowe,
Whereof these braunches fine doe growe.
Two bosses shine in siluer breast,
Nothing inferiour to the rest.
They be the hilles which doe inuite,
Gaye Venus darlings to delite.
On eyther side is finely dight,
Like armored scales shining bright.
Two rowes of Ribbes so euen and iust,
That when one mooues, the other must.
Next vnto this, the Waste so small,
Beneath her stately breast doeth fall,
That with a spanne might there be found,
The compasse of her middle round.
Beneath the hill, fayre Adons hill,
Whereof in Ida he did swill.
The pleasure sweete of loues desire,
Too rare to be a mould of myre.
Next vnto this the summe of all,
Which as I ought, I dare not call.
A seale of Virgin waxe at hand,
Without impression there doeth stand:
Then thyghes so fine, and smoothe as Iett,
Betweene the which a way is set,

---

29 **bosses:** breasts (literally, protuberances).

33 **dight:** placed, ordered.

39 **spanne:** hand's breadth.

41 **hill:** Considering its position, probably a euphemism for *mons veneris*.

41 **Adons hill:** Mount Libanus, where Venus visited Adonis. See Posie IIII.15n. Sidney, with similar suggestion, refers to "Cupid's hill" (line 78).

42 **Ida . . . swill:** Mount Ida was believed to give rise to fifteen rivers. "swill"=drink greedily or freely. It is unclear how line 41 connects with line 42.

45 **summe of all:** i.e., the female genitalia.

47–48 **A seale . . . stand:** Suggested by Sidney (lines 75–76): "A daintie seale of virgin-waxe, / Where nothing but impression lackes."

48 **Without impression:** i.e., still virgin (unstamped, unpenetrated).

50 **Betweene . . . set:** Suggested by Sidney (line 58): "Betwixt these two a way doth lie."

Of eyther side as soft as downe,
The readie path to high renowne.
Her knee so knitting legge and thigh,
Like Scalap-shell of Azure skie,
Doeth double beautie ioyne we see,
Which Venus mooues to ielousie.
The Kaulfe euen rising iust betweene,
The gartering place and small is seene.
As pointed Diamond Anckle bright,
Like droppes of dewe on Roses white. [B3v]
Her presse so soft with foote so fine,
That where she goeth scant grasse do twine.
Thus haue I framed her partes in kinde,
And yet the chiefe is left behinde.
Which last I left, though it be least,
Yet for memoriall to the rest.
Her hand is it, her hand in sight,
The glistering glasse of beautie bright.
Her lillie handes eche looker paines,
Embroydered with azure veynes,
By arte such workes did neuer passe,
Vnlesse her hand a sample was.
Her peble fingers long and small,
Tipte with yuorie beauties call,
Shin'd so bright as Titans rayes,
My penne wants skill to paint her praise.

76 praise.] praise,

58 **The gartering place:** From Sidney (line 99).

59 **pointed Diamond Anckle:** Cf. Posie I.14.

62 **scant . . . twine:** barely entwines or mats the grass. Cf. Shakespeare's *Venus and Adonis*, 1027–28, and Ovid, X.652–55.

63 **in kinde:** in their generic nature, in their natural order.

67–72 **Her hand . . . was:** The more or less final prominence given to the "hand" occurs also in Sidney (lines 121–29).

72 **sample:** ideal model.

73 **peble fingers:** fingers as white as rock crystal.

74 **beauties call:** call (them) beauties.

75 **Titans:** See Sonetto 13.1n.

The beautie of this pearelesse peece,
Surpasseth farre the Queene of Greece.
Whose countenance and Maiestie,
Doeth rule the sterne aboue the skie.
Yet curteous, modest with distaine,
That euerie rowling eye doeth paine.
Her loftie thoughtes and high desire,
Are neuer mou'd with fancies fire.
Who so hath seene, let him repent,
Who neuer her view'd, may well preuent.
For hope deceiues each one that proues,
In such a soyle to plant their loues.

---

79 countenance] countenace

---

80 **sterne:** (1) primum mobile; (2) governor (i.e., God).

81 **modest with distaine:** of modest coloring. *Q*'s "distaine" may, however, be a misreading of "disdaine," the phrase then meaning "not disdainfully overbearing.

84 **fancies fire:** burning of amorous imagination.

86 **preuent:** anticipate, look forward to.

87 **proues:** learns by experience.

[3] Moderatus (sigs. C3^{v}–C4^{v})

WHen lordlie Titan in his chiefest pride,
Ouer-spread Auroraes blushing countenance,
And Triton on his grayish steedes did ride,
In calmed Seas, on waues the Nayades daunce.
No duskie vapour couer'd the welkin cleer'd,
Phœbus (discouering ay the heauens) appear'd.

Here Iupiter presented no escape,
Then watcht by Argus hundreth waking eyes,
The Syrens then transformed no mans shape, [C4]
Nor to intrappe layd foorth their watching spyes.
And Proteus in his wonted shape remain'd,
For Nature would that nothing should be stayn'd.

Princes then walkt abroad for their delight,
Courtyers attend vpon their princes trayne,
Of tempestes Sea-men were not then affright,
The husbandman did hardly plye his gayne.
Dame Flora eke did couer the earth with greene,
Procuring hope most liuely to be seene.

Sung by Priscus, son and heir to King Lothus of Aemulia and bosom friend of Moderatus, who secretly watches Florida, daughter of Duke Devasco, with whom he has fallen in love, as she is bathing.

1 **Titan:** i.e., Phoebus Apollo; see Sonetto 13.1n.
2 **Auroraes:** See Posie I.3n.
3 **Triton:** See Passion V.3n.
4 **Nayades:** See Posie IIII.23n.
6 **discouering:** revealing.
8 **Argus:** See Sonetto 23.4n.
9 **Syrens:** See Posie XI.9n.
11 **Proteus:** a sea god, son of Oceanus and Tethys; best known for his ability to change his shape at will.
16 **hardly . . . gayne:** scarcely had to work for his livelihood.
17 **Dame Flora:** See Sonetto 11.2n.

Minerua then the Chaos did vnfolde,
Of these so farre vnordered terrene thinges,
That in good order you might all beholde,
Truss'd in a fardell vnder Fortunes winges.
  Well may I crie alacke and well away,
  That Fortune frayle did beare so great a sway.

It was the rusticke Goddes festiuall day,
When shepheardes quaint doe frolicke with their mates,
With stones blacke that time well marke I may,
For then begun all my disaster fates.
  Then with a smile fell fate did couer a fraude,
  To perfect which, Beautie made Fame her bawde.

Fame carefull then for to perfourme her charge,
Sounding due prayse, redoubled in mine eare,
Venus ouer-match, she blazed then at large,
Which stroke my bodie in a quiuering feare.
  This rare reporte being heard, I wish to see,
  If earthly Wightes affoorded such a shee.

I came, I sawe, nowe Cæsars fate I want,
For to ouercome: wherein I may dispayre,
Her statelie lookes my hoped hap doeth scant,
And day by day doeth still my ioyes impayre, [C4v]
  For that my minde lyeth in her princely bowre, [41]
  Whose beautie doeth excell Loues paramour.

---

19 **Minerua:** Greek goddess (also known as Pallas Athene) of wisdom, war, and the liberal arts.

19 **vnfold:** spread out (to make chaos orderly).

20 **terrene:** earthly.

22 **fardell:** bundle.

26 **quaint:** dressed in their best clothes.

27 **stones blacke:** black memorial stones (commemorating some unhappy "time"). "Stones" is two syllables.

28 **disaster:** disastrous.

34 **stroke:** struck (variant form).

37–38 **I . . . ouercome:** Cf. Julius Caesar's famous vaunt: "Veni, vidi, vici."

39 **scant:** stint, make scarce.

A liuing minde in dying corpes I haue,
My bodie here, my minde with her doeth stay,
A speedie death, if her I loose, I craue,
Whose sweete consent is euen that blisse-full Boy,
  Which onely is the harbour of my rest,
  In whose high thoughtes I wish to builde my nest.

Thou glistering Phœbus, hide thy shining face,
If euer thou view'st the beautie of this Dame,
Her brightsome hew will sure thy lightes disgrace,
The rarest wyght by her may blush for shame,
  Whose glorious lookes doe still present a iarre,
  Twixt fire and water there lyeth peace and warre.

O would I might (but what thereon may fall,
I knowe not well) once compasse her goodwill:
Or that I had not (nowe too late I call
The thing farre past) her knowen my ioyes to spill.
  Then had I liu'd and ledde a quiet life,
  Where nowe I pine with pure tormenting strife.

Sure shall desert there merite but disdaine,
Where high desire doeth lodge in loftie thought,
Seeing Loue and Fate doe still conspire my paine,
Voyde of all hope, I count my toyle for nought.
  Yet naythlesse hope for to obtaine thy loue,
  Not fearing aye the thing thou neuer didst prooue.

---

52 **by:** in comparison to.
53 **iarre:** discord, discrepancy (between appearance and reality).
55 **what . . . fall:** what as a result may happen.
58 **her . . . spill:** (had not) known that she would destroy my happiness.
66 **Not . . . prooue:** Not forever fearing that which (i.e., love) thou didst never experience. In its context the meaning is unclear.

[4] Moderatus (sigs. D2^{v}–D3^{v})

WHen Phosphorus declining West her tracke,
Commaunding Nox her charge to take in hand,
And for to spread abroad her curtaine blacke,
By Natures course to couer both sea and land:
  Then at her becke a clowdie vale in stept,
  And terrene thinges quite from our sight hath swept.

By this had Phœbus clearely made escape,
And Vesperus his action did assoyne,
Of Thetis Queene then cloyed with the rape,
With Lucina in coiture doeth ioyne:
  From whome he cleerely receiu'd alway his light,
  Least she should blush, being seene in such a plight.

Lucina then her budding hornes did stretch,
And borrowing of her Louer light, appeares,
When Morpheus presented to me poore wretch,

---

11 alway] away

A "Cansong" (from Italian *canzone*=song; Parry's form is not recorded in the *OED*) sung as a lament by Priscus, who has been repulsed by Florida, a lament overheard by his friend, Moderatus, who then attempts to comfort him.

1 **Phosphorus:** the morning star; in Greek mythology, he was the son of Astraeus and Eos.

2 **Nox:** Night.

5 **vale in stept:** veil intervened.

8 **Vesperus . . . assoyne:** The evening star made an excuse for what he (i.e., Phoebus) did.

9 **Of . . . rape:** then surfeited with the seizure of Thetis, the queen (of the Nereids and mother of Achilles by Peleus). In Greek mythology, Thetis was connected with Zeus, not Phoebus, and "rape" can only be associated with Peleus before he became her husband. In any case, the line seems to make little sense in its present context.

10 **Lucina:** Roman goddess who presided over childbirth; also one of the many names applied to Phoebe, goddess of the moon.

10 **coiture:** sexual copulation. Also a metaphor for Phoebus (sun) giving his light to Lucina (moon).

11 **alway:** always, ever. Q's "away" makes no sense in relation to "recieu'd." Gentrup (privately) queries whether "he" is a misreading for "she."

13 **hornes:** The moon was thought of as "horned" in its first and last quarters.

15 **Morpheus:** the childlike god of sleep and dreams.

A sight, which still my dulled senses cheeres:
  Ah cheeres: a wofull cheere: woe worth the time,
  That makes me thus to spend my golden prime.

What fancie moou'd, folly did put in vre,
And Queene Desire did straight appoint the game,
Which once begunne, no hope could helpe procure,
Beefore I loose, to giue it ouer were shame:
  Although Dispayre doeth say that I shall gaine,
  Nought for my toyle, but heapes of cruell paine.

Cupid then smyl'd such Clyent to possesse,
And thank'd Morpheus that procur'd the same,
Venus mislikte I should rest in distresse,
Least after I would ay renounce her game.
  Shee fitted me, with opportunitie
  To speake: alas I spake: all would not be.

All would not be, what then? ah dolefull chaunce,
Haue all the Fates confederated my fall? [D3]
Yes, yes: too soone I did my Barke out launce,
And eke commit my sayle to windes a thrall:
  Wherefore rowe backe thy barge to natiue porte,
  In earnest end, what thou begun in sport.

That thou begun in sport: a heauie sport,
Which is the worker of thy great annoye,
Thou canst not long endure in such a sort,
Exempt from hope of any earthly ioye:
  Vnlesse the Saint, that wrought this deepe distresse,
  Pityes thy panges; and doe thy paynes redresse.

Thy paines redresse, if not foorthwith, too late,
For Phebe thrice her wasted hornes renew'd,

---

17 **woe . . . time:** evil befall the time.

19 **vre:** operation.

20 **Queene Desire:** sexual desire thought of as an absolute monarch, a favorite image of Parry's.

32 **Fates:** See Passion VII.9n.

43 **paines . . . late:** redress thy pains, if not immediately, (it will be) too late.

44 **Phebe:** See above, line 10 n.

Since I was forc'st by spitefull frowning fate,
To come and seeke the sight I latelie view'd,
  Which viewe my paines, so destinie assign'd,
  For at her handes no hope of grace I finde.

No hope of grace I finde, woe me therefore,
Without whose grace my life can not endure,
Oh that I were not as I was of yore,
Free from the scathe which doeth my harme assure,
  Then would I keepe my finger from the fire,
  And quite renounce the Lawes of fond desire.

Of fond desire the Lawe, oh lawlesse Lawe,
Which doeth extreemes combine and ioyne in wrong,
And ministreth pilles, which will not from the mawe,
This from the eye, not from the desert is sprung,
  A fickle Iudge for to discerne the right,
  Which blinded is with force of beauties might.

The force of beauties might: a power-full might,
Which can compell the proudest to obey,
Whose meere report hath brought me to this plight, [D3v]
Deuoyd of hope: for sorrowe beares the sway.
  Wherefore as Fame me forc'st this paine to prooue,
  There I began, and there will ende my loue.

---

51 **yore:** formerly.
57 **will . . . mawe:** which the stomach cannot digest.
65 **prooue:** undergo.

[5] Moderatus (sig. G2)
VEROSAES song.

ANd must the Punie that learned Gammut scant,
Muse vpon Crochets trebled oft and oft?
Or who of Arte the perfect groundes doeth want,
To iudge thereof, shall he then clime aloft?
No, no: of trueth his cunning prooues but vaine,
And so herein shall I such merite gaine.

But seeyng your doomes is a commaund to speake,
I will not sticke, (yet blame me not therefore,
If I do erre) for that my skill is weake,
So that of right the blame is yours the more,
Appointing her of colours Iudge to be,
Who being so blinde, can therein nothing see.

For Cupids craft, euer fronted with a smyle,
Hath neuer pierst my panting virgins breast,
For I abhorre the Caytiffes crafty wyle,

A group—made up of Florida, Duke Devasco's daughter; Verosa, daughter of Perduratus, banished Duke of Florence, and sister of Moderatus; Cornelius, Duke Devasco's son; Priscus; Moderatus; and Pandarina, a gentlewoman of the house of Devaloyes—debates the nature of love. Each one, during the quite lengthy discussion, sings a song expressing his or her view of love. Verosa, who is called upon to begin, uses her song to explain that she is too naive to give an opinion on such a difficult and controversial subject and begs to be excused.

Title. **VEROSAES song.**

1 **Punie . . . scant:** novice that scarcely has learned the first or lowest note in the medieval musical scale.

2 **Crochets:** notes of half the rank of a minum.

3 **doeth want:** lacks.

4 **clime aloft:** achieve eminence.

5 **cunning:** knowledge, skill.

6 **so . . . gaine:** in this matter (pretending to "cunning" that I don't possess), I will gain an equally meritorious result (irony).

7 **doomes:** judgments, opinions.

13 **craft:** artifice, cunning.

15 **Caytiffes crafty wyle:** wretch's clever, deceitful trick.

Wherewith the Louers fond are euer opprest.
    I wish my friends neuer for to prooue such fate,
    Least vnto them repentance commeth too late.

For to repeate the Louers dreaming thoughtes,
If skill to me had taught the ready way,
Howe with loues frowne they seeme like dampned ghostes,
Were toyled too much, and eke would make you say,
    That I a foe were to humanitie,
    Therefore with this, I craue excused to be.

22 **Were toyled:** had struggled.

[6] Moderatus (sigs. G2^{v}–G3)
CORNELIVS song.

WHo aymes at honours worthy name,
And coueteth renowmed fame,
In no wise can thereto aspyre,
Without the ayde of Queene desire.
  Oh mighty Cupid, Venus boy,
  Accept of mine vnfayned ioy.

She sits triumphant in her seat, [G3]
And foes with furious lookes doeth threat,
Which do blaspheme with wordes vnmild;
Against her selfe and bonny child.
  Oh mighty Cupid, Venus boy,
  Accept of mine vnfayned ioy.

A child, whose force and mighty hand,
The great God Mars could not withstand,
That burneth like a lampe of fire,
In fleeyng thoughtes wing'd with desire,
  Oh mighty Cupid, &c.

Whose shining beames doeth plainly show,
The ready way for them I trow,
For to aspyre to dignitie,
If loyall Louers they will be.
  Oh mighty Cupid, &c.

Lo, here behold the honours due,
To amorous hearts that will be true,
But who dislodgeth from his bowre,

---

title CORNELIUS] CONELIUS
2 coueteth] coueteith

Cornelius, Duke Devasco's son and the would-be lover of Verosa, sister of Moderatus, criticizes her for taking an attitude toward Cupid (i.e., love) that will reduce her to the life of a nun unless she recants; Verosa does so "rather then loose so honourable a Seruant."

Title. **CORNELIVS song.**

2 **renowmed:** renowned (variant form).

14 **Mars:** See Sonetto 21.11n.

Shall soone perceiue his rodde is sowre.
O mighty Cupid, &c.

And that he may with force confound,
Each liuing wyght that goeth on ground.
All you that doe this God despise,
Flye from his reach if you be wise.
O mighty Cupid, &c.

But he that mean'th not to disdaine,
For pleasures sake to take some paine,
Ioyne with the rest that amorous be,
And to his Court to gaine your fee.
Oh mighty Cupid, Venus boy,
Accept of mine vnfained ioy.

---

26 **rodde is sowre:** instrument (of control) becomes distasteful or distorted; "rodde" here, perhaps, carries a phallic suggestion; Gentrup (privately) suggests a reference to Cupid's arrow.

29 **goeth:** walketh.

36 **fee:** reward.

[7] Moderatus (sigs. G3^{v}–G4)
FLORIDAES song.

LAtely when Aurora drewe
Curtayne, which was darke of hewe,
Which vnspred shewed light,
That couered was by Lady nyght:
And blushingly discouered ay,
Her loues bed wherein she lay,
Then Titan lordly in his seate,
Dryed vp moysture with his heate,
And chased hath the vayle darke
Of racking clowdes for his parke:
Fishes swamme in siluer streame,
And I vnripped seame by seame.
Circumstance of natures mould,
Which rare seemed to behold.
Gazing thus with eyes of minde,
There I could nothing finde,
Which pleased not curious eye,
And therewithall I gan to spye:
Narcissus that was so fayre,

---

7 lordly in] lordly-n

Described by Parry as an "Ode" (see Posie IIII, headnote), Florida's song caps Cornelius' song.

Title. **FLORIDAES song.**

1 **Aurora:** See Posie I.3n.

3 **vnspred:** folded, drew back.

5 **ay:** ever, always.

7 **Titan lordly:** See Sonetto 13.1n.

10 **racking:** wind driven.

10 **parke:** here, apparently, used for the "earth."

12 **vnripped . . . seame:** torn apart wrinkle by wrinkle.

13 **Circumstance . . . mould:** the result of action that arises from nature's shaping hand.

19 **Narcissus:** In Greek mythology, Narcissus, a beautiful youth, fell in love with his reflection in a fountain, thinking it to be the nymph of the place; being unable to gain possession of his supposed love, he grew desperate and killed himself. His blood was turned into a flower which still bears his name.

With his golden lockes of hayre,
Which of late had scorned all,
That were bent to Cupids call,
Viewing there the water cleere,
Where his beautie did appeare,
He thought it had another beene, [G4]
Whose like before he neuer had seene.
Thinking to embrace a shade,
(That of a substance scorne had made)
He consum'd in loues desire;
Of such force is Cupids Ire,
That prepares the bed of woes,
To all such as be his foes,
And to intrap, he snares doeth lay,
Such as doe him disobey.
When I sawe his doome so dyre,
To such as despis'd his fire:
At his flame I thought to warme,
Least I catch'd the greater harme.
Then in haste I came away,
Like aspyne leafe quaking ay,
For feare of the mighty God,
That all threatned with his rod,
That euer would disloyall be,
To his Mothers progenie,
His iudgement pronounced was,
With such terrour, that alas,
I heare it sound in mine eare,
Moouing body to pale feare,
Least I should incurre his Ire,
Which might yeeld me chiefe desire.

---

28 **That . . . made:** i.e., his scorn of love (Cupid) had made a shadow appear to him as a physical body.

50 **me:** Probably a compositorial misreading of "my."

[8] Moderatus (sigs. G4v–H1)
Moderatus song.

WHen golden Titan did the Ram forsake,
And warmed the Bull with force of greater heate,
Then foorth I walked the pleasant ayre to take,
Glad when I heard the silly Lambes to bleate.
  Pleas'd to behold the stormes of winters ire,
  (With quiet calme) at last for to expire.

As thus I mused vnder the silent shade,
The chirping birdes chattering their harmonie,
Pleasant slumber my sences did inuade,
And then I heard a voyce that lowd did crie,
  Woe worth the time that I did yeeld consent,
  To lawlesse Loue, which now I do repent.

The golden shafte that pearst my panting breast,
Came from the quiuer hang'd at blind Cupids side,
Which hath so full bereaued me of rest,
And therewithall againe he lowdly cryde,
  Woe worth the time that I did yeeld consent,
  To lawlesse Loue, which now I doe repent.

Phœbus reflecting beames from polished glasse,
Yeeldes not more liuely shewes then doeth her face,
That is the cause of this my harme, alas,
Well may I say, being hopelesse in her grace,
  Woe worth the time that I did yeeld consent,
  To lawlesse Loue, which nowe I do repent.

Moderatus, after praising Florida for being "so rare [a] demonstration of an excellent Poet, and exquisite Musitian," begins his "Cansong" with "a slow and soft voyce."

Title. **Moderatus song.**

1 **When . . . forsake:** When the sun (Titan Helios) passed out of the zodiacal sign Aries.

2 **Bull:** the zodiacal sign Taurus.

13 **golden shafte:** i.e., Cupid's golden arrow. Parry explains the reference in the following poem, lines 29–36.

19 **Phœbus:** another name for Titan Helios.

Whereat I wak't, but nothing could I viewe,
Which made me thinke a vision it should be,
And straight I rose to see what would ensue,
And then a nouell strange appeared to me,
  A frozen man being in a fierie flame,
  Another fryed in frost, (woe worth the same.)

Afore I could the meaning vnderstand, [H1]
This strange Aenigma vanished quite away,
Whereat amazed much I then did stand,
Thinking that wofull wyght did lately say,
  Wo worth the time that I did yeeld consent,
  To lawlesse Loue which nowe I doe repent.

28 **nouell:** novelty.

[9] Moderatus (sigs. H1^{v}–H3)

WHen Flora flourished in her prime,
bedeckt with gallant greene:
Had ouerspred the subtill soyle,
most liuely to be seene.

No wit could chuse but wonder much,
to see such gallant Dame,
Attyred so gay with Maiestie,
belonging to the same.

She trac'd abroad with pompous pace,
and troupes of royall trayne,
Both male and female followed her,
the Prince and Country-swaine.

Each one so placed in his degree,
as best did fitte his state,
Some pleased with his happy chance,
some cursed his frowning fate.

Before her went, but dare I speake,
what there I did beholde:
A Princely youth, a mighty King,
a God both stout and bolde.

His amber lockes so gaily twyn'd
like crysped wyers of golde,
His beauty so rauished my wittes,
I can it not vnfold.

---

21 lockes] lookes

Before Pandarina, whose turn is next, offers her song, she criticizes Moderatus' song, saying, "you began so poeticall, persisted so musicall, and ended so sophisticall." Florida defends Moderatus with whom she has fallen in love (unreturned by Moderatus). Pandarina had described Moderatus' attitude to love: "your darke description therof made mee thus much to descant."

1 **Flora:** See Sonetto 11.2n.

3 **subtill:** finely textured.

21 **lockes:** hair. *Q*'s "lookes" is an obvious misreading.

In one hand he did beare a bowe,
  the other carryed fire:
Which would consume the stubburne sorte,
  that seru'd not Queene desire.

And at his side a quiuer did hang, [H2]
  wherein was arrowes twaine:
The one with golde full finely typt,
  that Louers vse to paine.

The other leaden headed was,
  which makes disdayne in heart:
Who so is towch'd with this, of Loue
  shall neuer feele the smart.

He winges did beare, in token that
  who did his fauour require:
That he should beare aspyring minde,
  and wing'd with high desire.

But last, which doeth not payne me least,
  the worlde to him was darke:
He could not see to giue to each,
  according to desart.

Thus marched Flora in her pompe,
  chiefe Actrix of the game,
And ministred matter to the rest,
  delighting in the same.

She is the frute of pleasant Ver,
  most liuely to be seene:
Which glads the hearts of youthfull wyghts,
  and beautifies the greene.

She matter yeeldes to Cupids mates,
  for to effect their ioy:

30–36 arrowes . . . smart: On Cupid's golden and leaden arrows, see Ovid, I.470–6.
46 **Actrix:** this form of "actress" is not recorded in *OED*.
48 **same:** i.e., "the game."
49 **Ver:** spring.
53 **Cupids mates:** i.e., lovers struck by Cupid's golden arrow.

And he delightes within her bower,
her company to enioy.

This vnitie betweene these twaine, [H2v]
did boyle the feruent mynde,
And made each liuing thing to cleaue
by Nature to his kynde.

The God of Loue did fancy force,
and Flora frute did yeelde,
Conuenient to effect the same,
twixt pleasant groues in fielde.

Wherefore by heapes the Amorous troupes,
resorted to the place:
And followed still this Princely crew,
their pleasures to embrace.

Whose Maiesty when I beheld;
and stately countenance,
Not Mars in field seemed so stout,
with warlike bloody launce.

For presently he vaunc'd him selfe,
vnto a stately throne,
More gorgeously then euer was wrought,
in timber or in stone.

It was emboss'd with bordering bowes,
and brancht with knots of greene,
No wyght by arte could frame the lyke,
but flourishing Flora Queene.

About this seate where Cupid sate,
the chyrping byrdes did sing,
And his Venerian Clyents eke,
a dolefull knell did ring.

---

55 **he:** i.e., Cupid.
61 **fancy:** love.
63 **same:** i.e., "fancy" and "frute."
73 **vaunc'd:** aphetic form of "advance."
77 **emboss'd:** ornamented.

Some merrily did laugh and sport,
possessing heartes desire.
And others cryed for equity, [H3v]
being skorched with his fire.

This Chaos of confused sport,
did make me much to muse,
If that I should this God adore,
or so to doe refuse.

As thus I stood, not yet resolu'd
what course therein to take,
I had a summons to his Court,
my fealty to make.

Then did I seeke to wrest by force,
his will for to withstand,
All that I could, I striu'd: yet was
to weake my faynting hand.

Loe I which erst their follyes blam'd,
am now perforce constrain'd,
To yeeld obeysance at his barre,
which late the same disdain'd.

Wherefore I burne, and so must all
that dallieth with the flame,
Euen as the Flie turning about,
is perished in the same.

83 **Venerian Clyents eke:** Venus' patrons or customers also.

103 **barre:** tribunal

[10] Moderatus (sigs. H3^v–H4) *PRISCVS song.*

WHen Titan gan the Crancke for to ascend,
And touch'd the point ecliptike in the skie,
Each thing on earth did then him selfe defend:
Euen from his parching beames, that did welnye
  Consume all things, (with violent force of heate,)
  That walkt abroad in this terrestriall seate.

Princes did keepe within their princely bowres,
With bowes of greene their chambers hanged were.
Wherein they dallied with their paramours:
The windes lay silent in their concaue sphere.
  All sought that night (at pleasure) take their ease,
  Of raging heate the furie to appease.

The sillie swaynes (wo's me, the sillie swaynes)
Vnder a Pine in silent shade did rest,
Ah rest, which restlesse still my poore heart paynes,
Wherewith euen now my carkasse is opprest:
  Vnwitting then their secrets I ouer-hard,
  To what I did not taking good regard.

It was the great God Pans festiuall day,
When shepheards quaint do plod it with their kinde,

---

13 swaynes] swayues
17 secrets] seerets(?)

Priscus, whose turn is next, having been "once almost a sworne foe to Cupid and his Lawes," says that Pandarina's song "hath nowe altogether reclaymed me from mine errour, . . . wholly recanting mine heresie."

Title. **PRISCVS song.**

1 **Crancke:** winding path.
2 **point ecliptike:** high point or moment of eclipse.
10 **concaue sphere:** the so-called "cave of the winds" in which Neptune could imprison them.
18 **To . . . regard:** i.e., not giving proper consideration to what I was doing.
19 **Pans:** Pan was the god of shepherds, huntsmen, and all inhabitants of the countryside.
20 **quaint . . . kinde:** dressed in their best do trudge on this festival day along with their usual companions.

Of rusticke pipes they made a consort gay,
To honour Pan each sport they cald to minde:
Thus they did banket with their musicke rude,
When to the same my selfe I did intrude.

Where when I did intrude, my heart I pawn'd,
For floating fame did fill mine eares with praise,
Of Venus peere, whose becke is a commaund,
And then desire that is a spurre alwayes
(So fortune would) did pricke my wounded minde,
(But in her sight) that no where ease I finde.

A combat straight within my selfe arose, [H4]
Of that I should yeeld vnto Queene desire,
Knowing that fame is partiall as she goes,
So I might fall in seeking to aspire,
Then Ladie Loue said that I must obey,
Which sentence past, I durst not make delay,

Fortune thus fram'd the plot to mine annoy,
Fame blew the coales to kindle my desire,
Loue did command I should no rest enioy,
Till I were clens'd in Cupids purging fire,
Thus I doe range to seeke a remedie,
And though I liue, yet liuing daily dye.

Seing Fame of beauties pride could me enforce,
What maruell is't if beauty it selfe could moue?
But oh that beautie had not some remorce,
To yeeld me due, that feruently do loue,
Or at the least to pitie mine estate,
And not for loue to yeeld me deadly hate.

The God is blinde that workes this mysterie,
And doeth not worke according to desart,

---

23 **banket:** banquet (variant form).
32 **Of . . . should:** concerning whether or not I should.
33 **fame:** public report.
43 **beauties pride:** beauty's flower or best.
45 **But . . . remorce:** But, oh, that (very) beauty had not any compassion.
46 **To . . . due:** to give me what was due to me. *Q*'s "me" may be a misreading of "my."

But yet I yeeld me to his Maiestie,
In hope at last he will regard my smart.
In the meane time I banish quite despaire,
Expecting him my wracke for to repaire.

Repaire if that he will, long may he raigne,
Triumphing wise to gouerne both Gods and men,
If otherwise I can not griefe refraine,
But must seeke out a darke and dolefull den,
In deserts wilde to end my dismall dayes,
And Hermyte-like on rootes to liue alwayes.

[11] Moderatus (sigs. L2v–L3)

THe fluent streame that leades a swelling tyde,
When Aquilon the raging waues doeth reare,
Bounce not more oft vpon their bankes so wyde,
That with their force the stony rockes doe teare.
  Then panting doeth my heart her prison walles,
  Iumpe oft against, and iumping sudden falles.

The little current stealing through the vale, [L3]
Being stopt in course aboue her banke doeth swell:
So stealing loue suprest, doeth make me pale,
For why, in thought I feele a present hell.
  Thou maist direct the streame her course to keepe,
  And free my heart that lyeth in prison deepe.

The little shrubbes in downes stirre not at all,
And meane mens thoughts are seldom sauc'd with care,
When mightie Cedars shakt with windes do fall,
And noble mindes on chaunces hard do fare.
  Loue lookes not lowe on Idiots rustie ragges,
  Nor cares not much for Marchants welthy bagges.

But Loue (as Iuy claspes the tree) takes holde,
On vertue, which is seated in the minde,
And eke on Beautie pleasant to beholde,
Neuer hoping for a better hap to finde,
  Then for to yeeld when heart on hope is paund,
  And to obey when honour doth commaund.

As Priscus' friends conclude their visit to his sick-bed, Cornelius, Duke Devasco's son, who is in love with Verosa, Moderatus' sister, slips her a copy of the following love poem. After reading it, Verosa "began to feele her heart warmed, with a secret and priuie flame that lay wrapped in her bosome."

2 **Aquilon:** the north-east wind.

5 **panting . . . heart:** See Sonetto 9.9n.

17 **Loue . . . ragges:** i.e., Love does not stoop to concern itself with a clown in his rude rags (as "shrubbes" are not affected by the wind).

Your beautie sweete did claspe my tender breast,
My heart is paund your heast for to fulfill,
Loue in my secret thought hath built his nest,
Honour commaunds I must perfourme his will:
  Wherefore within your orient beauty faire,
  Doeth wholly rest my wracke for to repaire.

26 **My . . . fulfill:** My heart is pawned in order to fulfill your command.

[12] Moderatus (sigs. M2–M2^{v})

THe vaine delightes that please the curious eye,
By proofe I finde to turne vnto their paine,
Such obiectes rare do darke the sence: for why,
The beames thereof reflecting, pierce againe
With double force the faithfull Louers brest,
Vntill by stealth it robbes his quiet rest.

The pinching paine that doeth torment the minde,
Is more increas'd by glauncing of the eye,
Which can no where a quiet harbour finde,
But in the heart, such is his vrgent might.
The vertue then of a light rowling looke,
Vnder a baite doeth hide a hydeous hooke.

Like Iett attractiue, and like pearcing steele,
The heauiest things vnto it selfe it drawes,
Nothing so hard, but yeeldes: wherefore I feele
My heart is drawen vnto his proscript Lawes,
And pearced eke by force of subtill sight,
Wherefore I yeeld vnto his lawlesse might.

His might hath captiue tane my pensiue heart,
His might hath made my hauty brest to bend,
His might hath turned my iesting vnto smart,
His might enforst me scalding sighes to send
From skorched brest, where carefull thoughtes enioy
Hope of nought els, but liuing in annoy.

---

9 harbour] habour

Priscus, who, as we have seen, became ill when he was repulsed by Florida, is now visited by the ladies, among them Florida, whose disdain of Priscus has softened and who arranges a tryst with him for the following day in the private garden where he had first seen her. There, waiting for Florida, he falls asleep; when Florida comes, she sings the following song to the sleeping Priscus.

9 **harbour:** Probably a variant spelling of "arbor." *Q*'s "habour" is a compositional error.

13 **Iett attractiue:** Jet, when rubbed, exercised some magnetic force, attracting light objects; Parry, however, says it, like magnetized steel, draws the "heauiest things."

17 **subtill:** penetrating, keen.

When brutish beastes doe chew their cuddes in shade, [M2v]
Nought doe they care for barren winters foode,
Who knew but shallow foords, feares not to wade:
Euen so each louer in his merrie moode,
  (When fortune smiles and holdes him in her lappe)
  Thinkes not this calme doeth breede an after-clappe.

30 **after-clappe:** unexpected, surprising, unhappy result.

[13] Moderatus (sigs. M2^{v}–M3)

IF wearie sleepelesse rest
In nightes doe argue care,
And dayes with dole opprest
To them that louers are:
Then watchfull cares that with my cholour grew,
To heate extreme shall prooue me louer true.

Mee louer true, then trueth
Deserueth trust I trow,
Which motiue is too ruthe
In such as grace doeth grow.
No pittie then without desert I craue:
For what I bought I merited to haue.

To haue what faith may reape,
And loyall loue obtaine,
I ought to haue like cheape,
As I doe sell againe.
With loyaltie I purchase all my loue,
God graunt againe that others faithfull prooue.

If faithfull others prooue,
I prize my paine for nought,
If tryed trueth may mooue,
I haue the thing I sought.
If neither may take place, I pine with woe, [M3]
Dye had I leuer, then liue and liuing so.

---

5 cholour] colour

Being awakened by Florida's "Dittie," and delighted by what he has heard, Priscus immediately "pay[s] her her debt in the same coyne."

5 **cholour:** choler.
8 **trow:** believe.
9 **motiue . . . ruthe:** course of action is too compassionate or ruthful. *OED* does not record an adjectival use of "ruth"; the Scottish "routh" (=abundant, plentiful) only appears in English usage in 1791.
10 **grace doeth grow:** grow in attractiveness. The sense of lines 9–10 is unclear.
12 **bought:** (1) exchanged; (2) paid for.
15 **like cheape:** at a low price or bargain rate.
16 **As . . . againe:** were I to sell again. The meaning is again unclear in context.
24 **leuer:** rather.

[14] Moderatus (sig. O1)

None may this sharpe and cutting sword vncase,
But to redeeme the daughter of a King:
Nor any Knight this Armour bright vnlace,
Nor of his vertue bragge in any thing:
But he therewith that shall a Tigre tame,
For to defend a princely virgins name.

Moderatus has set out on his self-imposed "exile," which he had undertaken to remove himself from the court in order to give his friend Priscus a clear field in his wooing of Florida, Duke Devasco's daughter, who, unfortunately, had fallen deeply in love with Moderatus. He meets an old hermit from whom he learns of the false charge of sexual impropriety brought against Modesta, the daughter of King Lothus, by Count Delamure in revenge for her rejection of his marriage suit. The penalty is death, but King Lothus for love of his daughter allows a three-month period during which a champion may appear, who, by defeating Count Delamure in single combat, will prove Modesta's innocence. Moderatus at once determines to act as her champion. Being now without horse or armor, he is led by the hermit to a pine tree, on which a suit of black armor is hanging. In the bark of the pine, Moderatus discovers a "poesie" engraved that describes under what circumstances and by whom the armor, which is enchanted, may be worn. Recognizing that he and the occasion both meet the terms called for, Moderatus "dissolue[s] that inchauntment," takes the armor, and dons it; "in the place where [the pine tree] had bene appeared a very faire horse wel and richly furnished." Moderatus thus becomes the Black Knight, a disguise that conceals his true identity.

[15] Moderatus (sig. P3)

THe Ocean seas for euery calme present
A thousand stormes: so howerly doeth my minde,
While that I doe excogitate the euent
Of things, wherein great mysterie I finde.
With paine I prooue a treble dammage losse,
Sith Fate my heart in waues of griefe doeth tosse.

The wonder late I sawe, wherein I thought
A strange and rare effect for to containe,
Was, when I view'd your face, which in me wrought
Such deepe desire euer yours for to remaine.
That when I finde that hope forbids to prooue,
To seeke redresse, I languish for your loue.

But froward Fate too cruell dealt with me,
To ruminate vnto mine eares your fame:
Yet glad thereby that you redeemed be,
Though I do pine when thoughtes present your name.
In that I can not still possesse the sight
Of your sweete selfe, that sole may me delight.

Moderatus composed and sent this "fancie" to Modesta, whose honor he had vindicated by defeating Count Delamure, her false accuser, in single combat, by his squire, Perio, asking him to tell her that he would become a hermit unless she would grant him her favor.

3 **excogitate the euent:** think out the outcome.

11–12 **hope . . . redresse:** Hope forbids me to demand the truth by seeking compensation (for my sufferings).

14 **ruminate:** *OED* offers no meaning of "ruminate" that fits the context. Parry seems to associate the word with the verb "rumor" (i.e., circulate rumors).

15 **you redeemed be:** i.e., you have fulfilled your promise.

[16] Moderatus (sig. P4^{v})

HOw can I sing, and haue no ioy in heart,
In heart no ioy, a heauy dolefull iest.
A iest, God wote: that still procures my smart,
A cruell smart that breedeth mine vnrest.
Shall I then sing, and can not iest nor ioy,
Nay rather weepe thus liuing in annoy.

Why should I weepe, or heauie lot bewayle?
Why should I sobbe, and sigh with sobbing care?
For herein teares, sighes, nor sobbes can preuaile,
But hope may helpe to rid me from this snare.
The valiant minde condemnes such trifling toyes,
Though cruell loue bereaue his wished ioyes.

O balefull ioy reioysing in the sight
Of beauties flowre, a flowre like Cockeatrice.
Whose view doeth pearce the man of greatest might,
And doeth subuert the reason of the wise.
Such was the sight that did inthrawle my sight,
Such was the spight that wrought me deepe despight.

Haue I then pawn'd my credite to this end?
Haue I my life in ballance put therefore,
Her life to saue and credite to defend,
And brought my life to thraldome for euermore.
And may not hope this curtesie to haue,
Euen at her handes, her champions life to saue.

Moderatus, tortured by his growing love for Modesta, of whose equal love for him he is as yet ignorant, "warbled out this ensuing Dittie."

2 **iest:** mockery, joke.

14 **Cockeatrice:** a serpent or basilisk which was fabled to kill with a single glance (="view" in line 15).

20 **in ballance:** at risk.

23 **may . . . haue:** may not hope to have this favor or indulgence.

Despaire not man, thou hast not tryed her truth,
Doubt not before that she an answer giue,
Seeke first for fauour, women be full of ruth,
Though she denie, let no deniall grieue.
  Women will say, and will vnsay againe,
  And oft refuse the thing they would obtaine.

---

26 **Doubt . . . giue:** Don't doubt her (feelings) before she gives an answer.

30 **oft . . . obtaine:** Cf. the proverb, also applied to women: "Say no and take it."

[17] Moderatus (sig. S1)

HAue heauens conspired my balefull destinie?
Haue fates decreed my thraldome to prolong?
Will Mersa at all rue on my miserie?
Or shall I euer continue in this wrong?
  Woe worth the houre, wherein thou hast bene borne:
  Despayring thus like to a man forlorne.

Forlorne: for that thou darest not sue for grace
Of her, who sits like Iuno in her throne,
Driuing the lookers on into a maze,
To whom in vaine I daily make my mone.
  Yet at her handes no hope of grace I finde,
  That still torments my poore perplexed minde.

Liue long thou tree, wherein these lines I graue,
And witnesse beare of this my loyaltie,
And how I seeke of her some fauour t'haue,
Whose heart is framed in forge of crueltie:
  Then shall I liue though dead I be in graue,
  With louers true, and challenge place to haue.

---

12 minde] my minde

Priscus discovers some verses "ingraued in the barke of a tall Beeche tree" written either by Hymon or Philetas, "two louing swaynes [shepherds] that contended for Mersa [a beautiful shepherdess]."

1 **balefull:** unhappy.
2 **fates:** See Passion VII.9n.
3 **rue on:** take pity on.
5 **Woe worth:** may evil befall or light upon.
12 **my poore . . . minde:** Q's repetition of "my" following "perplexed" is both syntactically and metrically superfluous.
18 **challenge . . . haue:** i.e., lay claim to have my place (in the annals) of "louers true."

[18] Moderatus (sig. S1v)

WHat rare desart hath moou'd my mind
  to follow fond desire?
What fate so fell hath fram'd my fall?
  What fortune did conspire?

What platt was laid? what time doth worke
  to aggrauate the same?
What daunger thereof doth ensue,
  I attribute to fame.

For had not fame a blabbe bene found,
  for to extoll her praise,
That is the causer of my payne,
  then Mersas oft delayes

Had neuer disturb'd my quiet rest,
  for I my flocke had fed,
When I for ease, and they for food
  had better farre bin sped.

Priscus discovers a second poem addressed to Mersa "written on a Poplar."

5 **platt:** plot, conspiracy.

6 **aggrauate the same:** worsen the effect of (the "platt").

10 **for to extoll:** to magnify.

12 **oft delayes:** "delayes" is a noun meaning frequent hesitations (to reciprocate my love).

[19] Moderatus (sigs. S2–S3)

BY Vestaes tapers, and her holy fire,
By all her troupe of sacred Virgins kind,
Which vowed are to pure and chaste desire,
By Cybil's wise and sage presaging wind,
    Which turne her ordered leaues (as is decreed
    By heauenly powers) to good or bad with speed.

By Siluan Nimphes, oft troubled with great feare
In shunning of Siluanus raging lust,
Who still their flaring haires with griefe do teare,
Least rapes they be vnto this god vniust,
    Whose horned shape their dammage will procure,
    If he them winne to cease vpon his lure.

By the great care of Daphne, flying fast
From the pursuit of Bacchus hote desire,
Whose burning flames hath made the Nimph agast:

---

4 Cybil's] Cybll's

Priscus, hoping to catch a sight of the beautiful (and learned!) Mersa, overhears her singing "this Cansong following."

1–2 **BY . . . kind:** Vesta (Greek: Hestia) was goddess of the hearth and family; her holy fire (her symbol), said to have been carried to Italy by Aeneas, was watched over by six virgins belonging to her order in her temple in the Roman Forum.

4–5 **Cybil's . . . leaues:** The Delphic Sibyl, the best known of the ten Sibyllae, sometimes delivered her Apollo-induced oracles written on the leaves of trees blown thither by a kind of messenger wind.

7 **Siluan Nimphes:** Wood nymphs were semi-divine beings (female) who presided over rivers, woods, fountains, etc.

8 **Siluanus raging lust:** Silvanus was worshipped as the god who protected the woods, fields, herds, etc. He is often, as here, confounded with satyrs, who, like Silvanus, were half man (horned) and half goat, and were often represented as types of lustfulness.

10 **rapes:** persons to be raped.

12 **cease . . . lure:** seize upon or fall for his (1) trap, snare, (2) enticement.

13 **Daphne:** the beloved of Phoebus Apollo, who had been struck by Cupid's golden arrow, but Cupid struck Daphne with his leaden arrow (to punish Apollo), making her impervious to love; chased by Apollo, she flees and is turned into a laurel or bay tree (see Ovid, I.452–65). Parry appears to have substituted Bacchus for Apollo.

To turne whose shape the gods did then conspire,
To a Bay tree, which lasteth to her fame, [S2v]
And euer groweth greene in honour of her name.

By Procris rage and byting ielousie,
When by the same her death she did sustaine,
By all the rites of pure virginitie,
And by Dianaes chaste and holy traine
I sweare, (and that vnuiolate shall rest,
What euer mishappe or fortune me molest)

That first from Pontus waues, where Isters fall
In braunches seuen is to the raging sea,
Each one of these returne their courses shall,
And backewardes shape the same without delay
(Against the course and force of Natures seede)
To seeke the spring from whence they did proceed.

Before that Mersa mooued with fancies forme,
Shall make a shipwracke of her honestie,
I rather leaue the sicker Swaines to storme,
Then I should feele of loue the tyrannie.
I know not what it is, nor dare not prooue,
Who tryed may say: no heate to heate of loue.

---

19 **Procris:** the wife of Cephelus; she thought that her husband was being unfaithful when she heard him lovingly addressing Aura, his name for the cooling morning breeze. Procris, believing Aura to be the name of a nymph, cried out and Cephelus, thinking this noise to come from some wild beast, cast his javelin in the direction of the sound and killed his beloved wife.

22 **Dianaes:** Diana was the sister of Apollo, goddess of the hunt, a virgin and sacred to virgins.

25 **Pontus:** Pontus Maximus, the early classical name for the Black Sea.

25 **Isters fall:** Ister was the Latin name for the Danube.

29 **Natures seede:** natural growth.

31 **Before . . . forme:** before Mersa, excited by the (mental) image of amorous desire.

33 **sicker:** free from the danger (arising from giving in to amorous desire).

33 **storme:** complain loudly (about unrequited love).

34 **Then:** than that.

36 **Who tryed:** i.e., those who have experienced (love).

Although that Nictinen in raging wise,
Pearst with the shaft of the blind wanton boye,
Paid for her lust after too deare a price:
Yet meane I not so wantonly to toye.
I loue no Owles, nor yet their Musicke hoarce:
From such fond loues, I meane to make deuorce.

I like not Venus wanton toying trickes,
With Adon sweete her louing heart and ioy:
I loue not them whome fond desire still prickes,
Nor yet these simpring Dames that be so coy.
I hate their lust, I banish their desire, [S3]
I will not warme by their fond fancies fire.

No shapes transform'd to gold, to Swan, or Bull,
Shall pierce the fort of Mersas constant thought,
Nor euer my minde in follyes cradle lull
Such vaine delightes, I count them all for nought.
If euer I loue, I will not loue in haste,
Who seekes me so, in vaine his toyle doeth waste.

If ought may mooue my minde to stoope to loue,
Vertue thereof shall sure the conquest make:
No light desire veneriall actes to prooue,
Ne any thing my settled minde shall shake.
But tract of time by due desart me leade,
For more then this it booteth not to pleade.

---

54 waste.] waste

---

37 **Nictinen:** Nyctimene was the daughter of Nycteus who disgraced herself by tricking her father into committing incest with her: she was changed into an owl (see line 41) by Minerva just as her father, outraged by her deception, was attempting to stab her.

44 **Adon:** See Posie I.17n.

46 **coy:** disdainful.

48 **warme . . . fire:** warm myself by the hot desire of their foolish notions or whims.

49 **transform'd . . . Bull:** i.e., disguises adopted by Zeus (Roman: Jupiter) for his various amorous seductions.

58 **Ne:** nor.

59 **But tract of:** unless in the course of.

60 **booteth:** availeth.

[20] Moderatus (sigs. S4–T2)
HYMONS Song.

THou Hebe sweet which in the heauens doest stay,
And to the gods doest heauenly Manna bring,
Fly from the skyes, packe hence with speed away:
In earth below there is a fairer thing,
A Nymph it is, the fayrest of all fayre,
Who (thou being gone) must where thou art repayre.

For Iupiter being moou'd with her good grace,
Will thee despise, and her in stead prefer:
With enuie burst to be in such disgrace,
And dye for griefe. The goddes sometimes do erre,
Sith they so fickle seeme, and chuse to change,
When fancie stirres their wauering mindes to range.

Depart not yet, from heauen thou shalt not wend,
Vse diligence the goddes againe to please.
Let Mersa rest: sweet Mersa on earth attend,
My troubled thoughtes and pensiue cares to ease.
Without whose grace nothing can pleasant be,
Nor ought remaine a hearts rest vnto me.

How oft tuckt vp like Amazonian Dame,
With bowe and quiuer tracing these groues among,
Following the Deare, or els some other game,
And killing oft the fayrest in the throng.
The goddes them-selues being mooued with her loue,
To winne the same in vaine full oft did prooue.

---

13 Depart] Depatt

Sung by Hymon, one of Mersa's "two louing swaynes," at the request of Moderatus.

Title. **HYMONS Song.**

1 **Hebe:** Greek goddess of the spring and youth and cup-bearer to Zeus until she was displaced by Ganymede.

2 **Manna:** divinely supplied, spiritual sustenance.

5 **Nymph:** i.e., Mersa.

7 **grace:** charm, attractiveness.

12 **fancie:** caprice.

17 **grace:** favor.

They proffer kisses sweet and giftes in vaine, [S4v]
They garlands make of choyce and finest flowers,
They bring her fruit, but nought of her they gaine,
They smyle and sing, she looketh coy and lowres.
  Full of disdaine her tramels she doth shake,
  Which makes the stowtest of vs all to quake.

O would she were not so hard to be pleas'd,
O would she shewed more gentle fauour to me,
Happier then I, could nothing then be prais'd,
But she reiect'th my louing lasse to be.
  She doth despise my prayers, and griefs disdaynes,
  She flies from me, which still my poore heart paynes.

O Mersa stay, flye not so fast from me,
Faire Mersa stay, no Lestrigonian bruit,
Doth make pursuit to feed his lust on thee:
But one, if thou him knew, whose honest suit,
  Is worthy of the same he doth desire,
  And burnes for thee with chast and holy fire

And though my corps doth sauage seeme with haire,
And beard vnkempt an vgly thing to see:
Yet am not I deform'd, for beard is faire,
And hayres decent for such as valiant be.
  When strong men fight nyce meacocks they do feare,
  And Schools to daunce, and not to fence they reare.

If ought for wealth thou likest, a shepheards stocke
I haue, and few doth more then I possesse:
For heards I keepe, and eake full many a flocke,
A thousand kine do feed on finest grasse,
  Of swine great store, and cattell fat withall,
  And goates in rockes their bleating kiddes to call.

---

28 **coy and lowres:** disdainful and looks angry.

29 **tramels:** braids of hair.

38 **Lestrigonian bruit:** cannibalizing monster. *OED* does not record any adjectival use of "Lestrigonian."

47 **nyce . . . feare:** they terrify tender weaklings.

52 **kine:** cows.

Store of throme milke in season still I haue,
My chest is full of cheeses new and olde, [T]
Take what thou wilt, thou need'st not ought to craue,
For all I haue is thine, whereof be bolde.
  My selfe also (though thou the same refuse)
  Is at thy becke, thereof to take the vse.

If thou would'st daine to walke sometimes with me,
Gather I would the Apples mellowe fine,
And clustring grapes with full ripe figges for thee,
And Filberds kernels eake if thou were mine:
  With these I would thee cramme my prettie peate,
  For whome great store of bloody droppes I sweate.

Howe oft would I thy tender corpes then clippe,
And eke the same in folded armes combine,
With thousand kisses would I presse thy lippe:
Doubt not of these: to pittie eke incline,
  And come with me (least that my paine increase)
  To cure my care, and thraldome to release.

By pleasant springs our ease then we will take,
Embracing there sweete sleepe will vs depriue
Of wanton sport: when semblance we do make,
Not howe with gaine and lucre for to thriue,
  (In silent shades) but of meane mirth and ioye,
  When greatest minde we haue to wanton toye.

The hanging boughes and murmuring streame will striue,
Who best may please and worke our sweete content,
While raging force of Summers heate doeth driue.
Howe deare to me would be thy sweet consent?
  Alas thou nought doest weigh my giftes, nor loue,
  Whose heart faire speach, nor weeping teares may mooue.

---

55 **throme milke:** meaning uncertain; see *English Dialect Dictionary* under "thrum"= strong, healthy milk.

67 **clippe:** embrace.

68 **combine:** couple.

75 **semblance . . . make:** we make an (amorous) image or appearance.

77 **meane:** moderate.

78 **wanton toye:** play wantonly.

More cruell then the Hircan Tigre fierce,
More deafe then th'Images of Marble made,
More hard than stones that engines none can pierce, [T1v]
Art thou: in fine whose beautie sure will fade.
  Though nature did the same to thee ordaine,
  But not true Louers sute for to disdaine.

So vnder freshest flowers the Adder lay,
So Hyble hath honie commixt with galle:
Trust not to forme, which with ripe flowers decay,
Forsake thy pride, for pride wil haue a fall.
  And while the same in prime doth flourish most,
  Loose not the time in vaine, thou crau'st being lost.

Vse thy good giftes while thou hast time (each thing
By reason of his vse commended is)
For withered age deformity will bring,
Too late thou wailest when thou doest find the mis
  Of thy faire face, to wrinkled furrowes turnde,
  And thy bright hew with Phœbus beames being burnde.

How oft in glasse wilt thou behold the same,
And then condemne the follie of thy youth:
That would not hunt, while time affoorded game,
Then shalt thou find the prouerb old a truth,
  Which euer was, is, and so will be alwayes,
  That time and tyde for no mans pleasure stayes.

But why poure I my plaintes vnto the wind?
Why doe I throwe my seed to barren sande?
I striue in vaine, of fate some fauor to find,
That cruel is my hap for to withstand
  Fate, more than gold or gentry doth loue haile,
  This scornes the Prince, when subiects do preuaile.

---

85 **Hircan Tigre:** Hyrcania, a country in Asia, was famous for a variety of wild beasts.
88 **in fine:** in the end, finally.
90 **But . . . disdaine:** but (did not ordain) that true lovers should be disdained.
92 **Hyble:** See Posie I.43n.
93 **forme:** bodily appearance (i.e., "in prime," line 95).
100 **mis:** privation.
109 **vnto:** Parry frequently uses "unto" where we would expect "into."
112–13 **That . . . Fate:** So that it is my painful lot (always) to offer resistance to destiny.

And though more fyence then serpent thou be set,
Me to annoy that am thy carefull thrall:
For with thy frownes my inward soule doth fret,
Yet will I wait, and eke attend thy call, [T2]
  And loue thee still, which in my heart shalt rest,
  For Mersa alone in mind and mouth is prest.

---

115 **though . . . set:** The meaning of "fyence" is uncertain. J. J. M. Tobin suggests (privately) that "fyence" is a compositorial reading of "syence" (i.e., "science" meaning "wisdom") and that the line may be read as meaning: "Though (with) more wisdom than the serpent, thou art ordained (to be odious to me)." The obvious meaning of "fyence" is, of course, "fiance" (an aphetic form of "affiance" meaning "trust" or "confidence" that does not fit the context); reading "syence," however, seems to be supported by its apparent reference to Genesis 3:1. Gentrup (privately) suggests reading "fyerce," metrically an easier reading.

115 **be set:** beset.

116 **carefull thrall:** captive full of sorrow.

118 **eke attend:** in addition wait for.

120 **in . . . prest:** in thinking and speaking is ready.

[21] Moderatus (sigs. T2–T2^{v})
PHILETAS song.

MErsa, more white than flowre, or new burnt lime,
Or raging salt-sea fome, or milke reboylde:
More red than Cheries, ripe by force of time,
Or Beries yet with taint of blacke not soyld:
  More faire than flowring trees in spring of yeare,
  More sweete than figges, that new and ripe appeare.

Such pappes had Venus none, such rolling eyes,
Such cherrie lips, both sweet and fine in tutch:
Why should I praise her soft and wel made thyes,
For better were to feel than talke of such.
  Both Goddes and men therewith enamoured be,
  For with mine eies a Satyre I did see,

Pursuing her, whom tane, he forste to yeeld,
Shee clamor made, then aide I would haue brought,
But to defend my selfe I had no sheeld,
Against his force, that with his hornes me sought,
  Of such a Riuall fierce I durst not proue,
  The mighty force, though pining for her loue.

Oh then how oft with signes she beckt at me, [T2^{v}]
And when I came me clipt in tender sort,
Euen as the vine or Iuie claspes the tree,
And wanton-like did bite my lippe in sport,
  And flapt me on the mouth with decent grace,
  Firme vowing then none other to embrace.

---

17 durst] dnrst
21 Iuie] luie

Philetas, Mersa's other principal suitor, "was a bonier swaine, and more quaint than all the rest [including Hymon], & therfore [ironically] was more in countenance fauoured of Mersa"; he now offers his rather peculiar love song.

Title. **PHILETAS song.**

17 **proue:** test, make trial of.

23 **decent grace:** suitably proper or refined action or becomingness.

But what alas all this is now forgot,
And she againe recouered libertie,
I seem'd then fine, but now a foolish sot:
For that she weighes none of my miserie.
  To serue her turne my seruice could her please,
  But nought at all my bondage to release.

---

29 **seruice:** i.e., his love's devotion.

[22] Moderatus (sig. U3[v])

WHat fancies foule doth sillie maydes entise,
To like and loue the false and flattering wight,
What Viper would the selfe same thing dispise,
Which erst he sought with all his force and might:
But fond I was, and fickle his desire,
Like bauens blaze, that soone was set on fire.

Such fire it was that wrought my deep annoy,
Such foole I was, that credulous would proue:
And trust repose, in him that did but toy,
And full of lust would counterfeit some loue.
Loe to my care with griefe of heart I find,
His flattering words, which were but blasts of wind.

What Cockatrice, so pleasant once could smile,
And couer fraud with such a glorious baite:
Who would haue thought such beautie couered guile,
But Fowlers still their snares being laid, do wait,
And counterfeit, the sillie birds to trap,
So did this wretch, the more is my ill hap.

"[T]his ensuing fancie" is sung by Verosa, sister of Moderatus; she claims that Cornelius, Duke Devasco's son, has been unfaithful to his declared love for her and has deserted her, now preferring her cousin, Bysantia. In the end, Verosa marries Priscus, Moderatus' devoted friend.

6 **bauens:** bundles of brushwood bound with a single withe (twig).

9 **trust repose:** trusting him as a center of stability (i.e., constancy).

13 **Cockatrice:** See *Moderatus*, No. 16.14.

14 **glorious:** luring (i.e., tempting).

Appendix: Selections from Robert Parry's Manuscript Diary

MS Diary, 18-19

A true declaracõn of the sicknes last wordes & death of the kinge of Spaine Philipe the seconde of that name whoe died in his Abbey of St Lawrence at Escuriall seven myles from Madrid 13 of September 1598
Wrtyyen in a Spanishe l'tre & trulie translated.

To satisfie my promys, and to geve answer to you^{r} l'res requiringe my advertisment of thes p*re*sent occurrents; I pray you^{r} understande, that this yere 1598 The Royall ma^{tie} of of [*sic*] our Lord Don Phylip the thyrd, beinge then but Prince was vpon St Iohns daye, in the markett place at Madrid to behould the Bull baytinges & other pastimes wch weare there[.] At wch sportes the kinge his father (wch is nowe in heaven) was not p*re*sent by reason of the payne of the gout wch sore troblyd hym. his heighnes beinge retorned fro*m* the foresayde place descoursed vnto his father, all that he had seene, wheare vpon his ma^{tie} Answered, I am right glad to see thee so plesant, for thou shallt neu*er* so longe as I lyve see me have any ease or confort in this paynfull desease. And there vpon commaunded p*re*paracõn to be made for his removinge to Escuriall. Doctor Marcado one of his ordinarie phisisions tould hym, he ought not to sturr, lest the extreamytie of his payne should increase. The kinge answered seeinge I must be caried thether when I am dead, I had rather be caried thether beinge a lyve. So that in the end to satisfie his desire his footemen tooke hym vp vpon theire shoulders, and spent six dayes in goyinge those seven myles, wheare after that he cam, he was better for some fewe dayes, thoughe he was not able to stande, but was forced ether to sytt or lye. But p*re*sently the goute reseasinge hym, accompanied wth a fever, made hym far sicker then he was before, his phisisions shewyd all the skill they could to geve hym some ease[.]

But the extreamytie of payne so encreased, that p*re*sently he entered in to consideracõn of his soule by shrivinge & confessi[on] [*leaf torn*] and receavinge the sacrament at wch instant he [*leaf torn*] Garcia de Lugizor to be consecrated Archbushope [*leaf torn*] [p. 19] wch was p*er*formed by the popes Nuntio, wth all the solemnities & rites accustomed. There happined also to this good Kinge vpon his right knee a great vlcer or bile that could hardly be cured. vpon his laste admonition to his sonne he deliu*er*ed hym a lyttle whyppe w^{ch}

he had in a Cabinett kepte amongst Iewells of great worth. this whypp was [my *crossed through*] ymbrued wth his blood & his fathers blood also: for wth the same they dyd vse to dissipline them selves. This whypp he commended vnto hym as a Ieuell of great worth & wyshed hym to make vse thereof as he & his father before hym had done & gave hym speciall charge to serve god & to doe Iustice & god would p*ro*sper hym the better [.] after thes & the like admonitions havinge made hym self ready for that purpose he yelded vp the gost etc

The Essex rebellion.

MS Diary, 51-53

The sixt daye of ffebruarie [1600/1] beinge sondaye the Earle of Essex accompenyed wth a great troope of Noble men & gent yssued out of Essex howse wthout temple barr & he & his compeny in armes passed throughe fleet street & so to London Creinge aloude by the waye that Raughley would have murdered hym & that he fled to the Cytizens for saffgarde of his lyef. Wthin an howre after I hard hym proclaymed trayto^{r} by Temple barr in ffleet street & so went on wardes to London, the L. Burleighe caused the p*ro*clamacõn to be made wthin the Cyttie at wch tyme the Earle of Essex beinge in the howse of Thomas Symth Sheriffe of london yssued out and drove the sayde L. Burgley & his Compeny backe & on of his men weare slayne[.] And thus yt contynued[.] all the gates of the cyttie shutt & garded & proclamacõn vpon p*ro*clamacõn, the Court gate at Whyt hall shutt[.] a great rumou^{r} & hurly burly wthin and abouts the Cyttie & the Earle walkinge the streetes, not as much as one Cyttizen makinge head agaynst hym [till *crossed out*] fro*m* half an howre after x^{en} aclocke in the morninge till betweene 3 & 4 a clocke in the after noone not wthstandinge all thes p*ro*clamacõns, heerein the cyttizens for all this tyme stoode doubtfull whether syde to take as yt seemed [p.52] by theire behaviours heerein. In and betweene 3 & 4 a clocke in the after noone when he sawe the Cyttizens would not ayde him he cam towardes Ludgate to have passed that waye to Essex howse agayne as he p*re*tended but there he & his Compeny weare sett vpon by the Commaundment of the Bushop of London[.] In this Conflyct one Tracye gent of the chamber to the sayde Earle was slayne. Sr Christopher Blunt that had maried the Countesse the Earles mother was there dayngerouly hurte & so they weare driven to forsake that waye & turned backe agayne & tooke water abouts broken Wharffe together wth some of the noble men & gent wch did accompeny hym[.] the residue weare taken afore they could take water & to the nomber of xl^{ie} or L. gent Comytted to sev*er*all prisons. The Earle at his Comynge to Essex howse supposed hymselfe to be saffe because that morninge foure of the privie Counsell & nobilitie of the Realme vz The L. keep*er*. The Earle of Worcester Sr William knowles & the L. cheeffe Iustice were sent vnto hym the sayde Earle to exammen hym abouts some disobedience he had shewed towardes the Queene & the Counsell whom afore his dep*ar*ture out of Essex howse he had fast locked vp & commaunded Sr Gely merricke & others to guarde [Co *crossed out*] the howse & saffly to keepe them prisoners till his retorne[.] But Sr Fardinando Gorge after he had brought the Earle out of doores consideringe better of the matter retorned to essex howse agayne & wth a Counterfett token fro*m* the Earle caused the sayde noble men to be deliv*er*ed vnto hym & so he enlarged them & went wth them to the Courte. but the sayde Earle retorninge & myssinge the sayde noble men was in great despayre of the matter yet defended he his howse in warlilike maner till mydnight at what tyme he yelded hym selfe to the L. admirall. In this Conflyct in the howse was slaye [*sic*] [p. 53] wth a peece fro*m* the Street: Cap. Oowen Salusburie & one or two more hurte & some hurte and kylled in the street. In whiche After the sayde Earle wth the Earle of Sowthhampton weare condemned of heighe treason & Essex was behedded wthin the towre. Sr Charles Davers & Sr Chrystopher Blunte weare also behedded on the towre hill. Sr Gely m*er*icke & henrie Cuffe secretarie to the sayde Earle weare hanged & quartered at Tiborne. And one Capten Leighe was also executed[.] Div*er*se other noble men & gent weare condemned in the Starrchamber & putto [i.e., put to] great fynes. one Mr Iohn lyttleton a private gent fyned in tenne thowsande poundes others after the qualitie of theire offence & abilities weare likwyse fyned but I do not remember that any more weare executed. The fyrst sondaye after the Earle of Essex was comytted there was great feare lest the prentices would have rissen And streight watch & ward was [comytted *crossed out*] kepte the Towre garded & other speciall places of defence. And great charge geven that all the Cyttizens should keepe wthin doores all that daye so that at churches & s*er*mons weare fewe or no men that daye, but the weomen supplied that torne. Thomas Smyth Sheriffe of London was comytted for that he had suffred the sayde Earle to escape after that he had byn in his howse beinge p*ro*claymed Traytor and the Saterdaye folowinge a newe shiriffe was chosen in his place.

This account differs in a number of details from those of Stow or Speed.

Philip III of Spain has a son and heir; an unwelcome celebration.
MS Diary, 100

In the begin of Aprill [1605] a younge prince was borne in Spayne for the wch there was great ioye there and the newes cominge to the Spainishe Embassador in London he gott leave of the Counsell to make bonefires and some triunphe. And therevpon caused 4 pynacles to be errected in the Strand hard by Som*er*sett howse wherein he laye & thes pynacles havinge fyre workes wthin them burned very strayngly & sent out many tymes prety voleys of fleyinge squibbs. The Spainardes fro*m* the Battlements of the howse threwe money in great abondance amongst the people, whoe inveterated wth maleyce (as yt seemed) towardes the Spainards tooke occasion of discontent wth the Squibbs that flue abroade alledginge they myght doe harme & sett theire howses of [*sic*] fyer. And therefore insteed of the money wch was throwen to them they thrue stones at them & tore in peeces theire pynacles; but the pacience of the Spainards made an end of this tumult.

John Stow, *Annals or Summary of English Chronicles* (1615), 862, gives a very different and much more politic account of the celebration: ". . . for Ioy whereof Don Iohn de Taxis, the spanish Liedger, vppon Munday the 15. of Aprill at his house in the strand, made bonefiers, discharged diuers peales of Chambers, set vp a red crosse at his doore, with diuers great Cresset lightes, and the most part of the afternoone he continued throwing diuers soms both, of Golde, and siluer amongst the Multitudes: taking great pleasure to see the people catch one from another."

An execution.
MS Diary, 101

On Saterday the 23 of m*ar*che [1605] was brought to Tyborne amongst others to be executed one [*space left for a name*] whoe was condemned for supposed feleny whoe vpon his death made this p*ro*testacõn & confession folowinge viz. that he was inocent & guyltles of the felony for the wch he was condemned & that he had neu*er* in his lyef stolen any thinge to the value of a groate But confessed that this was a punishment vnto hym for his other synnes, & specially beinge a Catholike (as he then protested & died) he had in the late difference & controversy betweene the Iesuites & some of the discontented secular priests ben ou*er* forward agaynst the fathers of the Societie & had byn a great divulger of bookes & other prynted libells & phamphetts [*sic*] agaynst them, for the wch specially he dyd beleve that god suffered hym to fall to this end And dyd p*ro*test also that the maleyce of one of the Iudges whome he had often brybed & nowe wearie therew^th^ had stayed his hand, whoe by his maleyce had thus causles wrought his ov*er*throwe. After whose confession as ye have thus harde; the other that stoode in the Carte wth hym beinge heretickes fell to pray & singe salmes wch he publikly vtterly renownced & defied both them & theire fayth & prayed a part & so dyed very resolutly his face vncou*er*ed wth a most myld & sweet countenaunce wheare the other, beinge dead dyd looke most horrible & vgly.

First-Line Index

Poems in *Sinetes* are distinguished by signature notation (e.g., C1^{v}); poems from *Moderatus* by lyric number and signature (#1 [A3^{v}]); "Epitath for Mistris Katheryn Theloall" by CC and folio page.

International Advisory Council

Peter Beal, Sotheby's, London
Lukas Erne, University of Geneva
M. T. Jones-Davies, University of Paris-Sorbonne
Harold Love, Monash University
Sergio Rossi, University of Milan
Helen Wilcox, University of Groningen

Editorial Committee for *The Poems of Robert Parry*:
Steven May, chair
W. Speed Hill
Arthur F. Kinney
Arthur Marotti

The Renaissance English Text Society was established to publish literary texts, chiefly nondramatic, of the period 1475–1660. Dues are $35.00 per annum ($25.00, graduate students; life membership is available at $500.00). Members receive the text published for each year of membership. The Society sponsors panels at such annual meetings as those of the Modern Language Association, the Renaissance Society of America, and the Medieval Congress at Kalamazoo.

General inquiries and proposals for editions should be addressed to the president, Arthur Kinney, Massachusetts Center for Renaissance Studies, PO Box 2300, Amherst, Mass., 01004, USA. Inquiries about membership should be addressed to William Gentrup, Membership Secretary, Arizona Center for Medieval and Renaissance Studies, Arizona State University, Box 874402, Tempe, Ariz., 85287–4402.

Copies of volumes X–XII may be purchased from Associated University Presses, 440 Forsgate Drive, Cranbury, N.J., 08512. Members may order copies of earlier volumes still in print or of later volumes from XIII, at special member prices, from the Treasurer.

FIRST SERIES

VOL. I. *Merie Tales of the Mad Men of Gotam* by A. B., edited by Stanley J. Kahrl, and The History of Tom Thumbe by R. I., edited by Curt F. Buhler, 1965. (o.p.)

VOL. II. *Thomas Watson's Latin Amyntas*, edited by Walter F. Staton, Jr., and Abraham Fraunce's translation The Lamentations of Amyntas, edited by Franklin M. Dickey, 1967.

SECOND SERIES

VOL. III. *The dyaloge called Funus, A Translation of Erasmus's Colloquy (1534)*, and *A very pleasaunt & fruitful Diologe called The Epicure, Gerrard's Translation of Erasmus's Colloquy (1545)*, edited by Robert R. Allen, 1969.

VOL. IV. *Leicester's Ghost* by Thomas Rogers, edited by Franklin B. Williams, Jr., 1972.

THIRD SERIES

VOLS. V–VI. *A Collection of Emblemes, Ancient and Moderne*, by George Wither, with an introduction by Rosemary Freeman and bibliographical notes by Charles S. Hensley, 1975. (o.p.)

FOURTH SERIES

VOLS. VII–VIII. *Tom a' Lincolne* by R. I., edited by Richard S. M. Hirsch, 1978.

FIFTH SERIES

VOL. IX. *Metrical Visions* by George Cavendish, edited by A. S. G. Edwards, 1980.

SIXTH SERIES

VOL. X. *Two Early Renaissance Bird Poems*, edited by Malcolm Andrew, 1984.

VOL. XI. *Argalus and Parthenia by Francis Quarles*, edited by David Freeman, 1986.

VOL. XII. Cicero's *De Officiis*, trans. Nicholas Grimald, edited by Gerald O'Gorman, 1987.

VOL. XIII. *The Silkewormes and their Flies* by Thomas Moffet (1599), edited with introduction and commentary by Victor Houliston, 1988.

SEVENTH SERIES

VOL. XIV. John Bale, *The Vocacyon of Johan Bale*, edited by Peter Happé and John N. King, 1989.

VOL. XV. *The Nondramatic Works of John Ford*, edited by L. E. Stock, Gilles D. Monsarrat, Judith M. Kennedy, and Dennis Danielson, with the assistance of Marta Straznicky, 1990.

SPECIAL PUBLICATION. *New Ways of Looking at Old Texts: Papers of the Renaissance English Text Society, 1985–1991*, edited by W. Speed Hill, 1993. (Sent gratis to all 1991 members.)

VOL. XVI. *George Herbert, The Temple: A Diplomatic Edition of the Bodleian Manuscript (Tanner 307)*, edited by Mario A. Di Cesare, 1991.

VOL. XVII. Lady Mary Wroth, *The First Part of the Countess of Montgomery's Urania*, edited by Josephine Roberts, 1992.

VOL. XVIII. Richard Beacon, *Solon His Follie*, edited by Clare Carroll and Vincent Carey, 1993.

VOL. XIX. An Collins, *Divine Songs and Meditacions*, edited by Sidney Gottlieb, 1994.

VOL. XX. *The Southwell-Sibthorpe Commonplace Book: Folger MS V.b.198*, edited by Sr. Jean Klene, 1995.

SPECIAL PUBLICATION. *New Ways of Looking at Old Texts II: Papers of the Renaissance English Text Society, 1992–1996*, edited by W. Speed Hill, 1998. (Sent gratis to all 1996 members.)

VOL. XXI. *The Collected Works of Anne Vaughan Lock*, edited by Susan M. Felch,1996.

VOL. XXII. Thomas May, *The Reigne of King Henry the Second Written in Seauen Books*, edited by Götz Schmitz, 1997.

VOL. XXIII. *The Poems of Sir Walter Ralegh: A Historical Edition*, edited by Michael Rudick, 1998.

VOL. XXIV. Lady Mary Wroth, *The Second Part of the Countess of Montgomery's Urania*, edited by Josephine Roberts; completed by Suzanne Gossett and Janel Mueller, 1999.

VOL. XXV. *The Verse Miscellany of Constance Aston Fowler: A Diplomatic Edition*, by Deborah Aldrich-Watson, 2000.

VOL. XXVI. *An Edition of Luke Shepherd's Satires*, by Janice Devereux, 2001.

VOL. XXVII. *Philip Stubbes: The Anatomie of Abuses*, edited by Margaret Jane Kidnie, 2002.

VOL. XXVIII. *Cousins in Love: The Letters of Lydia DuGard, 1665–1672, with a new edition of* The Marriages of Cousin Germans *by Samuel DuGard*, edited by Nancy Taylor, 2003.

VOL. XXIX. *The Commonplace Book of Sir John Strangways (1645–1666)*, edited by Thomas G. Olsen, 2004.

SPECIAL PUBLICATION. *New Ways of Looking at Old Texts, III: Papers of the Renaissance English Text Society, 1997–2001*, edited by W. Speed Hill, 2004. (Sent gratis to all 2005 members.)

VOL. XXX. *The Poems of Robert Parry*, edited by G. Blakemore Evans, 2005.

MRTS

Medieval and Renaissance Texts and Studies
is the major publishing program of the
Arizona Center for Medieval and Renaissance Studies
at Arizona State University, Tempe, Arizona.

MRTS emphasizes books that are needed —
editions, translations, and major research tools —
but also welcomes monographs and
collections of essays on focused themes.

MRTS aims to publish the highest quality scholarship
in attractive and durable format at modest cost.